Understanding Public Management

Understanding Public Management

Kjell A Eliassen and Nick Sitter

Los Angeles • London • New Delhi • Singapore

SAGE Publications Ltd
1 Oliver's Yard
55 City Road
London EC1Y 1SP

SAGE Publications Inc.
2455 Teller Road
Thousand Oaks, California 91320

SAGE Publications India Pvt Ltd
B 1/I 1 Mohan Cooperative Industrial Area
Mathura Road
New Delhi 110 044

SAGE Publications Asia-Pacific Pte Ltd
33 Pekin Street #02-01
Far East Square
Singapore 048763

Library of Congress Control Number available

British Library Cataloguing in Publication data

A catalogue record for this book is available
from the British Library

ISBN 978-1-4129-0858-0
ISBN 978-1-4129-0859-7

Typeset by C&M Digitals (P) Ltd., Chennai, India
Printed in Great Britain by The Cromwell Press Ltd, Trowbridge, Wiltshire
Printed on paper from sustainable resources

Contents

List of Figures and Tables

Figures

Tables

Preface

Management in public organisation involves leadership within a range of different institutions, and it is shaped by external developments at three levels: macro change at the national and international level; organisational change of the public institutions themselves; and development of new management tools and practices at the micro level. Most textbooks on public management focus on one of these levels. This book represents an effort to integrate these three levels in a single volume, and to analyse how public management is a matter of managing the interaction between these levels. Even if broad common trends can be identified at the international level and many countries' reform programmes are informed by similar ideas and theories, important differences remain in the patterns of organisational development and management in the public sector across modern liberal democracies. This book explores both broad trends in public policy and local variations in public administration. Perhaps the single most important of the broad trends has been the 'information revolution' – or more specifically digitalisation and the development of the information society – which has shaped developments in public management at all levels. This trend cuts across the three levels, and therefore runs like a thread throughout the book.

At the macro level, the book focuses on globalisation and European integration. The recent wave of globalisation has been driven by the information revolution, and it has radically changed both the tasks of the nation state and the way states provide public services for their citizens. In Europe the development of the European Union and the extension of its Single Market to the public sector has been both a part of the globalisation process and a strategy for managing the effects of globalisation on the nation states. Consequently, the nation state of the 2000s is very different from the nation state of the mid-twentieth century. At the meso level the combination of globalisation and digitalisation on one hand, and of new developments in politics and economics on the other, have led to radical changes in the organisation of public service provision. Liberalisation, privatisation and the increased use of competition within the public sector have altered the dynamics of public management. Privatisation and liberalisation has led to a shift in the focus of public service provision, from ownership to regulation and results. Public sector reform has increased the importance of management in public administration. At the micro level, digitalisation, new models of non-hierarchical management, and new management techniques have radically altered the practical delivery of public services. These developments have generated increased demand for a new type of public manager, and more individual-oriented management techniques such as team leadership and coaching.

This book has been designed with two types of audience in mind, both as a textbook for full-time students of public administration and as a textbook for executive programmes in public management. The book covers theoretical aspects of the debates on globalisation and European integration, and discusses theories of public policy, privatisation, liberalisation and regulation as well as new public management and leadership. At the same time, the book also seeks to illustrate the rich variety of public service provision in modern liberal democracies by drawing examples from different organisational arrangements. It also points out models of best practice, and indicates a number of contemporary management techniques.

In writing an academic textbook, the authors inevitably rely on help and advice from a number of people. The present volume is certainly no exception. We therefore offer our thanks to colleagues in several countries and within our own department: the Department of Public Governance at the Norwegian School of Management. We would like to thank Inger-Margrete Svendsen in particular for her substantial contributions to Chapter 8 on 'Tools of Management and Leadership', a topic that is at the periphery of the core competence of both of us. Thanks also go out to the four students on the School's MSc Political Economy programme who have served as research assistants for the book: Lene Bratesveen, Roar Wold, Inger Hoff and Nils Tyssebotn. The Department of Public Governance generously provided financial support for part of this project.

We would also like to acknowledge the essential part played by Dr Verona Christmas-Best, who has helped manage the entire process from conception to publication. Without her help, inspiration and continuous encouragement this project would have remained at the draft stage.

Kjell A. Eliassen and Nick Sitter
Oslo, 2 August 2007

Introduction: Liberalising and Modernising Public Services

This book's central theme is that the provision of public services in liberal democracies has changed dramatically over the last two decades. In most of Europe the state's involvement in the economy is now better described as indirect and regulatory rather than direct and interventionist. This introductory chapter explores the economic and political philosophies that underpin the foundations for this change and the variations in patterns of change. Changing economic conditions, globalisation and regional integration caused much of the pressure for reform. Gradual trade liberalisation since the Second World War and the digital revolution of the 1990s both accentuated the need for public sector reform and opened up a series of new ways of delivering public services. However, the ideas that shaped the political parties' and governments' responses to these changes have deep roots. The political response to challenges to the state's capacity for governance developed along three broad lines. First, reform programmes were designed to reduce the scope of the state by privatising certain public services and introducing competition by liberalising monopoly markets. This involved a shift from the state to the market, and from centralised to less centralised control. Second, reforms were introduced to improve the efficiency of the services that remained under the auspices of the state. This involved an element of decentralisation of decision-making, as well as a shift from administration to management in the public sector. Third, states sought to strengthen international cooperation. This involved a shift from the state to the European level, or at least to shared competence between these two levels in many policy areas. The two first strategies, which amount to efforts to modernise public service provision, make up most of the subject of this book. The third strategy, European integration, is addressed in a separate chapter, although this theme returns throughout the book as and when it touches on public service provision.

The core of this book focuses on reforms that have been designed to reduce the scope of the state and to make the state work better. These two strategies became part of the mainstream political agenda most clearly in the UK and the USA during the 1980s, but were in fact adopted in one form or another by most European governments in the late 1980s and the 1990s. Many of the immediate challenges lay in the political and economic climate of the 1970s: the expanding size of the liberal democracies' welfare states and the worldwide economic downturn, which made meeting these increasing costs even more difficult. At the same time the current process of globalisation was beginning to take off, and in the 1990s it was dramatically accelerated by the digitalisation of both information and communication technologies and their convergence into the ICT industry. An increasing number of political actors saw protectionism not only as costly, but also as an anathema to free trade and prosperity. Regional integration in Europe helped the states regain some of their capacity for governance by way of joint problem-solving. In the second half of the 1980s the European Union project (still the European Economic Community at that time) was accelerated and turned in a clear free-market direction. Around this time many West European social democratic parties adopted a more liberal economic stance (most of the former communist parties of East Central Europe also turned liberal after the collapse of communism in 1989). In the 1990s, with several of its member states reducing the scope of the state's direct involvement in public service delivery, the EU took its 'public turn' as the Single Market was extended to cover many aspects of the economy that had until then been dealt with nationally, such as telecommunications. By the late 2000s, the twin processes of liberalisation and modernisation were well-established across Europe.

Political Economy and the New Right Challenge to the Welfare State

'Markets are created by governments, ordered by institutions and sustained by regulations' (Wilks 1996: 538). Wilks' comment provides a reminder that advanced markets are created by regulation. They are not spontaneous, separate from political institutions, or self-governing, let alone 'natural'. This observation lies at the heart of the political economy literature and explains much of the variation in markets across the world. It complements rather than contradicts the classical idea associated with Adam Smith (1776) that the 'invisible hand' of the market tends towards efficient distribution of resources by way of the price mechanism. Classical (normative) economics holds that the state should provide the institutions necessary to make the market operate, such as the legal system, property rights and some measure of internal and external security, and that it may, under certain circumstances, exercise regulation (see, for example, Phelps 1985). It is the extent of the two caveats that have been hotly debated: how far should the state go in providing institutions, infrastructure and public services; and what legitimates state intervention in the market?

The two classical responses can be summed up by invoking Friedrich Hayek and John Maynard Keynes. On the left, Keynes (1936) argued for substantial state intervention in the economy and for a comprehensive welfare state that was seen to be both necessary (to correct for market failures) and politically desirable (to redistribute wealth; see also Rawls 1971). On the right, Hayek (1944) warned that state intervention was likely to amount to a step on the *Road to Serfdom*, not primarily because it could not be as efficient as the market but because it constituted a limit on individual freedom.

Historically and today, Western liberal democracies all fall somewhere between these two responses. Both the market and liberal democracy rest on a series of institutions that provide for pluralism. The combination of several competing economic and political groups (the diffusion of economic and political power) and a legitimate regime based on the rule of law (accepted by all the major groups) amounts to a system in which uncertainty is institutionalised (Olson 1993, 2000). Modern liberal democracy entails competition among several different interest groups, none of which can achieve dominance alone (Dahl 1961, 1971). The legitimacy of both economic and political institutions rests partly on the fact that the outcomes of political and economic games are not, and cannot be, known in advance to any single group (Przeworski 1991).

Even the private firm is not so much a spontaneous organisation, as an institution that developed in the nexus between business and politics – regulated capitalism. As two *Economist* journalists put it in their history of the firm: 'No matter how much modern businessmen may presume to the contrary, the company was a political creation' (Micklethwait and Wooldridge 2003: 53). The central questions have not been whether the state should regulate economic activity or provide public services, but the extent to which it should do so. In other words, why regulate or supply public services? The answers that have prevailed in the USA and Western Europe fall into two broad categories: to correct market failures and to provide public services.

The first of these two justifications for public services and state intervention in the economy is the least controversial. It is based on the central argument of Thomas Hobbes' *The Leviathan* (1651): that the state is required to secure the rule of law and prevent anarchy. Moving beyond the matter of the state providing security and the legal order that is necessary for markets to function (notably property rights, police, courts), classical economic theory holds that there are some cases in which markets will not generate the most efficient outcomes possible, and that state intervention might therefore be warranted. Pareto (1906) gave name to the concept 'Pareto optimality' by focusing on sub-optimal situations in which one or more persons could be made better off without any other individual becoming worse off. These include situations in which there is inadequate provision of public goods, for example because nobody is willing to pay for something that they cannot be excluded from enjoying (such as clean air). Other types of market failure include some cases where voluntary transactions between two individuals have negative consequences for a third party that cannot be built into the cost of the transaction; where the nature of the industry (ever lower costs for producing each new unit) makes it possible for one firm to establish a monopoly; and where companies collude to fix prices or otherwise limit competition.

The second set of justifications for public services relies on the much more controversial notion that state intervention may be in 'the public interest', as defined by the government of the day. Examples of goals that most European governments have deemed worthy of pursuit at some point in time include regulation to ensure minimum quality (e.g. regulating the medical profession) and safety standards for products (e.g. seat belts in cars); consumer protection and liability laws that hold the producer responsible for flawed products; cross-subsidies (e.g. equal price for local telephone calls in a country); and access to services and security of supply (e.g. the right of connection to the water and electricity grid).

These kinds of goals may be deemed appropriate because of the complexity of the modern market, where the individual consumer lacks complete information. However, they may also be part of an effort to meet social goals determined through the political process, including redistribution of resources. Inasmuch as interest groups get involved in the policy-making process, the danger is that a group may lobby for regulation or intervention (particularly subsidies) that benefits the group but involves an overall cost to society. This leads to the danger that the cumulative effect of each interest group's demands on the state might result in public sector expansion or in regulation becoming increasingly complex and costly (Olson 1982). This was deemed to be the case in much of Western Europe by the late 1970s.

Although pluralist theories of the state and classical economics dominated western analyses during much of the twentieth century, there has been no shortage of challenges. In the more extreme versions, these were not only alternative analyses of politics, but alternative political systems that ranged from communism to Nazism. In their milder forms, elite theory and Marxism provided serious challenges to both the pluralist model of liberal democracy and classical economic theory. Perhaps the most influential mainstream critiques have been that there is no 'level playing field' between capital and labour in liberal democracy and that elites manipulate political agendas and constrain outcomes. Lindblom (1977) has emphasised the advantages of industry over trade unions that may result from differences in access to the political elites, media and capital resources, suggesting that once imbalances occur they might generate a vicious (or virtuous, depending on the point of view) circle that reinforces differences inasmuch as winners gain ever more resources. In *The Semisovereign People*, Schattschneider famously argued that 'the definition of the alternatives is the supreme instrument of power' (1960: 68), suggesting that the pluralist game is skewed by elites. In the end, however, from a present-day perspective, it is the *public choice* critique that has proven most influential. Public policy is increasingly seen not as a consequence of normative theories, but of political games in which the participants rationally pursue their (primarily economic) interest.

The New Right and public choice analysis of politics

During the 1960s and 1970s the band of thinkers that challenged the welfare state consensus from a free-market perspective expanded and developed into a fully fledged New Right assault on conventional public service models. Much of this drew on analyses that approached 'economic man' as a rational actor in pursuit of his or her interests (Dunleavy and O'Leary 1987). The New Right developed perhaps the most consistent and comprehensive critique of both the pluralist state and classical theories of public policy. In retrospect it has certainly proven the most influential. Public (or rational) choice theory raised questions about many of the assumptions inherent in pluralist political analysis and classical economic theories of public policy (Shepsle and Bonchek 1997, Muller 2003). The starting point is a dual challenge, based on assertions that the state cannot amass the necessary information and knowledge to act reliably in the public interests, and even if it could there is no reason to expect that it would. The first assertion is associated with the Austrian school and can be traced to Hayek's warnings that state intervention is an affront to individual liberty. The second is based on economic analysis of democracy that builds on assumptions about individuals' rational pursuit of well-defined preferences. It is associated in particular with the Chicago school and traced back to Downs' (1956, 1967) work at Stanford. Together, the 'small government' and public choice analyses laid the basis for a formidable challenge to conventional theories of public policy and regulation in the shape of the New Right.

Hayek and the Austrian school based the critique of big government on the incompatibility of individual liberty and state intervention in economic activity. The central point is not so much that economic liberty fosters democracy, as that state intervention is a challenge to both economic and political liberty.

When states start circumscribing economic liberty they are on a slippery slope towards limiting political freedom, on 'the road to serfdom'. There is therefore an a priori case against state intervention, even the kind of intervention that is compatible with classical economics, and a case for a minimalist state. In policy terms, this translates into recommendations to limit the role of states, to 'roll back the frontiers of the state' (Thatcher 1988), not merely to reform and modernise public governance.

The work on economic theories of democracy that laid the foundations for public choice analysis provided the theoretical foundation for a rational choice critique of big government and economic intervention. Its principal basis is not merely that governments cannot achieve sufficient information or that state action is a threat to liberty, but that careful analysis of the motives and opportunities of the agents of the state reveals that they cannot be expected to act in the public interest. Assuming that individuals pursue their own interests and observing that government agencies and civil servants often enjoy something of a monopoly of information about the costs and benefits of their own activities, Niskanen (1971, 1973) argued that bureaucrats will tend to maximise their budgets, not the utility to society. This shifted the focus from what ought to be done to who wants it done. This change from the normative question of what policies are required to correct market failures, to the positive question of who benefits from the current set-up, radically altered the fundamental questions in public policy analysis. The new question asked who had developed the present policy regimes and in whose interest: in other words, who wanted regulation? The answer central to much of the New Right literature was 'interest groups'. Groups or firms want regulation to protect them against competitors (Stigler 1971). Not all pressure groups succeed, and Olson's (1965) 'logic of collective action' analysis suggests that industry and labour are generally in a stronger position than consumers. In turn, elected politicians who seek financial support for re-election campaigns compete for interest groups' favour, and bureaucrats, seeking to expand their budgets, supply the regulation or intervention that these groups demand (Tullock 1976).

The main thrust of New Right analyses was thus that, in liberal democracies, the state has had a tendency to grow too big, and to expand its activities and public service programmes beyond the socially optimal point. These arguments are taken up and discussed in more detail in the chapters on privatisation, regulation and New Public Management (Chapters 3, 4 and 5). The key point here is that they formed the basis for many political party programmes on the right and centre-right in the 1980s and 1990s, not only in the USA and the UK but across Western Europe. One of the most widely cited links between theory and practice is the influence of the circle around Keith Joseph and the Centre for Policy Studies and Institute for Economic Affairs on Margaret Thatcher, who became UK Prime Minister in 1979 (Young 1989: Ch. 7).

However, the challenges of 'stagflation' (the combination of inflation and economic stagnation, or low growth) prompted a range of European parties to rethink their economic policies and approach to public service provision. The answers centred on the two ideas mentioned in the first paragraph of this chapter: to reduce the scope of state activity, and to make public service provision more efficient.

Beyond the New Right: the Institutional Turn in Public Policy Analysis and the Modernisation of Social Democracy

Although elements of public choice analysis and the New Right's political prescriptions formed part of the new political consensus in the late 1980s and early 1990s, both academia and politics developed considerably in reaction to the New Right challenge. In the academic debates, a number of North American and European political scientists employed public choice theory to arrive at conclusions that differed considerably from the core of New Right thinking. At the same time, the academic debate on public policy in the USA, EU and its member states increasingly turned its focus to the role that institutions play in shaping the outcomes of political games. This broadening of public choice analysis provided a part of the basis for extended debates on the modernisation of the centre-left (see, for example, Sassoon 1996: Ch. 24). Indirectly, these developments contributed to the 'renewal' of centre-left policies, from Bill Clinton's Democrats in the USA and Tony Blair's New Labour in the UK to the social democratic parties in the Netherlands, Scandinavia, Germany and even France. In the 1990s and 2000s, liberalisation and modernisation became part of the mainstream political consensus in most European states. The question for governments of both the centre-right and the centre-left became how to make liberalisation and modernisation work. This political debate has been developing in parallel with changes in the academic debate, both in terms of more diversified public choice research and a move towards research that focuses more on the role institutions play in public policy.

A broader public choice agenda

Public choice theory laid the foundations for a formidable challenge to pluralist theories of the state and classical normative economic policy analysis, and influenced the public policy debate on the political left as well as right. Critiques of bureaucracy and public policy based on rational choice are of course closely associated with the New Right, and direct links can be found between academic analyses and centre-right policies in the USA and UK, particularly under Reagan and Thatcher. However, the public choice literature extends across a broader political and academic spectrum, comprising analyses that do not reach the same conclusions as the New Right (Shepesle and Boncheck 1997, Scharpf 1997). Elaborating on rational choice analysis, and building on Downs' work, Dunleavy (1991) suggests that bureaucrats may have incentives to shape budgets according to their own preferences, rather than simply to maximise their budgets as a whole. LeGrand (2003) relaxes the assumptions about egocentric actors to allow for altruistic motivation and argues that cases for public service systems are sufficiently robust to take account of both kinds of motivation.

The institutionalist turn in public policy analysis

A broad political science literature has developed which focuses on the role institutions play in shaping political outcomes. The central point in the public choice literature is that outcomes are the result of the constellations of actors' interests, strategies and resources on one hand, and the rules of the game on the other. Or, as one textbook on EU politics put it succinctly: Preferences · Institutions = Outcomes (Hix 1999). An important caveat is that strategies may change, even if more fundamental goals and preferences remain more or less constant, and that games at one level are affected by games at another (Tsebelis 1990). However, the *new institutionalist* literature asks whether institutions have a more independent impact on political outcomes (March and Olsen 1989, Pierson 2004). In the words of the title of Weaver and Rockman's (1993) edited volume: *Do Institutions Matter?*, unsurprisingly given that the edited volume sets out to assess the effect of institutions, their answer is affirmative.

In the new institutionalist research, public policy is seen as a matter of institutional design and history. Regulatory regimes are shaped by the existing institutional set-up, even where considerable innovation takes place, e.g. to devise new and credible regimes. For example, the European Union has developed into a 'regulatory state', partly because its limited financial resources make regulation the most appropriate tool of governance (McGowan and Wallace 1996, Majone 1996). Regulation, rather than public ownership, planning and administration, has become the dominant form of state activity in Western Europe, at both the state and EU level (Majone 1994, 1997). For many states, EU-level policy-making consists in no small part of efforts to project their own (or preferred) institutions onto the EU level; to make sure EU rules and institutions are compatible with existing national rules (Eyre and Sitter 1999). Regulatory developments therefore 'reflect a pragmatic attempt to live with the constraints imposed by the EU, and, in particular, the inherent limitations in the Commission's executive powers' (Hancher 1996: 64). The central question, both at national and international level, is therefore not only why public services are needed or who wants them, but how the existing arrangements came about and whether they shape the option for future change?

The 'Third Way' and the modernisation of social democracy

During the 1990s most social democratic parties in Europe embraced a large number of the changes that were taking place in the public sector. In much the same way as the conservative and Christian democratic parties became party to the welfare state consensus in post-war Western Europe, the debates about and strategies developed to strengthen state capacity were not associated with one side of the political spectrum only. Even if the right (in the late 1980s) and the left (in the late 1940s) may have gone considerably further than the other side was prepared to accept, particularly in adversary political systems like that of the UK, some elements of the new reforms became part of the new consensus. In most European cases the political right started the shift from the state to the market (in an effort to reduce the scope of the state), as well as the shift from public administration to public management (the effort to improve public services). However, many of the measures taken were soon accepted by the political centre-left. Moreover, the accompanying shift from centralised control to decentralised service delivery, whether by local government or more independent agencies, was not as clearly associated with the right's political agenda as was privatisation. The general tendency of opposition parties to accept many parts of the *fait accompli* of the governments that they oppose and eventually replace, primarily because it is costly or impractical to reverse established reforms, is reinforced by the fact that most reforms are multi-faceted and that parties often reassess their policies when in opposition.

The most racial changes on the centre-left, in terms of both policies and electoral strategy, occurred in the USA and the UK. In the late 1980s the Democrats and Labour began to play down ideology in favour of more centrist and pragmatic approaches to politics. The processes thereby set in place would be developed with considerable success by Bill Clinton and Tony Blair and help them win office in 1992 and 1997 respectively. Both leaders adopted explicitly pragmatic and centrist ideologies, and Blair's 'New Labour' in particular was closely associated with the work of the sociologist Anthony Giddens (1998) on the 'Third Way' and the renewal of social democracy. For Blair, Giddens, and the New Labour party, the Third Way was principally an effort to go beyond what they saw as the neo-liberal orthodoxy or ultra-liberalism of the Thatcher years, which they deemed inadequate in a number of respects. However, this was to be accomplished without a return to the classical state-oriented economic intervention of the old Labour party. In this project Labour leader Blair built on his two immediate predecessors' shifts towards the centre ground in British politics: Neil Kinnock's isolation of the hard left and John

Smith's weakening of the party's links with the trade unions. Labour's new centrist ideology permitted the party to take on board some important elements of the right's reforms of the public sector, including a commitment to the newly privatised utilities, to further liberalisation in some sectors, and to managerialism and a degree of competition in the public sector. When Labour won office in 1997 the policy to reduce the scope of the state was thus not reversed, although the approach to regulating the liberalised sectors was altered somewhat. The shift from administration to management was maintained, although some aspects, such as compulsive competitive tendering and quasi-markets, were played down. The reduction in the central government's direct involvement in public service provision was, if anything, carried further, albeit because of Labour's commitment to devolution of power to regional and local government. In addition, a series of reforms were undertaken to improve governance as a whole, improve public sector funding, and to deal with a series of sector-specific problems.

In the more consensual European states, such as the Netherlands and Scandinavia, neither the right nor the left went as far from the political centre as in the UK. None of the centre-right parties in the Netherlands, Sweden, Denmark or Norway featured party leaders quite as radical as Thatcher, and in any case their tenure in power was tempered by their participation in minority and/or coalition governments. Consequently, despite an overall trend of a move from state to market and from public administration to management, the centre-left faced neither the same incentives nor the same *fait accompli* as their counterparts in the UK. The four social democratic parties have been part of the broad pattern of centre-left reform, though the Dutch and Danish parties went somewhat further than their Swedish and Norwegian sister parties (the latter lost a considerable number of votes to its far left competitor in the 2001 election, which it fought on a Blairite platform, but recovered when it took a more left-wing posture in 2005). Although similar trends in public policy reform characterise these four countries and the UK, and utilities privatisation and liberalisation developed as fast and as radically, these states have taken a more cautious approach to internal reforms of public service delivery.

Political and public policy developments in France and Germany have been less radical than in the Netherlands, Scandinavia or the UK. Although the centre-right parties were in office for considerable periods in the 1980s and 1990s, the critique of the existing public policy regimes and of the general role of the state in economic policy was much weaker than in the UK, and political change was in many ways more conservative even than in Scandinavia (for example, in terms of telecommunications and energy liberalisation). Although Schroder's Social Democratic Party did adopt a more Third Way type programme, and successive governments in the 1990s have been committed to reform, public policy modernisation and broader economic reform has met considerable obstacles in Germany. France has been an even more reluctant reformer. Although the Socialist's rightwards turn began as early as the 1980s, Third Way social democracy was still controversial on the centre-left in the 2007 elections.

In short, the politics of public sector reform and the debates on liberalisation and modernisation of public services to some extent reflected the differences in the types of modern capitalist regimes found in central and northern Europe (see Esping-Andersen 1990, Scharpf 1999, Hall and Soskice 2001). The 'liberal' welfare regimes (to use Esping-Andersen's label), here represented by the UK (and the USA), saw the most enthusiastic and radical employment of New Right theories in the 1980s, and the most thorough centrist move from the social democrat parties. The reduction of the scope of the state involved both general nationalised industry and many public utilities, and the shift from management to administration relied heavily on introducing competition and market mechanisms in the public sector. Decentralisation primarily meant hollowing out the role of the central government by shifting authority to independent agencies, rather than empowering local government (though this changed with the change of government in the UK). The 'social democratic' or 'consensual' model, in this case the Scandinavian states and to some extent the Netherlands, adopted a more mixed strategy, including radical liberalisation but less extensive use of market mechanisms for the services that remained in public hands. France and Germany, the 'corporatist' states, have seen somewhat less radical reforms, although the overall trend is in fact common to all EU states and the EU as such.

The Structure of this Book

The structure of this book follows the themes discussed so far: the first two chapters focus on the changing international context; the next two chapters focus on the strategies for reducing the role of the state (and relying more on the market) and the consequent challenges involved in the switch from direct intervention to indirect rule by regulation; and the last four chapters focus on the shift from public administration to public management. The core of the book therefore focuses on the liberalisation and modernisation of public service provision, but the two first chapters also address the overall framework for these reform processes: globalisation and the digital revolution. At the end of the book, Chapter 6 addresses the effects of digitalisation on public service organisations and service delivery, and Chapter 8 discusses the implications for leadership and organisational structures inside the public sector. The examples are taken principally from the seven European states discussed in this introductory chapter: the UK, Germany, France, the Netherlands, Sweden, Denmark and Norway. This selection allows a number of comparisons: across the three models of 'welfare capitalism' or 'varieties of capitalism'; between fast and slow reformers in terms of both the shift from state to market and from administration to management; between old and relatively new EU member states; and across large, medium, and small EU members, as well as the 'quasi-member' Norway.

The first section, which comprises Chapters 1 and 2, addresses the international context: globalisation and regional integration. At the macro level, international developments have changed the parameters for states' policy-making. This represents the starting point in analysing public sector reform and designing public management programmes: addressing the questions of how global and international developments have changed the context in which states operate and how this provides both challenges to and opportunities for modernising government. Chapter 1 on 'Internationalisation, Globalisation and Liberalisation – Strategic Challenges for Public Governance' therefore addresses the relationship between international developments and domestic government, including more detailed focus on the three central aspects of globalisation: technological change, the liberalisation and growth of world trade and finance, and the political dimensions of globalisation. Chapter 2 on 'European Integration – Recapturing Sovereignty and Institutionalising Liberalisation' turns to one of the main strategies European states have adopted to strengthen their capacity for governance: joint governance through the European Union. The EU also amounts to an institutionalisation of certain liberal policies, and places certain parameters on the member states' domestic policies related to public sector reform and management.

The second section, which comprises Chapters 3 and 4, turns to the first of the two broad national-level strategies for strengthening state capacity: reducing the scope of the state and shifting some public services over to the market. At the state level, developments in public administration and management are placed in the context of changing economic policy. New approaches to managing the economy and industrial policy have played important roles in driving forward public sector reform. Chapter 3 on 'Liberalisation and Privatisation' therefore addresses public and private ownership, developments in economic policy and management of industry, and the resulting processes of privatisation. This includes focus on the theories that form the basis for privatisation and liberalisation, with particular focus on utilities: telecommunications, electricity, rail transport and postal services. Chapter 4 on 'Regulation and Competition Policy' turns to the challenges for the state that this shift from direct intervention to indirect rule by regulation involved. As it turned out, both in the USA and Europe, privatisation and liberalisation warranted re-regulation rather than deregulation. Establishing rules for a fully functioning liberalised utilities market requires far more complex regulation than a state providing public monopoly services. Theories of regulation, deregulation and regulatory change are covered, as are the wider public policy implications of privatisation and liberalisation.

The third section, which comprises Chapters 5 and 6, turns to the second broad strategy for stronger state capacity: making the public sector work better. This section is dedicated to the macro level of public sector reform: ideas and technology. It addresses public administration reform programmes and the technological developments that helped drive the agenda of public sector modernisation. Chapter 5 on 'Modernising Public Administration: To New Public Management and Beyond' discusses the theoretical bases for reforms, drawing on the public choice literature on public administration and bureaucracy that formed the basis for a wide range of public sector reforms collectively known as 'New Public Management'. NPM has become the most prevalent model for public sector reforms across the world, and the attributes of NPM are therefore analysed here. The chapter then proceeds to address the implications of NPM reforms, and the changing types of government that are now known as 'governance' – modernised, and lighter, more flexible methods of public management. Chapter 6 on 'Modernising Government – *e*Government' turns to the modernisation of public management in the light of technological change (addressed under the topic *e*Government) that has permitted a new form of more user-oriented, accessible public services.

The fourth and final section, which comprises Chapters 7 and 8, continues the theme of making the public services work better and turns to implementation and management. Chapter 7 on 'Organisational Design and Institutional Governance' addresses the meso-level of change: reform of organisations involved in public service delivery. The focus is on the services that have remained under the auspices of the public sector, either through direct public provision or by contracting out to private or semi-private providers. This includes education, health and selected local government services such as refuse disposal and care for the elderly. Chapter 8 on 'Tools of Management and Leadership' proceeds to the micro-level. The roles and tools of public sector management and leadership are a central issue here, as is the question of the extent to which strategy and theories developed for private sector management are relevant to the public sector. This includes discussion of the challenges involved in implementing policy in rapidly changing environments, including change and project management, decentralisation and delegation, and knowledge-based organisations. It also examines the differences between management in the public and private sector as well as considering the range of tools available for improving management and leadership at different levels; from formulating visions to inspiring subordinates.

Further Reading

Dunleavy, P. and O'Leary, B. (1987) *Theories of the State: The Politics of Liberal Democracy* (London: Macmillan). Provides an excellent overview of the major theories of liberal democracy. Chapter 3 on 'The New Right' elaborates on many of the theories discussed in this chapter.

Fukuyama, F. (2004) *State-Building: Governance and World Order in the 21st Century* (Ithaca: Cornell University Press). A short book on the national and international role of the state. Chapter 1 on 'The Missing Dimensions of Stateness' provides a good overview of the functions of the state and how to strengthen 'state capacity'.

Richards, D. and Smith, M.J. (2002) *Governance and Public Policy in the UK* (Oxford: Oxford University Press). An introduction to public policy in the UK, which provides good coverage of public policy reforms and debates in the 1980s and 1990s. Chapter 5 on 'The Internal Challenges to the State: The New Right' is particularly relevant.

Newman, J. (2001) *Modernising Governance: New Labour, Policy and Society* (London: Sage). Covers the modernisation project of the Labour government in the UK. Chapter 3 on 'The Third Way: Modernising Social Democracy' provides a good introduction to the modernisation of social democracy.

Hood, C. (1998) *The Art of the State: Culture, Rhetoric and Public Management* (Oxford: Oxford University Press). Takes a long term perspective and provides an excellent introduction to the dynamics of public management reform. Chapter 2 on 'Calamity, Conspiracy and Chaos in Public Management' discusses the kind of problems and challenges different public management systems are likely to encounter.

ONE

Internationalisation, Globalisation and Liberalisation – Strategic Challenges for Public Governance

Since the Second World War, the world has seen the gradual but continual development of free trade, to the extent that we may today speak of operating within something close to a global free trade regime. This chapter analyses the development of globalisation and liberalisation, and the consequences this has had for the public sector in the nation states. From a highly protectionist starting point just after the Second World War, the political and economic world changed substantially over the next half-century. By the turn of the twenty-first century, global free trade had become politically accepted as the norm for trade relations among most, if not all, states in the world.

The free trade regime exploits the effects of the distribution of labour principle in the economy: goods and services are produced where it is cheapest to do so, and sold where the highest price can be obtained. This politically and economically driven trade liberalisation process constitutes an important part of the globalisation process. In addition, a raft of bilateral, regional and inter-regional trade liberalisation arrangements have been developed, in the form of regional organisations, free trade areas and custom unions, and inter-regional organisations. Globalisation and regional (as well as inter-regional) integration are two very closely related processes. Whilst regional integration deepens trade liberalisation for the members of the regional organisation, the same regional cooperation also protects the member states from at least some of the effects of global trade liberalisation. Thus, although regional integration to some extent reduces state sovereignty at the national level, it also increases the combined (or 'pooled') sovereignty of the member states in the regional organisation.

This chapter will introduce the processes of trade liberalisation and globalisation and point out the more general dynamics of regional integration. More detailed analysis of the European Union as the prime example of a well-developed and comprehensive example of a regional organisation follows in Chapter 2. The present chapter first discusses the concept and dimensions of globalisation, as well as presenting globalisation's main institutions. It then proceeds to analyse the impact of globalisation at the national level, and finally discusses the relationship between globalisation and regional integration in more detail.

Globalisation

Gradually – since the Second World War, but in particularly in the last decade or so – the scale and scope of global interrelations have grown enormously in almost every aspect of human life: politically, economically, culturally, socially and regarding everything from environmental hazards and cooperation to military intervention and global arms trade. World-wide economic integration has linked the fate of nations, communities and households across regions and on the global level in such a way that crises in one country usually take a toll on jobs, production and investments in the rest of the world. A central factor in this process is the international, or transnational, firm. Transnational corporations account for between 25 and 33 percent of world output, 70 percent of world trade and 80 percent of international investment; overseas production by these firms considerably exceeds the level of world export; and every day more than 1.2 trillion US dollars is handled at the foreign exchange markets (Baylis and Smith 2005: 20–21). This makes such firms key players in global trade, investment and production, whilst effectively operating outside the control of their nation states and even regional or international organisations. At the same time, the external effects of their decisions on investment, production and trade had to be dealt with by the nation states through their welfare and regional development policies.

The second central factor is the context and environment in which production and trade takes place. The collapse of communism in Europe in 1989 and the end of the Cold War brought about radical changes in the international political and economic system. As Thomas Friedman (2000) put it: the world went from playing chess to playing Monopoly. The end of the Cold War, the bi-polar world and the ideological struggle between capitalist liberal democracy and communism removed some of the biggest constraints on trade and interaction between states as well as non-state players.

The third important factor behind this wave of globalisation is the digital revolution. Digitalisation has created a completely new global communications infrastructure with enormous capacity and flexibility, and brought about the convergence of telecommunications, communication and IT into a strong and powerful ICT base for a new global information economy and information society. This influences everything from running businesses to the spread of new hits in the music industry. Without this digital revolution, the present wave of globalisation could not have been so forceful, let alone had such radical consequences.

Globalisation is not merely a post-Second World War phenomenon; we have witnessed periods of globalisation in earlier times. Most obviously, the period between 1880 and the First World War was also a period of globalisation, with perhaps a more extensive integration of the world economy than today (Dicken 2003). At that time the nation states were not as developed as today and there were far fewer restrictions on the free movement of individuals. Depending on the definition of globalisation, other periods in world history with a rapid expansion of political or economic regimes could also be characterised using the term globalisation: for example, the Roman Empire and some of the early phases of colonialisation. What is certainly different with this late twentieth century and early twenty-first century globalisation is the interrelation between the global reorganisation of production (both of goods and services) and the territorial opening of free trade among most of the countries in the world. It should also be noted that during the 1970s the cost of sea freight was dramatically reduced, which greatly contributed to a rapid increase in the free movement of goods in this wave of globalisation. This was due both to new technology and new logistic systems. More than 80 percent of world trade in goods is done via sea transport. Moreover, the digital revolution has played a big role in the (potentially) global integration of intangible commodities in the form of ideas, knowledge and services. The impact of these two developments is also felt in areas like culture, environment, military and migration etc.

Understanding globalisation

What, then, is globalisation? How can it be defined, and how has it developed? The focus here is on the concepts and processes of globalisation, how these developments are perceived by different actors and the effects of globalisation on national, regional and local public policy-making. Globalisation has been the new buzz word both in politics and in academic debate in this decade. There are, however, several definitions and understandings of what it is, how it comes about and what is new about it. The simplest definition of globalisation is that it is a process driven by technology *and* ideology in which geographical distance becomes irrelevant for cultural and economic relations. In the literature, globalisation has been defined in many different ways, for example as 'the intensification of worldwide social relations which link distant localities in such a way that local happenings are shaped by events occurring many miles away and vice versa' (Giddens 1990: 21) or simply as 'the integration of world economy' (Gilpin 2001: 364). Others have stressed changes in space and dismantling of borders like 'de-territorialization or [...] the growth of superterritorial relations between people' (Scholte 2000: 46), and 'time-space compression' (Harvey 1999).

Globalisation is also closely linked to regional integration and the development of multilateral and bilateral free trade agreements. The aim of these more limited agreements – from a geographical point of view – is both to reap the economic benefits of distribution of labour among the participants, and to protect them against some of the negative effects of globalisation.

Since the turn of the century, globalisation has become perhaps the most important framework for national and local politics and policy-making. The globalisation process has dramatically reduced the freedom of governments and other publicly elected bodies to make unilateral decisions. The development of free-trade regimes and reorganisation of global companies, and the prominent role played by global and regional regulatory regimes have had a direct impact on national and local companies. This also has political implications. One could argue that the globalisation process has created two types of democratic deficit. First, the political influence of the democratic institutions in the nation states may be reduced, and second, new global systems of governance are established outside direct democratic control. The end result is both increased pressure on the national welfare states and, at the same time, a desire for the development of better and stronger global regimes. However, the establishment of such regimes requires unanimous agreement among the states involved. This has proven very difficult in trade, environment and most other global issues.

Even if growing consensus on the newness and very comprehensive impact of the current wave of globalisation exists, there are still at least three distinctly different approaches to this phenomenon. These approaches differ on how they interpret both the characteristics and the potential impact of globalization. They also serve as a more theoretical introduction to analysis of the various dimensions of globalisation.

First, *hyperglobalists* see globalisation as a development which fundamentally reorders the framework of human action and undermines the role and functions of the nation state and its democratic institutions. State governments will no longer be capable of controlling their own societies and economies (Ohmae 1995, Scholte 2000). According to this interpretation of the world, the dominant features of globalisation are the creation of global capitalism, global governance and a global civil society (Held et al. 1999). The driving forces behind this development are capitalism and technology. The result is denationalisation of economies through the establishment of transnational networks of production, trade and finance, and the erosion of old national and regional hierarchies.

Second, the *skeptics* view globalisation as just another instance of internationalisation and regionalisation, where states and regional organisations still play the dominant role. The dominant features of this development are trading blocs, regional blocs and somewhat weaker geographical control than in the earlier periods. The driving forces are states and markets. Thus, internationalisation depends on state acquiescence and support – and states and geopolitics still remain the forces creating world order (Krasner 1999, Gilpin 2001).

Third, the *transformationalists* view globalisation as the reordering of inter-regional relations. The central assertion is that there is no clear distinction between international and domestic, external and internal affairs. The state remains the central actor, but its role is changing. The supporters of this view argue that both the *hyperglobalists* and the *skeptics* exaggerate their main analyses and arguments. The world is going through complex changes that combine several forces including modernisation, global integration and fragmentation. Thus, the total picture becomes complex and multifaceted. Politics becomes global and politics is everywhere. There is no lack of government, but the logic of politics and the arena on which it is played out are changing. In fact, both the nature of the state and the international system has been changing, sometimes at a faster pace and sometimes at a slower pace, for the last five centuries (Bobbitt 2002, Cooper 2003).

In this volume globalisation is seen as a gradual transformation process – not new today, but different from any previous internationalisation and globalisation process. The rapid integration of the world economy and most aspects of socio-cultural activity may be desired by political parties, voters or governments – even if all the consequences have not been anticipated or are universally popular. The process is technologically driven, and extremely difficult to fundamentally reverse.

Characteristics of Globalisation

Globalisation has become a common name for a wide range of different aspects of economic and political developments that have a world-wide reach. The most important task here, however, is to try to identify and analyse the different aspects of this concept, and how and to what extent the different aspects of globalisation influence the functioning of national political systems. A simple definition of globalisation might be: a technologically and ideologically driven process in which geographical distance becomes irrelevant for socio-cultural, political and economic relations. This highlights both the dual roots of the present globalisation (driven by the deliberate acts of politicians and the effects of digitalisation) and the cross-border perspective of this venture. More or less along these lines, Held defines globalisation as 'a stretching of social, political and economic activities across frontiers such that events, decisions and activities in one region of the world can come to have significance for individuals and communities in distant regions of the globe' (Held et al. 1999: 3).

This definition implies boundary permeability or transcendence. The importance of borders has been reduced dramatically. Frontiers have been opened through international agreement on free trade in goods and services, as well as agreements on the (effective) free movements of persons – at least as tourists. At the same time the digital revolution has made it impossible for one country to prevent all news and information from reaching their citizens. Satellites and the internet have made information available for citizens everywhere at little or no cost. Companies can have customers and suppliers all over the world, and the number of participants in any social setting is almost limitless.

All these developments increase the need for robust and flexible governing systems at the national, regional and global level to cope with the rapidly changing political, economic and cultural environment. The growing number and increasing diversity of participants creates severe problems for governments, for example, how to control, how to stimulate and how to tax! Taken together, these developments have brought about rising complexity and uncertainty in all countries of the world, and this in turn has created problems of political instability and change.

Why does the current wave of globalisation contain all these forceful elements? What are the main characteristics of the process? Politically, the current globalisation process is characterised by a fairly continual and gradual development toward a free world market not only in goods, but (from the mid-1990s) also in services and capital. The rise of neo-liberal ideology resulted in widespread liberalisation, deregulation and privatisation. The basic assumption is that increased world trade generates faster economic development. Regional development is a complement to globalisation, as both take advantage of opportunities to produce goods and services where associated costs are lowest, and sell them where they fetch the highest price. There are more than 170 regional organisations in the world. Organisations such as the EU, EFTA, APEC, NAFTA and ASEAN promote freer trade among their members, and thus contribute to economic growth (even if they may protect their members from some of the effects of global free trade). There has also been a proliferation of international and transnational regulatory regimes, such as the WTO, but these tend to be somewhat weaker because of the need to reach agreement among a large number of states. The result has been a multi-layered system of governance, and a diffusion of political authority that involves sub-national regions, nation states, regional organisations and global institutions. Chapter 2 explores the working of the most advanced of the regional organisations, the EU, in greater detail.

At the economic level, the last half-century has witnessed a continuous development of economic and trade liberalisation, which has led to a practically free global market for goods (excluding agricultural products) and a truly global financial system. The financial system is the most liberalised today. This has been a step-by-step process, governed by the results of the different trade rounds in GATT, and later the WTO, and of a large number of bilateral and multilateral trade agreements. Recent WTO negotiations and many bilateral agreements have come to include services from telecommunications to shipping. However, the degree of liberalisation varies from agreement to agreement and between different countries. In any case, the result at the global level is increased economic interaction among all countries, rapidly growing world trade, and greater economic interdependence.

Globalisation is also reflected in defence and military matters. There has been a shift in the nature and impact of global and regional conflicts. Attempts have been made to establish, or develop, or change the focus of, regional regimes for cooperative security and collective defence such as NATO, the OSSE and the EU's security and defence capacity. The end of the Cold War brought about new rivalries and security concerns, and a totally new pattern of global and regional threats. At the same time, armaments production and procurement has become more internationalised, and the US industry has emerged as hegemonic in this sector.

As in all previous periods of globalisation, there have been large waves of migration between countries, and even regions. In the current wave, the movement has primarily been away from war-zones, failed states and poor living conditions and poverty. Economic migrants in search of a more prosperous life may be highly skilled individuals such as doctors, nurses and engineers, but there are also a growing number of unskilled persons fleeing to the Western world from unbearable living conditions at home. This comes in addition to increasing numbers of international asylum seekers, refugees and displaced persons.

Cultural globalisation is an effect of globalisation, particularly in the Information and Communication Technology (ICT) field, but is also an important cause of further globalisation. The means of cultural transmission and reception are diffusing around the globe in the shape of TV, radio, satellite communications, mobile telephony and the internet. Many national media markets feature a degree of foreign ownership and control. This runs in parallel with a globalisation of content, from football and music to films and news, which has, if anything, developed even faster than the mediums themselves. Like so many other aspects of globalisation this is a double-edged sword: it helps create cultural trends which become truly global, whilst presenting new channels for the spread of alternative cultural messages (including anti-globalisation platforms). So far, the threat has been primarily to closed societies of the totalitarian or authoritarian kind (whether communist, fundamentalist or military regimes). The extent to which globalisation can be perceived as a threat to national cultures is hotly debated in many liberal democracies.

In the same way as culture, environmental problems can be seen both as a driver behind and a consequence of globalisation. Free trade has exacerbated some environmental problems, but others can arguably only be addressed at the international or global level. For example, increased global warming and ozone depletion is partly as a result of the increased transportation required for free movement of goods and persons. On the other hand there has also been a large increase in international environmental laws, treaties and regimes.

Compared to the previous waves of globalisation, the current pattern includes five features which are new or have not been fully developed before. The first is the somewhat unique international situation brought about by the end of the Cold War, which Fukuyama (1992) hailed as the *End of History*. Fukuyama's central point was the end of the ideological struggle between liberal democracy and its authoritarian rivals, and the near-universal acceptance of the ideals of democracy and markets. For the first time since the modern state system emerged in the seventeenth century, the major states are not locked in ideological contest. The collapse of communism in Eastern Europe and the USSR, coupled with China's market-oriented reforms, promoted the extension of Western liberal capitalist institutions towards a global reach. Existing international institutions such as GATT (the General Agreement on Tariffs and Trade) developed further and wider, to become the World Trade Organisation – and with a potentially global membership. New international institutions have been established, again with a potentially global reach, whether to ban landmines or combat climate change. Some, including the WTO, have been strengthened and take on what could be termed supranational features such as binding judiciary rulings.

Second, the present wave of globalisation has been characterised by a global development towards deregulation and limits to public monopoly provision of public services. This trend can be found across the world, but is particularly prevalent in the English-speaking democracies and the European Union. The processes of privatisation, liberalisation and introduction of competition between private and public suppliers of public services are analysed in the later chapters of this book. At this juncture it is sufficient to note that the establishment of markets and competition in sectors previously dominated by monopolies has led to more demand for regulation at the national, regional and international level. The liberalisation of national markets tends to attract competition not only among national companies, but also from foreign firms. Although liberalisation is often followed by the privatisation (fully or partial) of the former state-owned monopolies, they may face competition from foreign companies which enjoy a monopoly position in their own home markets. The possibilities of market regulation and the establishment of strong regulatory institutions at the global level is limited by the need to get agreement among all countries involved. The EU is perhaps the most successful regional regulatory institution, with both regional and national regulatory institutions and rules in place. As we will see in Chapter 2, this is partly because of its provisions for majority decision-making, an independent judiciary and the European Commission's ability to act as an independent agent.

Third, the technological dimension is stronger in this wave of globalisation than in the previous one. The basic technology that has made rapid economic integration possible in the current wave of globalisation is the digital revolution, which has led to dramatic improvements in telecommunications and the conversion of telecommunications, communication and information technology into an integrated ICT sector. The result has been a dramatic increase in capacity and in declining costs. This is perhaps the single most important reason for the strength of the current wave of globalisation. The information society or the new economy is characterised by its truly global reach; it favours the intangible (ideas, information and relationships), has interlinked network economies and tends towards mediating technologies. The essence is that the more plentiful or widely available things become, the more valuable they are – in stark contrast to the business logic at work in other industries. The sector is dominated by a vast array of players, rather than a few conglomerates: the customers (subscribers) are empowered by the breadth of choice available, and industry actors include the IT companies (hardware, software), telecommunications and information industry, network providers (electricity, cable, satellite etc.), other network industries (bank, insurance, travel agencies, airlines etc.) and content providers (publishers, media, entertainment industry). Again the effect is double-edged: on one hand are the new jobs, growing markets, new strategies for firms and governments (eCommerce, eBusiness, eGovernment); increase in the quality of life (more convenience, better services, better access); increase in the quality of work-life (convenience, increased job flexibility, hi-tech work environment); and improved education (eLearning). On the other hand there is the emergence of the 'digital divide' at international and intra-national levels. All these developments present serious challenges for national governments, regional and global political institutions.

Fourth, financial globalisation represents another important factor behind the current globalisation process. To some extent financial globalisation can be seen as the result of the core globalisation process itself: of free trade. At the same time it is a forceful engine for future expansion of the global economy. We already have a world where currencies and financial instruments can be traded globally with few, if any, restrictions on currencies, and fewer and fewer restrictions on financial instruments (at least for companies). The EU has substantially deepened the free trade regimes in goods by creating a truly single market and in financial services by the establishment of a free market that is gradually being extended to individuals.

Fifth and finally, the development of global companies represents something more than the creation of international or transnational companies. Previous forms of international activity centred on expansion of companies through export, foreign establishment and production and, eventually, international mergers and acquisitions. The present wave of globalisation has seen the creation of truly global companies, as a result of mergers of large companies from two or three continents. These companies do not have a single home country but act on a truly global basis. This move towards a limited number of large actors can be found across a range of industries. In some cases a single operator dominates, as Microsoft does for computer operating systems, or a few players dominate the global market, as in the armaments and settlement industries. This tendency creates severe problems in terms of political control of the companies, and their market behaviour. There is no global competition authority comparable to those which exist at the national and EU levels. Therefore, the only way to gain a degree of control over the behaviour of these firms is through some kind of cooperation among the competition authorities in the biggest economies, in effect the USA and the EU. Global companies also create other challenges for governance linked to, for example, public policy aspects from environment to tax payment.

The Institutions of Globalisation: From GATT to WTO

The global trade regime was developed in the years following the Second World War by the establishment of the General Agreement on Trade and Tariffs (GATT). The GATT was based on a few simple procedures and rules designed to promote the idea that if someone in one country can produce something that people in another country want to buy, they should have the right to sell it to them. This heralded the beginning of a global trade system based on rules and regulations that seek to promote economic exchange between countries, despite the temptations for or pressure brought to bear on national governments to protect their own industries. GATT was one of the three institutions established by the Bretton Woods conference in 1944, alongside the World Bank and the International Monetary Fund (IMF). However, at this point the establishment of a proper International Trade Organisation failed, largely due to resistance in the US Congress. Only in 1995 was the World Trade Organisation (WTO) established, based on the GATT. GATT was not originally intended to function as an organisation, but due to the lack of other instruments, the need for a structure and the rapid development of global trade it ended up serving as the world's 'trade organisation' for nearly half a century.

The basic principle of GATT and the WTO is the prohibition of discrimination, in the form of the most-favoured-nation (MFN) principle. This holds that any advantages, such as lower tariffs, that a state grants to one other state must be extended to all states that enjoy MFN-status. When a foreign product has entered a country and all duties are paid, it should be treated on a par with local products. The rules also stipulate that all other quantitative and non-tariff barriers to trade are prohibited – although this principle is often violated in practice. The anti-dumping rules make it illegal to sell a product in another country for a lower price than the cost of production in the home country. In general, the GATT favoured continuous liberalisation of global trade as well as transparent and predictable trade rules. The GATT also contained weak dispute settlement procedures.

Uruguay Round and the WTO

The GATT system was established to promote a process of gradually removing restrictions on trade. Its success came slowly over several rounds of trade negotiations, from 1947 until the Uruguay Round started in 1986. Thus far, GATT had focused almost exclusively on goods (including some agricultural products), even though services grew to make up a substantial part of world trade. The Uruguay Round changed this. It covered almost all aspects of trade in goods, including both tariffs and non-tariff barriers, and ranged from natural resources to textiles and agriculture, and from anti-dumping measures to subsidies. It covered services, intellectual property and investment measures. It developed a dispute settlement mechanism, and eventually, the WTO. Negotiations took nearly seven years, and were only concluded at the end of 2003. This agreement represented a substantial shift in the framework of international trade. The establishment of the WTO was of great symbolic value, but it also made international trade liberalisation work better. The total system of trade rules and regulations was made more coherent and comprehensive. Special trade policy reviews for the member countries were established. The developing countries were fully integrated into the world trade negotiation system for the first time, even if they still complained that their influence was limited. At the same time the dispute settlement procedures were considerably strengthened and have, to a very large extent, been respected by the parties involved in various dispute settlement cases which have arisen since this time.

With regard to goods, the Uruguay Round meant further (binding) reductions in tariffs, close to zero for most products. The average tariff on industrial goods among developed countries was reduced to less than five percent

(Winham 2005: 103). In agriculture, a fairer global market for farm products was established and import restrictions shifted from quotas to tariffs. Agricultural tariffs were to be reduced further in subsequent trade rounds. However, many developing countries complained that the basic global trade regime was not substantially changed during this round and they would like to see real changes in their favour in the next trade round. This is set to remain the central issue after the Doha Round. For textiles, the Uruguay Round represented the end to quotas and finally created a full market opening in the Western countries, which in turn promoted strong complaints from affected interest groups in the USA and the EU.

The inclusion of services in the world trade regime was perhaps the most important result of the Uruguay Round in terms of content. The new General Agreement on Trade in Services (GATS) in principle covers all types of services. The MFN principle is applied through mutual commitments between countries for different sectors. These arrangements were difficult to get into place, and the GATS negotiations resumed after the Uruguay Round had been completed. Telecom negotiations were finally concluded after the EU agreed their own internal telecommunications liberalisation package in February 1997, and financial services in late 1997. Negotiations over maritime services were suspended because of disagreement between the USA and the EU.

The second important new element in the Uruguay Round was the inclusion of intellectual property protection and enforcement (copyright, trademarks, geographical indications, industrial designs, patents, lay-out designs of integrated circuits, undisclosed information-trade secrets etc.). In a world of digitalisation and globalisation of information this would be a cornerstone in safeguarding payment for digital content. Enforcement has, however, turned out to be a very challenging problem.

A third important element was the full inclusion into the agreement and the employment of basic WTO rules of tariffs instead of quotas in the agricultural sector. Up until the Uruguay Round there had been few serious attempts on agricultural liberalisation and even in this round – hailed as the breakthrough of liberalisation in trade with agricultural products – not much was gained regarding, for example, export subsidies which was, and is, of critical importance for the developing countries. This was one of the reasons for the strong stand of these countries to actually receive some fundamental concessions in the next round of trade negotiations.

The WTO is a consensus-based organisation which has proved successful in managing the global trade regime after the conclusion of the Uruguay Round. The work is carried out in committees, and supported by a small secretariat. The trade policy reviews, the use of the dispute settlement mechanism and the preparation for new trade rounds have been the most important activities in the last decade. However, the start of the new Doha Round demonstrated the seriousness of the conflicts facing the WTO – between the EU and the USA, and between these two players and the developing countries – and it illustrated the difficulties involved in making progress in a consensus-based organisation.

The meeting in Doha in November 2001 was the second attempt to start this round, and two years after the formal deadline in December 2004 a comprehensive deal had yet to be agreed. The most difficult issue is agriculture. The developing countries argue that they did not get what they were promised in the Uruguay Round, and this time they are demanding substantial concessions from the rich countries on this issue. The EU and the USA cannot agree on their offer, and thus the negotiations continue. One of the most important effects of the lack of progress in the multilateral negotiations has been the rapid growth of bilateral and multilateral Free Trade Agreements (FTA), both between countries and between regional organisations. This creates a very fragmented global trade pattern, and is hardly supportive of the basic idea of common and equal treatment of all trading partners in the world.

The Effects of Globalisation at the National and Regional Level

The need for FTAs and other intra- and inter-regional trade arrangements is spurred by the rapid globalisation process. The different countries and regions of the world need to protect themselves against some of the negative effects of the globalisation process and to exploit the benefits of free trade further, at least among their most important trading partners. This section of the chapter turns to the types of effects globalisation has on the state; and the next section turns to the link between globalisation and regional integration.

The state level

Globalisation affects states in several ways. First, it makes it difficult to isolate or insulate national politics, governance and authority from the international scene. The input into national policy-making is increasingly linked to or driven by global or regional political and economic organisations such as the WTO and the EU, or is derived from ideologies and events at these supranational levels. A proliferation of international and transnational regulatory regimes is taking place, and regulatory decisions often involve interaction between different levels of government. At the same time, a decision in one country is likely to have direct implications for other countries. This makes the analysis and understanding of public sector management in one individual country much more challenging.

Second, globalisation affects not only the decision-making processes at the national level; it also has a direct effect on policy content. Most sectors in most states, from labour market regulation and welfare state policy to international competitiveness and de-industrialisation. Globalisation may restrict the policy options available to any given state government, whether through formal agreements or the effects of increased trade. Globalisation alters the allocation of resources, and may generate pressure on national labour markets and even unemployment in some sectors. It can also increase the pressure on nation states to reduce welfare costs because of problems with footing the bill for the changes in the labour market, or alternatively to use an increased proportion of GDP for welfare expenditure. On the other hand, many countries, particularly developing economies, experience increased competition for highly demanded competencies, such as medical doctors. This in turn generates pressure for more international cooperation, for example, in the form of demands for international regulation on labour standards (in the EU, and perhaps in the future within the WTO). Proposals have been put forward in many industrial countries for taxes or import duties to compensate for the low welfare costs in developing countries, or measures to restrict trade with countries with less strict labour market regulation.

Third, globalisation has a direct impact on business and industry at the national level. Global companies account for a steadily increasing proportion of the world economy, and to some extent they operate beyond the control of any single national government – even in their home country. These huge companies make decisions which directly influence the policies of the nation states and national economic policy. These decisions also increase global competition, and thus have an even broader impact on the confidence in national companies and labour market stability. All in all this raises questions about the role of foreign direct investment and multinational companies in determining or shaping national economic performance, and about the future balance between corporate and state power. States have perhaps always had difficulties in dealing with genuinely global problems, but today these problems are more challenging than ever.

Regional integration

The processes of globalisation and regional integration are closely interrelated. Regional integration can be seen both as a consequence of and a response to globalisation. Regional integration encourages intensive trade and investment relations among the members of a regional trading bloc or organisation. Although regional organisations primarily benefit their own members, and discriminate in their favour, they can be accepted by the WTO as long as they liberalise further than the WTO rules require and follow certain procedures laid down by the WTO. The aim is usually to strengthen regional efficiency and competitiveness (on a global scale), and economic growth in the region, but they also tend to contribute to global trade liberalisation in the long term by developing an advanced area of free trade that can form the basis for more global regimes at a later stage.

There are some 200 regional organisations or trade agreements in the world, and most if not all members of the WTO are members of one or more of these. They range from loose groupings of a handful of states that come together in free trade associations such as the European Free Trade Association (EFTA), to the European Union, the world's most developed and advanced regional organisation. Most are accepted as compatible with WTO rules, though some 70 (out of the 200) have yet to be recognised by the WTO. The EU is the only regional organisation which is itself a member of the WTO: in WTO negotiations the European Commission negotiates on behalf of the EU member states. The words regionalism, regional integration and regional organisations are often used interchangeably. Regionalism could be understood as a formal process of intergovernmental collaboration between two or more states. For most of the post-war period the term regional economic integration was used to cover cases of three or more states cooperating. However, recently the number of bilateral agreements, often between states in different regions, has expanded dramatically. This is, at least partly, a response to the slow progress towards global trade liberalisation. Insofar as it can become an alternative to global trade deals, these developments can be seen as a threat to global free trade. Such bilateral free trade arrangements also have to be accepted by the WTO. In addition we find there are a growing number of interregional trade regimes like Asia-Pacific Economic Cooperation (APEC) and ASEM between Asian countries and the EU. As it stands, more than half the world's trade is covered by regional or bilateral trade agreements.

Regional organisations are established for both political and economic reasons; often primarily for political rather than economic reasons (Ravenhill 2005: 120). The classic case is the European Coal and Steel Community (ECSC), which formed the basis for the European Economic Community/The European Union. Security concerns were prominent among the original motives for the establishment of the ECSC, which established supranational control of resources that were central to the state's military capacities and in turn bound France and West Germany closely together. In South East Asia the ASEAN was established partly with political motives, to strengthen these links between the member states against the threat of communism. However, economic arguments necessarily lie at the centre of most regional organisations. These arguments come in two principal forms. First of all, regional integration can be developed in order to deepen the global free trade regime, as is the case with most free trade agreements. Second, it can be used as a mechanism to protect its members against the negative (or feared) effects of global free trade.

Regional agreements come in a range of shapes and forms, from simple agreements on trade cooperation, through more comprehensive free trade areas, to customs unions, common markets and fully fledged economic unions. Common market regimes, such as the EEC, often develop through the other stages: from free trade to customs union to common market. The more advanced the trade cooperation and the more areas of economic activity covered, the greater the need for intergovernmental or supranational governing structures. This has proven exceptionally difficult to achieve in most cases, and the EU is the only organisation that comes close to advanced market integration (as of course does, to some extent, the EEA, the EU's agreement with the three EFTA states of Norway, Iceland and Lichtenstein). Governments are normally reluctant to give authority to supranational institutions.

The changing role of the state, and the politicisation of globalisation

Given the increased role of global and regional organisations, what then is the role of the state and the distribution of power between the national, regional and global level in different aspects of public sector activity? In the twentieth century the state was the primary regulator of the (national) economic system. Today the national economic system is regulated in a multi-layered political and economic system. The nation state has seen its sovereignty reduced. There is greater economic and political interdependence, both at the global and regional level. This holds particularly true in Europe, where the development of the Internal Market and European Monetary Union has been combined with substantially increased regional cooperation in nearly all fields where the state plays a role (with the exception of religion!).

What, then, is the role of the state today generally in the world, and especially in Europe? First of all, the states are resilient. There are still large national variations in business practices. In the foreseeable future, these differences will continue to influence the role and functioning of businesses. The state also remains an important regulator of economic activity, even if the EU member states increasingly share this role with the EU-level institutions. Several states have also sought to fight back and try to regain some control over economic activity and business development. Some countries are perhaps better equipped to fight globalisation tendencies than others, due to their size or at least the size of their domestic market (e.g. the USA), their cultural identity (e.g. Iceland or Israel), their control over important resources (Russia) or due to membership in strong regional organisations such as the EU.

Second, there are a number of political movements that seek to limit or reverse globalisation and/or regional integration. Some oppose international arrangements on principle. A number of parties and organisations reject existing efforts at international cooperation because they regard them as fundamentally flawed. Some of these organisations, and often their sections that are linked to interest groups, also oppose such agreements because they run counter to their economic interest. Organisations like *Attac*, and the coalitions of anti-globalisation groups seek (sometimes with considerable success) to disrupt G8, WTO and EU meetings, and tend to take a principled stand against globalisation, often combined with criticism of the (international) capitalist system. They therefore also oppose most existing forms of regional cooperation. Others, including a number of new left parties in Europe, oppose or criticise both the EU and international organisations because they see them as flawed, although they are open to international (and even supranational) cooperation in principle. Over the last two decades, globalisation has become increasingly politicised, in the sense that it has become politically contested.

Opposition to globalisation and regional integration also has a nationalist dimension. Across the political spectrum, from the far left, through the centre and to the political right, several organisations and political parties take the view that democracy can only operate properly in the framework of the nation state, and that supranational democracy is a contradiction in terms. In this view, international cooperation ought only to be inter-governmental: each decision should require the agreement of each and every government involved and not to be subject to binding rulings by international courts. Most of these groups and movements have had only limited influence, and have largely been reduced to opposing and occasionally halting or postponing international agreement. Inasmuch as they draw support from disparate groups, united only in what they oppose rather than presenting an alternative, their influence is set to remain limited. The more influential groups have been those that oppose specific deals on the grounds that they threaten the groups' economic interests. Farmers in the original EU member states oppose reform of the Common Agricultural Policy, whilst Norwegian farmers oppose EU membership. Public sector unions across the EU regularly speak out or demonstrate against further liberalisation, and French unions played a considerable role in limiting the directives on energy liberalisation in the 1990s. In the last two decades, broad campaign movements have succeeded in mobilising voters in referendums and defeating governments' efforts to engage in closer European integration not only in Switzerland and Norway, but in several other EU member states including Denmark, Ireland, Sweden, France and Germany.

Although the globalisation process may seem irreversible, or at least very difficult to reverse, the resilience of the state and the emerging political opposition to globalisation indicates that it is not an unstoppable process with inevitable consequences. States not only retain control of important aspects of their economies, but they also maintain their differences in business practice. Political opposition to globalisation is limited, but it has proven sufficient to derail individual deals and prevent some countries from joining certain international organisations.

Nation States, the EU and Global Governance

This chapter has focused on how globalisation is changing the total framework of modern public management in nation states all over the world. Globalisation is an evolving process, and the last two decades may merely be the start of the substantial development of a more radical process which changes the environment in which the nation states operate. The changes discussed in this chapter have been driven by both politics and technological change. The most important technological driver behind globalisation is digitalisation and the development of the information society, and the most important political driver is the belief held by most politicians in the world that increased trade liberalisation spurs more rapid economic growth. However, an important caveat is that globalisation has hardly been an even process – some parts of the world are considerably more 'global' than others. So far, the result has not so much been a 'globalised world', as a globalising international economic system. In several ways globalisation – and regional economic integration – represents a reduced and changing role of the state, and new public management is one type of state response to this process.

What are the possible developments in the future of the globalisation process? The present situation suggests that truly global companies are emerging (through mergers and acquisitions) in several important industries. Regional, inter-regional and global political and economic cooperation is necessary to regulate these companies and industries. The present trajectory is towards full liberalisation of world markets for goods and financial services, which in turn is likely to create further externalities and increase some of the burdens on the nation states as they seek to compensate for some of the effects of globalisation. One answer to this challenge is, of course, stronger global economic and regulatory regimes, but as the GATT/WTO story demonstrates, building world-wide international organisations tends to be a very gradual process. The rapid increase in the burdens on the national political systems and the need for better national public sector governance and public management has therefore promoted states to look to other, complementary, initiatives.

The most successful alternative to global organisations has been regional cooperation (and subsequently, inter-regional arrangements). The winners in the globalisation process and quest for better capacity for governance have been the well-developed regional organisations and their member states; the losers have been the smaller, poorer and more peripheral regions and states. One key player in the global and inter-regional game is the European Union. The EU is especially interesting because of its role as a model for regional integration and possible relationship between nations, regions and the global economic and political system. It is also interesting as a unique case for studying the effects of an advanced level of regional response to global politics on the management of public sector at the state level. The next chapter therefore turns to the European Union.

Further Reading

Dicken, P. (2007) *Global Shift: Mapping the Contours of the World Economy,* 5th edition (London: Sage Publications). An excellent analysis of globalisation and liberalisation as it explores the changing world economy. Particularly useful is Part Three, 'The picture in different sectors', as it outlines the process of industrial change world-wide in various industries. Moreover, drawing upon the theoretical foundation presented in Parts One and Two this book makes the complexity of globalisation easier to grasp.

Baylis, J. and Smith, S. (2005) *The Globalization of World Politics* (Oxford: Oxford University Press). A comprehensive textbook in the field of international relations which covers everything you need to know at an introductory level. Of particular interest are Chapters 7–12 which provide excellent overviews of theories to international relations and Part Four, 'International Issues', which covers topics such as European integration and regional cooperation, and Global trade and finance.

Ravenhill, J. (2005) *Global Political Economy* (Oxford: Oxford University Press). A readable textbook with an emphasis on contemporary issues and theoretical approaches to the field. A supplement to this chapter could be Chapter 4, 'The evolution of global trade regime', which provides an overview of the development of WTO, and also Chapter 5, 'Regionalism', as it discusses the economic consequences of regionalism.

Held, D., McGrew, A., Goldblatt, D. and Perraton, J. (1999) *Global Transformations: Politics, Economics and Culture* (Stanford: Stanford University Press). A fact-packed textbook dedicated to the topic of globalisation. Chapter 3, 'Global Trade, Global Markets', provides a good overview of the development and progress of global markets from the late eighteenth century up until today.

TWO

European Integration – Recapturing Sovereignty and Institutionalising Liberalisation

For most political and economic actors, European integration is a double-edged sword; at the same time a challenge and an opportunity. National policy-makers sometimes see the EU as a threat, but it can also be a source of protection. This duality dates back to the establishment of the European Union institutions in the 1950s, in the form of the European Coal and Steel Community, Euratom and the European Economic Community. These organisations were established partly to 'rescue the nation state' in Europe (Milward 1984, 1992) after two world wars, and partly to bind the West European states together and institutionalise interdependence (Haas 1958), thus preventing future wars. On one hand, the economic and political institutions that were established in Western Europe after the Second World War limited the formal sovereignty of their member states. On the other, membership increased the states' abilities to achieve objectives through joint action. It has therefore been common to talk of the EU states agreeing to place some limits on their legal sovereignty in order to increase effective sovereignty, or of 'pooling' sovereignty. This dual character of the EU has only been strengthened since the end of the Cold War, with increased globalisation. The EU can be seen as one of the drivers behind globalisation, but at the same time it is also as a bulwark against globalisation's more extreme effects on each member state. In either guise, the EU has profoundly affected the public policy of its member states.

With the establishment of the Single Market in the early 1990s, there are now few areas of public policy that are not touched by EU law. This is not only because the Single Market bans barriers to the free flow of goods, services, capital and labour within the EU. The EU has also expanded to cover a series of policy areas from health and safety at work to environment policy. The Single Market took a 'public turn' in the 1990s, and now covers much of the public sector. In addition, the effects of EU membership are increasingly felt at the regional and local level, and this development is reflected in the increase in the number of local governments represented in Brussels – from a handful in the 1980s to more than 300 today. Since the 1960s, EU law has been superior to national law, and it has a direct effect in the member states. Areas that were once thought exempt from EU law, from recycling of beer bottles to women-only university appointments, have been subject to rulings from the European Court of Justice. New legislation in the member states can be problematic if it is formulated in ways that contravene EU rules, even when the goals are not in direct conflict. This has generated considerable debate among academics and practitioners as to whether there is an ongoing process of 'Europeanisation' of member state public policy, as well as what 'Europeanisation' means and how far it actually extends.

The European Union constitutes both a constraint on, and a source of, member state public policy. If Europeanisation is defined as the member states' adaptation to European integration, all West European states have undergone a high degree of Europeanisation of public policy. The member states share a common set of rules, organisations and to some extent even goals, even if there is still much room for national variation. Today the vast majority of public policy initiatives in the member states are based on EU decisions or linked in one way or another to EU initiatives. This chapter first provides an introduction to and an overview of the EU as a political system, before it turns to the question of the impact of European integration on public policy in the member states. The first section explores the nature of the EU as a political system, and assesses rival claims about the principal drivers behind European integration. The second section provides an overview of the central EU institutions and the policy process, from agenda setting through the legislative process to implementation and supervision. The third section turns to the EU's core policy areas, and the fourth returns to the impact of European integration on national public governance and the extent to which the EU shapes public policy in Europe.

Understanding the Political System of the European Union

The roots of the European institutions lie in a very specific context: the challenges that the West European states faced after the Second World War. This included not only post-war rebuilding, but also promoting liberal democracy and securing peace among the former combatants, not least by tying West Germany into a supranational system. This helps explain why such robust institutions were established. Upon its establishment in 1951, the European Coal and Steel Community (ECSC) represented more than a deal to establish a common market for coal and steel; it also subjected vital war materials to supranational control and addressed French concerns about German industrial strength (Milward 1984). The High Authority, the executive body of the ECSC, on which the Commission of the EEC was later modelled, was therefore a far stronger and more supranational organisation than any other international body at the time. Yet it was balanced by the Council of Ministers, where the governments of the six member states were represented, which made the final decisions about legislation. An Assembly provided representation from the six national parliaments, but it had limited powers. This set-up was very much a compromise between the two main strategies for re-building Europe: on one hand cooperation above and beyond the direct control of the states, and on the other, state control of the new organisations. The same design was used for Euratom and the EEC, and the compromise remains at the core of the EU political system today.

The principal theoretical debate about the nature of the EU reflects these political divisions of the 1950s. It divides those who regard the EU primarily as an organisation designed and operated by the member states from those who argue that the system is shaped by a wider set of forces. Although the ECSC, Euratom and the EEC were the result of compromises, these organisations reflected the argument that economic ('functional') cooperation might gradually expand and tie the states together in what Mitrany called a 'working peace system' (Mitrany 1946). *Neo-functionalists* Haas (1958) and Lindberg (1963) went on to argue that the tasks assigned to the EEC were 'inherently expansive'; that solving one task or problem would often put new tasks on the agenda. This kind of 'functional spillover' was complemented by 'political spillover' whereby business and organised interests were expected to shift their focus, or even loyalties, to Brussels. The main rivals to the neo-functionalist accounts of integration held that the states dominated the integration process. *Realist* scholars had long argued that states should be understood as unitary actors that pursue economic and security interests in an anarchic world, and that the states are the key actors on the international scene. Stanley Hoffmann (1966) thus argued that there were clear limits beyond which European integration was unlikely to proceed. States might agree to cooperate on 'low politics' such as trade, always in pursuit of their long-term interests, but would remain sovereign when it came to more important 'high politics' questions such as defence or taxation. By the mid-1990s, three distinct models of EU politics had emerged from this debate about integration theory.

First, the most straightforward approach to understanding European integration is to start from the realist assumption that states design international organisations in order to pursue or protect their interests, and that the EU is basically a normal international organisation (albeit a very well-developed one). In *intergovernmental* models, states can be understood as rational principals that establish agents to carry out activities on their behalf, but sometimes struggle to control these agents (Pollack 1997). There is a number of reasons that a group of sovereign states might want to grant powers to a supranational agent, and agree to comply with its rulings. They might establish an agent with powers to enforce agreements, oversee compliance and deal with problems of incomplete contracting; or even to secure long-term policy consistency. This casts European integration as a relatively unthreatening project as far as member state sovereignty is concerned. It also has clear implications in terms of identifying the central actors and the manner in which public policy is made: decisions reflect the interest of the member states, and particularly the larger and more powerful states. The main focus is therefore on the Council of Ministers, and how national governments pursue fixed and well-defined preferences. Hard bargaining and negotiation is the key to understanding EU legislation. The power of the Commission and the European Court of Justice is limited, because the states ultimately have the power to change the institutional set-up. However, treaty negotiations and ratification processes in the 1980s and 1990s demonstrated that state interests are hardly fixed. Consequently, some state-driven analyses were refined to take account of how domestic politics shapes states' interests (Putnam 1988, Moravcsik 1991, 1999, Tsebelis 1994), and Moravcsik coined the term 'liberal intergovernmentalism', where the adjective 'liberal' signifies that the domestic dimension is included.

Second, many scholars have argued that the European organisations represent something new and unique, or *sui generis*. Although several prominent neo-functionalists revisited their work when European integration seemed to stall in the 1970s (Haas 1975), the Single European Act in 1987 revived the debate again (George 1985, Taylor 1991, Tranholm-Mikkelsen 1991). Drawing on both neo-functionalism and comparative politics, several models were put forward that emphasised the EU's unique character (Marks, Scharpf et al., Schmitter and Streeck 1996, Sandholtz and Stone Sweet 1998). Perhaps the most influential concept has been multi-level governance: analysis of the EU as a political system where the supranational, national and sub-national levels are interlocked (Marks et al. 1996). Wessels (1997) presented this as a matter of the states being fused with the EU system. In many of these analyses the focus is as much on ideas and norms as on states' rational pursuit of fixed interests. Constructivists emphasise the importance of ideas in defining a common understanding of reality (Christiansen et al. 1999, Checkel 1999): actors can and do shape each others' preferences, and discourse itself can be seen as an instrument of policy-making (Rosamond 2000). The EU is seen as a system of 'polycentric governance': 'a unique attempt to regain the action potential of the state which has been lost in the course of the internationalisation of functional systems' (Jachtenfuchs 1995: 129–30). The key to understanding policy developments and new legislation is ideas, norms and organisational culture, rather than rational actors' pursuit of fixed and immutable interests, and the Commission's leadership role is therefore more important than in intergovernmental models (Cram 1997, Héritier 1999).

Third, from the late 1970s onwards, much scholarly attention turned from integration to policy-making, and several analyses came to treat the EU as a state-like political system that can be compared to other political systems (Wallace et al. 1977, 1983, Sbragia 1992, Andersen and Eliassen 1993, Bulmer 1993, Hix 1994, Richardson 1996). The EU is both *pluralist* and *plural*: pluralist because a larger number of actors influence decision-making, and plural because it is made up of member states with very different cultures, political traditions and administrative systems. The comparative politics literature on the EU has developed into several strands, which reflect different approaches to the study of public policy (Hix 1998, Bulmer 1998). On one hand, a series of rational choice models have been developed, many of which draw on studies of US politics and formal models of decision-making (Tsebelis 1994, Garrett and Tsebelis 1996, 2000). Here the central focus is on how the combination of actors' preferences and the rules of the game (institutions) shape policy outcomes, but there is little agreement on whether the states remain in control of EU policy-making or not. Other strands have drawn on the *new institutionalist* turn in political science (March and Olsen 1989), for example, analysing the EU as a regulatory regime (Majone 1994, McGowan and Wallace 1996). Pierson (1996) argued that the combination of consensual politics and the states' short time horizons (as governments tend to focus on the next election) allow the other actors considerable freedom, which in turn means that the EU institutions develop beyond the states' control.

To be sure, each of the three approaches presented here overlap to some extent. They are not fully separate, incompatible models, but rather ways of understanding the EU. It is often suggested that different models are appropriate for the study of different aspects of EU politics. Taylor (1991) argued that different theories explain the pressure for and resistance against further integration; Keohane and Hoffman (1991) argued that the EU should be understood as an international organisation when studying treaty-making, but as a political system when the objective is policy analysis; and Richardson (1996) argued that different stages of the policy process warrant different theories. Because the present volume focuses on public policy and administration, the approach to the study of the European Union taken here is very much based on understanding the EU as a political system. The central focus is on the roles that the institutions and actors of the EU play in policy-making, and the evolution of the public policy agenda at the EU and national level, as well as the effects on public policy and administration in Europe as such. The next section turns to the institutions of the EU, and provides a brief introduction to who does what in the EU.

The Principal Institutions of the European Union

The Single European Act (SEA), which came into force in July 1987, inaugurated two decades of treaty changes that have altered the EU's political set-up considerably. Before the SEA, the policy process reflected the one established with the ECSC treaty, which could be summed up succinctly: the Commission proposes, the European Parliament advises, and the Council of Ministers decides. The member states were in full control over the legislative process. The European Parliament's (EP) legislative powers were limited to issuing an opinion under the *consultation procedure*, although withholding its opinion constituted a weapon of delay. The SEA introduced the *co-operation procedure*, a two-reading legislative procedure that grants parliament the right to adopt amendments (subject to Commission approval), and provides the EP with limited veto power: its amendments required support from the Commission, and could only be overruled if all member states agreed in the Council. The Maastricht treaty, which entered into force in November 1993, elevated the EP to something like the status of a second legislative chamber for most Single Market legislation, as it introduced the new, three-reading, *co-decision procedure* that grants the EP a veto and nearly-equal status to the Council. The treaty also extended the use of the cooperation procedure beyond Single Market legislation. The Amsterdam treaty of 1997 (which entered into force in May 1999) made adjustments to the *co-decision procedure* and applied it to further policy areas, which removed the last imbalances between the EP and the Council. On the other hand the European Parliament is unlikely ever to get the final legislative power of the kind we see in the member states. There is no desire among the member states to turn the EU into a fully fledged confederal (let alone federal) state in the foreseeable future. The 2001 Nice treaty (which entered into force in February 2003) modified decision-making rules further, primarily to cope with eastern enlargement, as a stop-gap until the next treaty. However, the Constitutional Treaty, which included further adjustments, was rejected in referendums in France and the Netherlands in 2005. A replacement paired-down Reform Treaty was being negotiated at the time of writing, in 2007. The result has been that, within the EC pillar (and even to some extent with respect to the Area of Freedom Security and Justice; but not in Common Foreign and Security Policy), the EU now operates somewhat like a confederal bi-cameral system: the Commission proposes new legislation and the Council and Parliament jointly decide.

The European Commission

The Commission of the European Communities fulfils three roles that are often held by different institutions in national police systems. First, it plays a political role as the executive government of the EU. This part is played by the College of Commissioners, which consists of one Commissioner appointed by each member sate and confirmed by the Parliament. This includes presenting proposals for legislation and defending (and amending) them before the Council and Parliament, as well as day-to-day management of the EU's finances and programmes, discretionary rule-making, supervision of implementation, and external representation of the EU. Second, the Commission fulfils a bureaucratic role, comparable to that of the civil service in the member states, which includes drawing up proposed legislation. This is carried out by the Commission's 37 (at the time of writing) Directorates General and Services. Third, and often more controversially, the Commission plays a regulatory role. Its Competition Directorate General has long been acting like an independent 'federal' agency, carrying out the EU's competition policy and playing the role of both police and prosecutor (McGowan and Wilks 1995, Gerber 1998). Only in the last few years has the Court begun to overrule some of the Commission's competition policy decisions (they are formally taken by a majority vote in the College of Commissioners). Beyond these three formal roles, the Commission is often seen as the guardian of the EU's legal framework and a key driving force behind pressure for further integration.

However, the Commission is in fact less cohesive than the picture that is painted in the classical model (Cram 1994, Ross 1995). Disputes between the various Directorates General (DGs) involved in a single proposal are not uncommon, particularly if the more independent Competition Directorate is opposed by DGs of more *dirigiste* leanings (Nugent 1997). For example, energy policy directly involves not only liberalisation (DG Competition, DG Internal Market), but also security of supply (DG Energy) and environment protection (DG Environment). Particularly in cases that centre on the Single Market and liberalisation, the dividing line often runs between the more interventionist and more free market Commissioners (Christiansen 2006). Because the Commission's decisions are taken collectively, by majority vote in the College of Commissioners, the *Cabinets* that support each Commissioner carry out considerable policy coordination.

The Council of Ministers and the European Council

The Council of Ministers' formal role is legislative. When the European Community institutions were designed, the executive functions were assigned to the Commission, whereas the decision to adopt legislation was left to the representatives of the member state governments in the Council of Ministers.

In the early decades this meant the foreign ministers, but in the 1970s the Council changed to its current format of specialised functional Councils attended by the relevant ministers acting on behalf of the foreign ministers. It is supported by the Council Secretariat, a permanent organisation of EU-level civil servants; as well as by permanent and ad hoc committees and the member states' permanent representations to the EU in Brussels (which consist of member state civil servants). The Presidency rotates between the member states on a six-month basis, although the Reform Treaty is set to change this. Since the SEA, the Council's legislative role has increasingly been shared with the EP, at least within the EC pillar.

Beyond this formal role, the Council plays a central role in negotiating compromises and protecting the interests of the member states. Since the 1970s, the European Council, the regular summits of heads of state and government, have taken over part of the Commission's role in providing political leadership. Issues that cannot be resolved in the Council of Ministers are sometimes 'kicked upstairs' to the European Council, although the latter lacks any formal decision-making power. In the Council itself, consensus has tended to prevail over hard bargaining and confrontation. Despite the provision for majority voting, votes are rarely taken in the Council (though this may be changing now that the Council consists of 27 representatives). Most compromises are worked out at the lower levels in the Council. Discussion of legislative proposals first takes place in working groups, made up of experts from the member states (usually national civil servants). Some 85 percent of all decisions are agreed at this level, or in the Committee of Permanent Representatives (Coreper) (Hayes-Renshaw and Wallace 1997: 78). Divisions vary considerably across issues, and pit liberalisers against more interventionist governments, big countries against small, centre-left governments against centre-right, and increasingly also states that are net contributors to the EU budget against net recipients.

The European Parliament

If the Council is one part of the EU's bi-cameral legislature, the European Parliament has become its second, and almost equally powerful, chamber. Since it became directly elected in 1979, if not before, the European Parliament (EP) has certainly aspired to the role of the general representative body of the people of the EU. Like most parliaments, the EP has the 'power of the purse', or the power to reject the budget. However, its power to amend the budget is limited. On a few matters, such as enlargement of the European Union, its assent is required under the *Assent* procedure. On other EU legislation its power ranges from negligible (in the CFSP and some AFSJ matters), to limited or partial (under the *consultation* and *cooperation* procedures), to joint power with the

Council (under the revised *co-decision* procedure). Unlike many national parliaments, the EP's role as a supplier of personnel for the government and its role in holding the executive to account are rather limited. The Commissioners are appointed by national governments, not recruited from the EP. As for holding the Commission to account, the EP has formal powers to censure the Commission and has expanded its role in vetting incoming Commissioners. Most famously its threatened censure precipitated the resignation of the Jacques Santer Commission in March 1999. In 2004, the choice of Jose Manuel Barroso as Commission President was seen partly as a reflection of the centre-right's victory in the EP elections, and criticism levelled against the Italian appointee Commissioner caused the candidate's withdrawal and prompted Barroso to adjust the make-up of his College of Commissioners.

Because it is directly elected (by proportional electoral systems, in the member states, every five years) the EP is usually seen as the EU's main repository of democratic legitimacy. However, this does not mean that it is the same kind of arena for political competition as the member state parliaments. Although the federal parties at the EU-level have strengthened somewhat since direct elections were introduced three decades ago, the EP is still some way from voting along party lines. Research on roll-call voting (the votes for which it is recorded how MEPs vote), reveals that the parliament divides on 'more vs. less integration' lines as well as on left vs. right lines (Hix 1999). Moreover, MEPs from a party that is in power in the national capital may be reluctant to vote against a compromise that 'their' government has helped broker, even if their federal party colleagues in the EP oppose the policy. Consequently, although the EP has a track record of supporting liberalisation, this has been driven as much by some MEPs' general support for European integration or policies pursued by their government as by liberalisation per se. There is therefore a prospect that as the EP increasingly shifts from adopting new policies to adjusting existing ones, left vs. right politics may become more prominent (Gabel and Hix 2002).

The European Court of Justice

The European Court of Justice (ECJ) is perhaps the closest equivalent to its counterparts in the member states, particularly in federal states such as Germany. Like most constitutional courts, its central role is interpreting the 'constitution', or rather the Treaties. In the ECJ's case this includes interpreting the treaties, from ruling on the applicability of EU law, to the competences of the institutions or the legality of their actions. This may include ruling on conflicts over the appropriate Treaty base for Commission proposals, which in turn determines which decision-making processes apply or even whether the proposal is legal. For example, the UK took the Commission to Court over the

1993 directive on Working Time, arguing that the Commission had used the wrong treaty base and thus deprived the UK of a veto (the UK lost). Not only EU institutions and governments can initiate cases: individuals, organisations or firms may also bring action before the court. Judges are appointed by the Member States for six-year terms, and make their rulings by majority vote.

Although the Court is sometimes considered to be pro-integration, this does not by any means guarantee pro-integration judgements. Wincott's analysis concludes that it has played a considerable role in shaping the EU legal system and the balance of power in the policy-making process, but not in the development of substantive policies (1996). State-oriented theorists tend to focus on how reluctant the Court is to rule against the interest of big member states, arguing that it only does so when it is confident that the states will accept its rulings (Garrett 1995, Tsebelis and Garret 2000). Pluralist theorists, on the other hand, have argued that the Court has played a major role in driving forward integration, citing the cases that established the primacy of EC law and its direct effect, as well as the principle of mutual recognition (Burley and Mattli 1992); others suggest that its role has developed more in partnership with the member states and their courts (Weiler 1991).

The evolution of the EU's institutions and the relationship between them has brought the EU closer to the kind of political system that one finds in federal states. The Commission's political and civil service roles are clearly distinct, and the political role has been taken over to some extent by the European Council and the Presidency of the Council of Ministers, at least when it comes to broad political leadership. On the other hand, the Commission's role as an independent regulatory agency, its supervision of implementation of EU law and its execution of EU competition policy has strengthened continuously since the late 1960s. In effect, the Commission can be said to play the role of the executive to the Parliament and Councils' legislature. In this sense the EU has grown into the role as a regulatory state that is inherent in the treaties: a rule-making system of governance, as opposed to one based on direct intervention, public ownership and control or redistribution of resources. This is often seen as a shift in the driving and guiding force behind policy development in the member states, from politics to EU-based regulation. During the 1980s and 1990s this went together with a shift in public policy and administration in the member states. The 'regulatory state' is therefore not only an EU matter; it refers to the combination of developments at the EU and national level. The EU political system remains characterised by consensus, and expert policy communities play a strong role. With a few key exceptions, notably competition policy, implementation is generally left to the member states. Much of what the EU does is as much about regulating the national regulatory agencies, as about direct market regulation. The next section provides an overview of the EU's core policy areas, with a focus on the development of the EU as a regulatory state.

The Dynamics of European Integration – The Development of a Regulatory State in Europe

The EU is often described as a 'regulatory state', because its primary instruments for governance are legal regulations rather than direct intervention in the economy or redistribution of resources. Its political and economic system is centred on strong and independent supranational institutions: the Court and the Commission. The EU budget is limited, and this constrains the EU's ability to intervene in the economy through direct means such as subsidies, redistribution or government ownership of industry. Throughout its existence the EU has therefore primarily been concerned with rule-making. In the 1980s and 1990s this type of economic regime became better aligned with the member states' economic policy, because most of them embarked on programmes of public policy reform that involved considerable privatisation and liberalisation. Majone (1994, 1996, 1997) thus argues that the 1990s saw the development of a regulatory state in Europe, both in the individual West European states and at the EU level. In McGowan and Wallace's words (1996: 565): 'the treaties can be read as mapping out a particular economic blueprint, on which, it turned out, fitted the political and economic climate of the 1980s rather better than it had the 1950s'.

Once established, the EEC rapidly acquired its own dynamics of evolution. Yet the pattern has been uneven. The early 1960s saw the establishment of the primacy of EU law; the second half of the decade saw the states reassert their control of EU policy. A period of stagnation followed in the 1970s, before a raft of new initiatives was launched in the 1980s and 1990s. The main treaties and developments, and enlargement to new member states, are set out in Table 2.1. The EU's development has taken place unevenly, along three dimensions. First, the term *deepening* is commonly used to refer to more intense (deeper) integration. Deepening usually implies that the EU becomes a more supranational regime, but in a few cases deeper integration has also been combined with a stronger position for the states at the expense of the Commission. Second, over the decades the EU has not only deepened integration in existing sectors, but also *expanded its scope* or reach to cover new sectors. Third, the EU has admitted new member states, expanding from six to nine, 12, 15 and now 27 member states; a process commonly described as *widening*.

Deepening

The process of deepening has perhaps been the least linear of the three patterns. Early developments in the first decade conformed more or less to the predictions of neo-functionalist theories of integration: the supranational

Table 2.1 EU membership and competences, changes over time (Treaties are in bold type)

	Members	European Community	Foreign and defence policy	Police and justice policy
1951	Belgium, France, Germany, Italy, Luxembourg, the Netherlands	**ECSC** **Euratom** **The EEC**	Nato and WEU **Eur. Defence Community** (not ratified)	
1973	+ Denmark, Ireland, the UK		Ad hoc cooperation	Ad hoc cooperation
1981	+ Greece			
1986	+ Spain, Portugal	**Single European Act**	European Political Cooperation	Schengen
1995	+ Austria, Finland, Sweden	**Maastricht**	CFSP	JHA
		Amsterdam		Schengen in to the EU
		Nice	Most of the WEU in to the EU	
2004	+ Estonia, Latvia, Lithuania, Poland, Czech Republic, Slovakia, Hungary, Malta, Cyprus	**Constitutional Treaty** (not ratified)		
2007	+ Bulgaria, Romania	Agreement on **Reform Treaty**		

organisations pushed for deepening and extension of the EEC. In 1963 and 1964, European Court of Justice rulings established that EEC law has direct effect in the member states and the EEC law is superior to national laws. This effectively established the primacy of EEC law. However, the new organisation's first and most serious crisis came in 1965–6, when the French government reacted to a series of Commission proposals for reform by boycotting meetings of the Council of Ministers. This 'empty chair' crisis was brought about by several questions, but the most serious was the plan to increase the use of Qualified Majority Voting in the Council. In the end the resolution to the crisis included the 'Luxembourg compromise'; and agreement that the states would not outvote each other on matters of vital national importance.[1] Although this is sometimes seen as the member states putting the brakes on the integration process, the crisis actually left the member states somewhat more willing to pursue closer integration because they had established that they were firmly in control of the process (Taylor 1996: 17–20).

---

[1] This is the usual expression; in fact the actual term is 'very important national interests' (Hayes-Renshaw and Wallace 1997: 14).

During the 1970s the question of strengthening the EC's capacity for effective decision-making and governance was largely a matter of improving the state-dominated aspects of the EC machinery. After the 'empty chair' crisis the quest for consensus in the Council assumed a central role in EC decision-making. The Committee of Permanent Representatives (Coreper) became the central venue for negotiations. In 1974 the ad hoc meetings of heads of state and government were institutionalised in the form of the European Council. This further strengthened the states at the expense of the Commission. Yet the supranational institutions were also strengthened. In 1967 the EEC, Euratom and ECSC executives were merged into the Commission of the European Communities. By the end of the decade, in 1979, direct elections were introduced for the European Parliament, thus strengthening its claim to legitimacy and power. The Court's rulings strengthened the Commission's powers to vet mergers and made it difficult for states to use non-tariff barriers to protect their own producers. The most celebrated case is the 1979 *Cassis de Dijon* ruling, which effectively established the principle that a product sold in one country cannot be barred in another ('mutual recognition'). Some therefore consider the 1970s as the decade in which the Court's influence was at its peak (Weiler 1991, Burley and Mattli 1993).

The 1980s is often described as the most important decade in the development of the EU. The Single European Act sought both to deepen and to extend the scope of the EEC. In terms of deepening, the introduction of new decision-making procedures gave the parliament a stronger role in the policy process and opened the way for actual use of Qualified Majority Voting (QMV) in the Council. This altered the formal power of the institutions and radically changed actual policy-making, and provided the EP with considerable powers if and when it enjoyed the Commission's backing (Tsebelis 1994). The simple logic of the new *cooperation procedure* was that in order to adopt the 300 or so new directives that would be required to meet the 1992 deadline for establishing the Single European Market, the national veto in the Council of Ministers had to be set aside and QMV actually used. If this were to be the case, approval by the European Parliament would be required, to lend legitimacy to a directive adopted without the unqualified support of each and every member state. However, this relatively simple principle would soon be amended beyond recognition in the quest for full co-decision power for the Parliament, and the development of the eponymous procedure. Come the Amsterdam treaty in 1997, the guiding principle for Single Market legislation was that the European Parliament and the Council of Ministers more or less made decisions as joint and equal partners. This also increased the role and importance of the Commission as a mediator, helping to draft compromises between the council and the parliament (Stacey 2003).

Scope extension

Like deepening, the process of extending the policy scope of the EU has been gradual, running in fits and bursts, and often entailing 'shallower' integration in the new policy areas. The two processes have gone hand in hand. The strengthening of the Court's powers in the 1960s and the Commission's capacities with regard to competition policy in the 1970s went hand in hand with the development of the common market. The Court's elaboration of the principle of mutual recognition of goods became an alternative to harmonisation of laws and standards, and this in turn became a key stepping stone toward the Single European Market. The SEA brought about more supranational decision-making, in order to extend the scope of the EC – the Single Market programme and flanking policies in the fields of health and safety, environment and regional policy. In the 1990s, it was the Commission's new-found willingness to use its monopoly-busting competition policy powers (then Article 90, now 86), upheld by the Court in the face of member state complaints, that permitted the 'public turn' of the Single Market. During the 1990s, the Single Market was thus extended to cover telecommunications, and eventually other utility sectors that had previously been dominated by state monopolies.

However, this relationship is not as strong outside the core policy areas. Even in policy sectors closely related to the Single Market, such as environment policy, the full 'deep' instruments were not introduced immediately but only gradually, both in the Maastricht treaty and (even more so) in the Amsterdam treaty. Some important matters, notably tax harmonisation, still require unanimity in the Council, and in these areas the integration process lags substantially behind. In matters outside the EU's core, such as foreign policy, security, defence and judicial or police cooperation, the relationship between deepening and extension is even more tenuous. In fact, at Maastricht, the incorporation of the two new pillars that, in addition to the EC pillar, made up the EU was predicated on the use of the old 'shallow' methods of decision-making. Although some supranational decision-making has been introduced in Justice and Home Affairs, decision-making in Common Foreign and Security Policy is almost exclusively by unanimity. Part of the reason for this is, of course, that the states are reluctant to cede control on these matters, but part of the reason may also be that integration in these fields started out as ad hoc cooperation between governments. Many of the initiatives that now come under Common Foreign and Security Policy, European Security and Defence Policy and the Area of Freedom Security and Justice were first developed as initiatives outside the formal EU institutions. This includes efforts to combat organised crime and terrorism, the Schengen arrangement for passport union and justice cooperation, and foreign policy cooperation.

Widening

The process of widening has been more linear. The British Conservative government decided to apply to join the EEC in 1961, with Denmark and Ireland quickly following suit. Norway prevaricated, while Sweden opted not to seek membership. In any case, Charles de Gaulle vetoed enlargement as long as he remained president of France. The UK, Ireland and Denmark joined in 1973, but Norwegian voters rejected membership in a referendum. A second wave of enlargement followed after the fall of the military dictatorships in Spain, Portugal and Greece. Greece, which had only seen a short period of dictatorship, joined in 1981; the two others followed in 1986. Meanwhile the democratic non-EC members in the European Free Trade Association (EFTA) sought closer relations with the EC. In 1984, the EFTA states sought to participate in the Single Market on a more systematic and multi-lateral basis, without joining the EC as full members. The result was the European Economic Area (EEA). In the meantime communism collapsed. The fall of the Berlin Wall in 1989 altered geo-political realities on the continent, and opened the way for the neutral countries of Austria, Sweden and Finland to join the EC, which they did in 1995 (Norwegian voters saying 'no' a second time, in 1994). Incorporating the former communist states took a little longer, but eastern enlargement soon became all but inevitable. In 2004, Poland, Hungary, the Czech Republic, Slovakia, Slovenia and the three Baltic states joined the EU (notably, the first time enlargement had taken place on 1 May rather than 1 January), alongside Malta and Cyprus. Bulgaria and Romania joined in 2007.

The main question concerning enlargement, apart from accepting new members, has long been its effect on deepening. The argument that deepening and widening reinforce each other rests on the logic that the bigger the group of states involved in decision-making, the less practical the veto and the more important it is to have effective mechanisms for decision-making. The move to use QMV in the Council came as the EU enlarged, from 9 to 10 to 12. The most pressing matter on the agenda for both the Amsterdam and Nice treaties was institutional reform to cope with enlargement to 25 and beyond; as it was in the negotiations on the Constitutional Treaty and in 2007 for the draft Reform Treaty. By a similar logic, enlargement has made the EU more diverse; in the past this has meant that new policy instruments have been developed to cope with diversity. Southern enlargement prompted new redistributive policies, notably regional policy, rather than extensive reform of the common agricultural policy (CAP). When it came to enlargement to include the post-communist states, new mechanisms were likewise developed to achieve gradual extensions of financial support mechanisms to the new members, and to ensure that they would be capable of enforcing EU law. At the same time the introduction of the single currency (the Euro), and cooperation among finance ministers from the Euro-zone, has created a new platform for further informal harmonisation of policies among the Euro-countries, for example, in difficult areas like taxes and social security which are vital to maintaining a common currency. The Euro could be seen as an alternative to formal institution-based deepening among the Euro-zone members after expansion to the east.

Enlargement has also raised questions as to whether all the member states in a larger EU can move ahead at the same speed. So far, most measures have been temporary, such as the derogations used to limit the access of new member states' labour force to the EU, both in the Mediterranean and East European enlargements. In 2004 the new members did not immediately qualify for full participation in EMU or Schengen. Moreover, a few states have sought exemptions from EU initiatives for political reasons, despite otherwise qualifying for participation. This group principally consists of Sweden, Denmark and the UK with respect to EMU; the UK, Denmark and Ireland with respect to Schengen; and the neutral countries with respect to the West European Union (another exemption, no longer in operation, was the UK's non-participation in the Social Chapter during much of the 1990s). The result has been a somewhat uneven development of the EU in terms of member state participation across policy areas.

The development of the regulatory state in Europe

The development of a 'regulatory state' in Europe is the product of the combination of the rather uneven development of the EU itself, and developments in public policy at the member state level. By the time the Maastricht treaty was negotiated (in 1991) the EU was institutionalised as a political system that relied on rule-making as the primary tool of governance, in which the Single Market was at the core of the project, and the Commission played a key role as regulator of the market and driver behind liberalisation. It had expanded to 12 member states, and looked set to more than double over the next decade or so. At the same time, most of the West European states, whether EU members or not, had either embarked on or were moving towards major public sector reform. The ideas associated with New Public Management, that the state's capacity for governance might be improved by privatisation, liberalisation and reorganisation of state agencies, were taking root across Western Europe. This had provided the common denominator for the SEA: the quest for a single, liberalised, market. In the late 1980s and the 1990s this context allowed the Commission to take the lead in liberalising telecommunications across the EU; liberalisation of electricity and gas markets followed. The confluence of developments at the EU level and in national public policy helped make the EU the central arena for liberalisation.

The Single Market has become the core of the EU's activity, and in retrospect, removing barriers to trade always was. The EU has relatively limited fiscal resources (max 1.27 percent of GDP, but usually less), and these are devoted mainly to the CAP and regional policy. Although the EU does engage in some economic redistribution, its primary activity is regulation. Competition policy is the Commission's key tool, partly because the Treaty has always provided the Commission with strong instruments and partly because the Court has (until recently) generally upheld the Commission's effort to expand its competition policy competencies. The main answer to 'What does the EU do?' is: regulating for competition and operating the Single Market, whilst developing flanking policies and large programmes in areas such as education, research and support from small and medium-sized businesses. In addition, it carries out some economic redistribution. For the countries that use the single currency it also provides the central bank, and sets some parameters for fiscal policy. To be sure, over the last two decades the EU has expanded its role in foreign and security policy, and it plays a steadily increasing role in policies related to immigration, judicial and police cooperation, and combating organised crime and terrorism. However, its core activity remains the establishment and maintenance of the Single Market and its flanking policies.

Yet if the 1980s and early 1990s saw the EU consolidate as a regulatory state, centred on liberalisation, the SEA and the Maastricht treaty also ushered in another dimension of EU regulation. Whereas the Single Market programme was primarily a matter of what Scharpf (1999) calls 'negative' integration, or the removal of barriers to the free flow of goods, services, labour and capital, it also paved the way for 'positive' integration in the shape of common EU-level standards for environment, health and safety, and even, to some extent, social regulation. Liberalisation not only required a considerable amount of new regulation to make competition work, it also warranted common standards for both products and production processes to avoid 'social dumping'. Briefly put, countries with tighter environment and health and safety regulations were concerned that industry might relocate to countries with lower regulatory standards – the so-called 'Delaware effect' (from Delaware's ability to attract industry because of its light regulatory framework, and the pressure this generated on other states to lower their standards). However, as it turned out, the EU has been characterised more by regulatory cooperation among states than regulatory competition between them. The final section duly turns to the impact of the EU on national politics and public policy.

The Impact of EU Politics and Policy on the State's Public Governance

Although the EU can be seen as a political system that was established by the member states in order to increase their capacity for governance, this brief review of the institutions and the evolution of the EU suggests that it has developed to a stage where much EU policy is beyond the control of any single state. At the very least, a number of laws have been passed either as a result of compromises between the member states or by way of Qualified Majority Voting in the Council. The first and most direct way in which the EU influences member state public governance is therefore through EU legislation and the consequences of European Court of Justice (ECJ) decisions. This is seen clearly, for example, in decisions on utility market liberalisation, where EU directives require member states to open, for example, gas markets to competition. These rules in turn assign rights to individuals and companies. Second, and more indirectly, the EU influences member state public policy through more indirect ways of coordination, benchmarking, target-setting and monitoring. This has come to be known as 'the open method of coordination' (OMC). Third, similar initiatives have also developed outside the EU formal framework, prompted by the Single Market but not directly driven by it. Examples include the impact of cross-country comparisons and coordination in education policy.

First, the EU developed as a legal system of the French type based on attempts to standardise member states through legal measures. The Single European Act shifted the emphasis from standardisation to harmonisation and mutual recognition, but the central instruments have always been EU directives and member state implementation. Gradually, especially in the North European countries, some directives have also been implemented through other national-level measures such as regulations, instructions and agreement among 'social partners', which have rendered EU policy even more flexible and adaptable to local variations and different policy traditions.

The broad common theme over the last two decades has been that the EU drives, or at the very least reinforces, the wave of liberalisation, privatisation and New Public Management in most member states. Rule-based Europeanisation of public policy has therefore, to a large extent, been about breaking down barriers to trade within the EU (negative integration). At the same time, however, other parts of EU regulation also try to introduce a basic level of protection against the effects of the market forces for workers, consumers and the environment. This 'service public' aspect of EU policy has remained somewhat weaker than the drive towards more free market competition, as has indeed the EU's 'social dimension' (which remains mainly a matter for the member state level). The EU has been criticised by trade unionists and anti-globalisation forces on both counts.

Although EU law may drive privatisation and liberalisation, it says little or nothing about state ownership (apart from prohibiting discrimination and subsidies). With a few significant exceptions, like Denmark, most EU states have long histories of major state ownership, particularly in the utilities sectors. The privatisation programmes that have characterised the last decade or two in Europe may go hand in hand with liberalisation of the European market, but they have been carried out by the member states. To be sure, the Commission issued legislation to break up member state monopolies, but although it directly prompted privatisation in some states, it did not require it. EU legislation thus provides frameworks and rules for how public ownership is exercised, how the former monopolists should behave in a liberalised market, and bans subsidies and discrimination.

With this heavy emphasis on rules and regulations, the EU drives (or at least reinforces) a tendency towards law-based, rule-driven governance in the member states. It assigns rights to individuals and organisations, which are often used against a government's priorities and policy decisions. For some, this is considered an excessive limit to governments' discretion and ability to make decisions about the directions in which society should develop and the appropriate means to be used. The role of national political decision-making is reduced, and some politicians in the member states often feel overruled by the EU legal provisions. The EU and the national systems have, however, more or less tended to develop in tandem, in broadly the same directions. Both the ECJ and the national courts have seen their roles increase over time, with this shift toward more rule-based governance and the two levels work in cooperation rather than competition. Both in effect strengthen the legal framework of national policy-making and implementation in the EU.

The result of this legal success story is a substantial increase in the impact of the EU on national public governance in at least three dimensions: the scope of the decisions affected, the different levels of national government affected, and the sheer volume of legislation passed. Today the EU directives and initatives not only affect the agenda of every minister in the national government, but also represent by far the main source of influence for national political initiatives. Three decades ago this was hardly the case in any ministry; in some sectors the EU is now the main source of initiatives. At the same time a majority of the legal acts passed by the EU affects not only or mainly the national level, but increasingly the regional, local and municipal level. The regional and local authorities have become the winners in the Europeanisation process as the EU has transferred power and resources from the national to the local level. Today regional and local governments are key actors on the European scene. Finally, the total volume of EU legislation in itself constitutes a challenge for governments on all levels: how to handle this growing set of legislation and at the same time honour the demands for flexibility, diversity and local influence?

Second, the broader result of developments in EU policy has been that the EU system exposes protected sectors to a degree of competition, if only by encouraging cross-country comparison of public administration practices, for example, from the health care to the education sector. Even here the ECJ has a potential, but not yet fully realised, impact inasmuch as it could decide to interpret the Treaties in a more expansive fashion. In the 1990s and 2000s, however, the main impact in these policy sectors, which remain at the member state level, has been indirect. This is part of a broader trend toward more indirect governance in the EU, which culminated in the Open Method of Coordination (defined at the Lisbon council in 2000). The four basic mechanisms are: establishing common goals with guidelines and timetables; establishing indicators and employing benchmarking; setting national targets (taking into account local variations); and organising monitoring and evaluation processes. It has been used not only for the Lisbon agenda, establishing a more competitive EU, but also for an increasing number of other issues. Environment policy, for example, mixes 'hard' and 'soft' instruments.

This shift towards increased reliance on 'soft' instruments in the 1990s has supplemented rather than replaced the emphasis on legislation and rule-based governance in the EU. It was first used with respect to the targets that states had to meet to qualify for participation in Economic and Monetary Union, with mixed success. Its subsequent popularity may be due partly to the weaker Commissions after the Delors era of the 1980s, partly to more assertive member states and the establishment of the 'subsidiarity' principle (decisions should not be taken at a higher level than necessary) and partly to the fact that with the Single Market in place, the EU is moving into policy areas where legislation is difficult or inappropriate, or in cases where many member states wish to limit or roll back the reach of the EU. Hence the suggestion that the OMC is a 'second best' solution, often used where it is difficult to use formal legislation. There are several reasons for the EU's reduced ability or willingness to use legislation as a policy-making tool: the recent Commissions have been somewhat weaker than their predecessors and European integration has become more politically controversial; the legislative programme linked to the Single Market has been completed in many sectors, and is giving way to minor revisions of existing legislation; the new challenges linked to competitiveness are difficult to address by regulatory measures; and making policy for an EU of 27 member states warrants more use of flexible instruments.

Third, and finally, the EU member states have developed a series of initiatives outside the formal EU framework. Some of these involve Europe-wide processes of policy harmonisation that are more far-reaching and efficient than EU legislative measures. These initiatives are developed on an intergovernmental basis, and completely voluntary, but no less effective for that. Decisions are implemented through legal and administrative measures in the member states, practically as if they were based on binding directives from the EU. The most prominent example is the Bologna process in higher education, but similar mechanisms can be found in other sectors such as vocational training or health care. These efforts draw on long-standing cooperation among national institutions and officials within EU committees, albeit in sectors where there is no legal basis for developing such initiatives. Thus, a new intergovernmental process is established, which is related to and partly driven by, but not formally part of, the EU.

To return to the opening theme of this chapter, the EU represents both a constraint on and an opportunity for national policy-making in Europe. Globalisation and European integration make up the most important parameters within which national public policy is made, but developments both at the global and EU level have also been shaped by the states. Over the last two decades, the key theme in public policy has been the effort to strengthen the capacity of the state, by reducing its scope through privatisation and more use of markets; by making the state more efficient through public service reforms and more use of competition; and by improving public management. Having set out the main sources of pressure on the state and the main parameters within which the European states operate and make public policy, the next three sections of the book turn to these three themes.

Further Reading

Nugent, N. (2006) *The Government and Politics of the European Union* (London: Palgrave). A classic textbook, now in its sixth edition, which provides an excellent overview of the working of the EU's institutions. Chapter 20 on 'National Influences and Controls of the European Union Process' is particularly relevant because it deals with relations between politics in the member states and EU policy.

Hix, S. (2005) *The Political System of the European Union* (London: Palgrave). A very readable account of the EU political system (now in its second edition), which takes a comparative politics perspective on the EU. Chapter 2 on 'Executive Politics' and Chapter 3 on 'Legislative Politics' provide a comprehensive overview of the EU decision-making process and review of the relevant literature.

Wallace, H., Wallace, W. and Pollack, M.A. (eds) (2005) *Policy-Making in the European Union* (Oxford: Oxford University Press). A comprehensive collection of chapters on a series of policy sectors (now in its fifth edition). Chapter 3 by Helen Wallace on 'An Institutional Anatomy and Five Policy Models' provides a good introduction to the main types of policy-making in the EU.

El-Agraa, A.M. (ed.) (2007) *The European Union: Economics and Policies* (Cambridge: Cambridge University Press). A classic edited textbook (now in its eighth edition) which combines economic and politics analysis of the EU and its main policy areas. Chapter 7 by Brian Ardy and Ali El-Agraa on 'The Economics of the Single Market' is particularly relevant.

Bulmer, S. and Lequesne, C. (eds) (2005) *The Member States and the European Union* (Oxford: Oxford University Press). A particularly relevant book because it focuses on the relationship between the EU and its member states. Chapter 16 by Vivien A. Schmidt on 'The Europeanization of National Economies' links this to varieties of capitalism and discusses trends over time.

THREE

Liberalisation and Privatisation

The introductory chapter outlined three strategies that states have developed in order to improve governance: to reduce the scope of what the state does, to improve the efficiency of what it does, and to cooperate with other states in doing it. Chapter 2 addressed international cooperation, focusing on European integration. This chapter and the next turn to the question of whether the states can do less, and how to regulate activity that is transferred from the public to private sector. Chapters 5 to 8 then turn to efforts to make the state more efficient. The central questions in this chapter concern how to reduce the scope of the state and introduce a degree of competition in public services – privatisation and liberalisation; Chapter 4 then turns to debates about regulation that have accompanied these changes.

The central aspect of the effort to make the state smaller has been to shift some activities from the state to the market. This means not only changing ownership, from public to private, but also ensuring that competition in the privatised sectors works efficiently. *Privatisation* – the transfer of assets from state to private ownership – therefore goes hand in hand with *liberalisation* – the introduction of competition to sectors that were previously dominated by a single or a few suppliers. This book's core focus is on public services, and the following discussion is therefore largely confined to privatisation and liberalisation in sectors that can be classified as public services. Although swathes of European industry have been nationalised over the last 200 years, for any number of reasons including ideological commitments to state ownership, arguments that the state ought to control strategic industry, or simply the case of a state taking over bankrupt firms, the focus here is on the core sectors involved in providing public services: telecommunications, provision of electricity, rail transport and postal services. All four are 'network utilities', and state ownership or control has generally been justified on the grounds that these are 'natural monopolies'. Across Europe these four services have been or are being liberalised and privatised, albeit to different degrees.

This chapter starts with a review of the main challenges to Western democracies' capacity for economic governance, in the context of different models of capitalism – the liberal, corporatist and social democratic models introduced briefly in the introductory chapter. The second section addresses the question of why liberalisation followed the particular trajectory that it did. It charts the progress of privatisation and liberalisation across the three broad varieties of capitalist states, starting with the liberal UK and proceeding to the Netherlands and the three Scandinavian cases (the social democratic states) and France and Germany (the more corporatist cases). The third section explores the spread of privatisation and liberalisation in four utilities sectors across the EU and its member states: telecommunications, electricity, rail transport and postal services.

Privatisation, Liberalisation and the Quest for Efficiency

Although liberalisation and privatisation processes are often associated with strong ideological agendas, linked to the ascendance of the New Right, most of the actual privatisation processes have been shaped by practical concerns and political games. This determined the 'what' and 'where' of privatisation. It is, for example, no coincidence that telecommunications was chosen as one of the first sectors to be liberalised in almost every case. Technological change combined with the comparatively low costs of failure and the relatively high potential for benefits made this a likely choice. Technological development made a series of services possible that went well beyond mere voice telephony, from answering services (voicemail) to caller ID and data transfers. The social cost of a failure in the telecoms network was likely to be far lower than a failure in electricity or gas supply; the consequences of going without telephone services for a day are far less severe than deprivation of electricity or heating, let alone water. The potential for new services made telecoms a promising market in terms of potential profits in the 1980s. In short, telecommunications was the least risky and most promising utility to privatise. As for the 'where' question, UK and US political institutions made the two countries strong candidates for radical reform: Margaret Thatcher and Ronald Reagan's electoral victories in the UK and USA in 1979 and 1980 respectively provided the political catalysts. Although many of the same challenges – derived from globalisation, economic stagnation and technological change – affected the OECD states, the different governments' responses varied according to how political games were played out.

Efficiency questions for the public sector – size, inefficiency and complexity

The common challenge for the Western liberal democracies in the 1980s was the size, inefficiency and complexity of the public sector. If this had been concealed by economic growth during the 1950s and 1960s, it was recognised as a problem almost universally across the OECD by the late 1970s. A new combination of inflation and economic stagnation permeated Western Europe and North America during the 1970s and gave rise to a new term – stagflation. The OECD proved the central forum for cross-country comparisons, and its reports both reflected and helped generate a broad consensus on some of the causes for Western Europe's economic problems. These OECD discussions were highly influential in shaping academic and professional understanding of the causes of the contemporary predicaments as well as setting out some potential solutions to the problems of state capacity (Fukuyama 2004). The central problems that were identified could be divided into three main types, as well as a fourth, more controversial, argument.

First, the public sector was becoming large. The public sector had expanded for almost three decades in most Western democracies by the late 1970s. The mere size of the public sector had reached a point where the sustainability of further growth was increasingly questioned, not only by academics but also by political parties. In Norway and Denmark the 'earthquake elections' of the early 1970s saw the emergence of populist anti-tax parties on the right. Sweden saw its first non-socialist government for 40 years in 1976. Thatcher's radical brand of conservatism triumphed in the UK election of 1979. France saw less debate about the size of the public sector in the 1970s but, even there, a light version of this debate would emerge in the 1980s. In Britain and the Netherlands, and to a lesser extent in Germany and Scandinavia, the centre-left's policy changes in the 1990s turned the ideas about the need to reduce the scope of the public sector into a broad consensus. In France, a similar development followed in the 2000s, but more controversially and less unequivocally.

Second, the economic downturn in Western Europe in the 1970s raised questions about the cost and efficiency of the public sector. Until the late 1970s, the question of efficiency in the public sector had largely been ignored, and in many cases the cost of delivering specific public services could barely be documented. The central charge in economic theory is that public companies tend to be less efficient than private ones because they are not subject to strong pressure in the shape of the profit motive. Even if they operate in competitive markets, the state-owned companies' governance structures and sources of finance permit a certain amount of slack. The core argument is that only the discipline that private, profit-maximising owners bring can prevent managers from pursuing their own agenda (Vickers and Yarrow 1988). In short, even if an economic activity takes place in a competitive market, private companies are presumed to be more efficient than state-owned ones. This has, of course, been contested, and efforts to assess the effect of state ownership as such have been inconclusive (Megginson and Netter 2001). However, the idea that private ownership is more efficient than public ownership formed part of the basis for the debates about privatisation in the 1980s.

Third, public sector organisations are sometimes charged with a series of tasks beyond mere service provision. Even if 'service provision' is meant to include secure and accessible public services, the goals of a public service provider may be much wider than to merely provide services securely and at affordable rates. The effect of the organisation's activities on, for example, employment, redistribution of resources or even counter-cyclical spending may be taken into account by state-owned enterprise or public service organisation. Privatisation, and the division of large organisations into functionally separate units, was (and is) therefore often seen as a strategy for making the goals of the organisations clearer. This, in turn, should make supervision and evaluation easier, and therefore reduce the scope for slack. In other words, large complex organisations that pursue multiple goals are often seen as a source of inefficiency (both in the private and public sector).

Finally, a more controversial fourth point is directly associated with the New Right analysis of bureaucracies: the hypothesis that the management (and indeed employees) in state-owned businesses and government bureaucracies are not primarily concerned with the efficiency of public service delivery, let alone with its effectiveness. Neither are they concerned with delivering service at the lowest possible costs, nor with actually evaluating whether the service 'works' (in the sense of delivering what the users want). The arguments about budget maximisation are discussed in greater depth in Chapter 5, on New Public Management. Suffice it to note here that much public choice analysis suggests that because the profit motive is weak or absent in the public sector, there is insufficient information for the politicians to be able to control and evaluate what the bureaucracy does (Downs 1967). In addition, in the absence of a quest for profit, many bureaucracies pursue maximum budgets and expansion of their offices or activities (Niskanen 1971, 1973). In short, public choice analysis suggests that, unless it is checked by scrupulous politicians, the bureaucracy has an in-built tendency to expand. This point has proven more controversial than the three previous ones (Dunleavy 1991), but it informed much of the debate on how to reform public services.

By the end of the 1970s the economic rationale for reform was thus becoming increasingly powerful, and it was strengthened by the political rationale for reform. At this time it was becoming apparent not only that the public sector in Western liberal democracies tended to be large (and getting larger), inefficient and complex, but also that it tended to escape control by politicians, let alone be independently regulated or overseen. Much of the necessary information was simply not there. For example, Nigel Lawson (1992) later revealed that in the early 1980s nobody knew if Britain's state telecommunications operations made or lost money. Three broad political reasons for reform complemented and reinforced the economic rationale for reform.

First, both voters and political parties shifted to the right in much of Western Europe. This included a turn toward neo-liberal economic policies on the part of many centre-right political parties and party leaders. This trend was strongest in the UK, but it could also be seen in Scandinavia and the Netherlands, and even to some extent in Germany and France.

Second, the rising cost of the welfare state put pressure on public finances, which in turn prompted politicians across the political spectrum to focus on the cost and efficiency of public services. This was part of a broader reassessment of the role of the state in the economy, which took place across the three types of capitalist regimes – liberal, corporatist and social democratic.

Third, the European states' treaty commitments to free trade principally, but not exclusively, through the EEC/EU reinforced any neo-liberal tendencies that were developing at the national level. The Single European Act and the effort to establish a single market and extend this to the EFTA states was the key development. In a sense, European integration has had a ratcheting effect: although it is difficult for the member states to agree new policies, it is even more difficult to go back on agreements once they have been reached. The EU principally drives the economy in a free market direction, because states need to cooperate to enable free trade, but can engage in protectionism on their own. The long-term effect of European integration has therefore been to push the member states toward dismantling barriers to trade.

In short, both political and economic developments meant that there was much common ground for economic policy change in Western Europe in the 1980s. Yet the differences in economic and political institutions (capitalist diversity) ensured that a range of different responses emerged across Western Europe.

The twin processes of privatisation and liberalisation

If many political actors, particularly but not exclusively on the centre-right, concluded that the public sector was rapidly becoming too big, too inefficient, too complex and increasingly difficult to control, part of the answer lay in reducing the scope of the state. Privatisation – the transfer of assets from state to private ownership – provided the common answer. It would, by definition, reduce the size of the public sector. Private ownership would provide the discipline that firms needed to focus on profit. A broad set of goals would be replaced by the profit motive. The combination of the profit motive and the transparency that the price mechanisms involved would make it easier for owners to control their firms, and replace bureaucratic control with corporate governance. Ideally this simplification and transparency would strengthen control and accountability, as the state replaced direct but inefficient control mechanisms with more limited but also more effective systems of control and oversight based on market mechanisms. In practice, it involved a shift from what we might call the public utility model to the regulatory agency model (Eyre and Sitter 1999).

Although ideal-type privatisation may involve a full transition from a state-run utility to a fully private company operating in a competitive market, most European cases of utilities privatisation have involved one or more transitional stages. In a number of cases it was (and still is) far from clear that full privatisation would ever be the goal. Several governments have focused on the *liberalisation* of utilities markets rather than on *privatisation* of the old monopoly operators. In effect, therefore, many privatisation processes have been partial. The common starting point for the utilities has been their operation as an integrated part of a government department. The first step on the path to privatisation has therefore been 'corporatisation' – the separation of the utility from its parent department. In most of the cases considered here, including the UK cases, the utilities had operated as government-owned enterprises or corporations for a period of time. Such state-owned corporations are often covered by special legislation, which may accord them particular privileges over private and commercial companies, such as protection from bankruptcy and favourable access to credit. The second step is to move from a state-owned entity covered by specific legislation to a fully fledged limited company, legally separate and fully exposed to market law. This is feasible even without privatisation. However, this is normally only a short step from stock-market listing and partial privatisation. The third step involves mixed ownership, with the state's share ranging from overwhelming to a minor share. This mixed model includes four major categories: firms that are predominantly state owned; majority state ownership; significant minority state ownership; and negligible state ownership. This last category is, for all intents and purposes, the same as taking the final step to full privatisation, unless the state retains some form of 'golden share' that allocates it a veto over major decisions.

These stages of privatisation involve changes in the way the state seeks to control the utility sector in question, and the specific company. When the service is operated as part of a fully integrated government department, it is covered by executive decisions, the state budget and administrative law. With the separation of utility services into separate legal entities, the balance of the government's control inevitably shifts, with reduced (or at least clearly delineated) avenues for direct political instruction, but considerable scope for influence through budget allocation or other financial requirements. Corporatisation and partial privatisation involves more radical changes, as the government is left with a combination of the tools that any company owners enjoy (financial requirements, appointing the board, structuring the incentives for the CEO) and the tools it enjoys by virtue of executive and legislative power. In other words, control is changed from direct centralised political control to indirect control by regulation and exercise of ownership rights. Although the original aim in the UK was that even the utilities companies might eventually operate in a fully fledged competitive and liberalised market – governed primarily by competition law – the experience with utilities reform across Europe has been that sector-specific regulators are needed. The regulators established for the UK utilities may have been intended primarily as a transitional measure, but they quickly became a permanent fixture on the regulatory scene.

Although liberalisation and privatisation have tended to go hand in hand, and have been motivated by similar concerns and driven by the same set of economic theories, they are two analytically and practically distinct processes. Whereas *privatisation* refers to the transfer of assets from the state to private (or part-private) ownership, *liberalisation* refers to the introduction of competition into a sector that has been dominated by a monopoly or in which competition has been severely restricted. This involves four major changes in patterns of government control, which amount to a shift from detailed direct control to lighter, more indirect, regulation.

1   Liberalisation has tended to involve a change from direct political control by the minister responsible for a particular sector to independent regulatory authorities. In Europe, and in the case of utilities liberalisation, this is a formal requirement of EU law (independent regulation is required, by a sector regulator or the competition authority, and the norm has been to establish national regulatory agencies – NRAs).
2   This shift from political instruction to regulation renders it much more difficult for the government to pursue active and interventionist economic policy. Utilities liberalisation is part and parcel of a broader trend of a shift from interventionist industrial policy to more liberal competition policy in Europe.
3   Liberalisation usually entails a shift in focus from the incumbent operator (the old monopoly operator) to its new rivals. Liberalisation involves a shift from protecting the incumbent to promoting competition, even if promoting competition is not the same as promoting specific competitors.
4   Liberalisation is often seen as warranting increased use of (sector-blind) competition policy rather than sector-specific regulation.

We will return to this debate about the consequences of privatisation and liberalisation for regulatory change in Chapter 4. Suffice it to note here that, far

	Operator	Primary task	Regulator	Competition policy
Public Utility Model	Single vertically integrated monopoly	Service provision	Utility and/or ministry	Limited impact, utilities may be exempt
Regulatory Model	Multiple private companies	Profit maximisation	Regulatory agency	Utilities covered, shared competence

Figure 3.1   Transformation from public utility model to regulatory agency model

from leading to de-regulation, privatisation and liberalisation requires substantial regulatory reform (Levi-Faur 2006). The change from the public utility model to the regulatory model is set out in Figure 3.1.

Varieties of Capitalism in Europe – and of Patterns of Privatisation and Liberalisation

How to interpret the challenges of size, inefficiency and complexity was as much a matter of politics, or more specifically political ideology, as of economics. This was mediated by political traditions and institutions, which meant that even the seven states considered here had quite different points of departure. Although broadly similar reform projects developed across the OECD, the OECD states started from very different bases. The reforms in the UK brought about by the Thatcher government demonstrated that party politics can play a central role in how and how far reforms are carried out. However, in consensual democracies such as Scandinavia or the Netherlands, the reform programmes of the 1980s drew on considerable cross-party consensus. In Germany, the change from a centre-left coalition government under Helmut Schmidt to Helmut Kohl's centre-right government in 1982 also brought about more neo-liberally oriented economic and fiscal policies. Even in France the socialist government during the early years of the Mitterrand presidency turned to a more liberal course, reversing its more traditional left policy in 1983. Moravscik (1998) argues that this was the crucial step that lay the foundations for the Single European Act inasmuch as France, Germany and the UK now adopted compatible economic and monetary policies. This provided the window of opportunity for the Single Market programme, as all the big member states could agree on the lowest common denominator: removing all obstacles to cross-border trade. The solution was that free movement of goods, capital, services and labour would take place on the basis of 'mutual recognition' (goods that are sold in one state may also be sold in another), not harmonisation of laws at the EU/EEC level. Capitalist diversity was thus maintained, but at the same time the EU system helped institutionalise the liberalisation processes that were taking place at the national level. Once markets were opened, it would be difficult for any one state to close them without leaving the EEC/EU altogether.

The literature on European political economy in general, and the literature on economic policy and welfare regimes in particular, often divides the European countries into several groups or broad types. We follow the patterns established in Esping-Andersen's *The Three Worlds of Welfare Capitalism* (1990), discussed briefly in the Introduction, and place the UK alongside the USA in the category of 'liberal' states, France and Germany closer to a more 'corporatist' type, while the Netherlands and the Scandinavian states represent a type that Esping-Andersen labelled 'social democratic' to reflect the significant role the centre-left parties played in establishing these specific welfare state regimes. We borrow the label 'consensual' from Lijphart (1984) for this last type, to reflect the more con-sensual style of political decision-making in these four countries. Other classifi-cations, such as Schmitter's (1974) distinction between neo-corporatist and pluralist regimes, draw on economic policy in general and the structure and role of organised interest groups in particular. Hall and Soskice (2001) take the pri-vate firm as their starting point, and like Schmitter they arrive at two types of regimes, which they label 'liberal' and 'coordinated' market economies. In all cases, the UK and Ireland represent contrasts to the continental European regimes. However, as Scharpf (1997, 1999) has pointed out, some of the differ-ences between the corporatist and Scandinavian (consensual) welfare regimes also have considerable implications for public policy and administration. The dif-ference is not only that the liberal regimes are more market-oriented and have weaker trade unions than the two other systems. The different welfare systems shape the challenges: the liberal regimes with more limited welfare spending face less formidable cost problems; the corporatist systems tie both welfare and its costs to labour in the private sector; whereas the Scandinavian systems fea-ture larger public sector employment and load the cost onto the general tax-payer (Scharpf 1999). The Scandinavian systems, which de-couple welfare and work, may have permitted them to engage in considerable privatisation and lib-eralisation inasmuch as they seek to protect the individual's welfare rather than individual jobs (Hagen 2006).

These three types or varieties of capitalism are ideal-types, and not a precise description of any of the regimes mentioned. They are better understood as patterns of change. The UK system in particular is quite far from the liberal model with respect to parts of the welfare state. The central point is rather that the practical politics and economic philosophy behind the existing regimes and effort to introduce reforms have shaped the trajectories of privatisation and liberalisation (and, as Chapter 7 will show, of organisational change within the public sector). Three broad patterns of liberalisation and privatisation fit these three broad patterns of types of economic regimes:

1 The liberal UK was the first and most radical mover in terms of privatisation of state-owned enterprises, but slower on liberalisation.
2 The consensual states were slower off the mark, but embraced radical liberalisation.
3 The more corporatist Germany and France have been more reluctant liberalisers and privatisers.

Despite the common frameworks laid down in EU regulation, regulatory regimes also vary considerably among the three patterns and seven cases discussed here. The Mediterranean states are often considered a variation on the corporatist pattern, though in terms of privatisation, liberalisation and regulation they are closer to the formerly communist EU member states inasmuch as their present regimes have been shaped by the EU regime (because they had less developed regimes for competition policy before EU law required that regimes be established). Moreover, closer analysis of these broad groups of states reveals 'varieties of capitalism' within the groups. Bohle and Greskovits (2007) find that the Baltic States have opted for a more neo-liberal approach, whereas the Central European states have 'embedded' their neo-liberalism in stronger welfare states and industrial policy, while Slovenia alone has taken a more neo-corporatist approach. The remainder of this chapter returns to the seven countries and the three broad patterns of reform.

The liberal pattern of privatisation and liberalisation – the USA and the UK

Privatisation and liberalisation may have been discussed in political, administrative and academic communities as the 1970s progressed, but it was the USA and the UK that would embark on the most radical reforms. Because these two countries featured clear and strong ideological driving forces and their governments were in a position to implement radical reform programmes, and because they therefore provided the 'purest' examples of liberalisation and privatisation, they receive disproportional attention in this chapter. In both countries, elections tend to produce clear majorities for one of the two main parties, in contrast to the multi-party systems and coalition governments that tend to characterise continental Europe (Lijphart 1984). In the USA the possibility that Congress and the Presidency are controlled by different parties limits executive power somewhat, but in the UK the governing party usually has a comfortable majority in parliament. In the USA, President Reagan worked with a democratic Congress. In the UK, Margaret Thatcher's electoral victory in 1979 provided a secure majority of 43 seats (of 659), and, after victory in the Falklands War, the 1983 election saw her return to power with a more comfortable majority of 144.

From the Reagan administration's view, and in the New Right's analysis, the central problem in the USA was not excessive state ownership, but over-regulation. During the two preceding decades, both federal and state legislatures had intervened in economic activity to an unprecedented degree, an expansion in state governance that was particularly associated with President Lyndon B. Johnson's effort to create 'the great society'. More specifically, the core of the critique of what was seen as left-wing 'big government' (notwithstanding the Republican Nixon and Ford administrations' continuation of these policies in the first half of the 1970s) was that heavy regulation of business reduced its flexibility, and therefore slowed productivity and economic growth. Privatisation in the USA therefore meant three broad sets of reforms:

1 Deregulation – the main thrust of the Reagan administration's reforms was the removal of 'unnecessary' federal regulations concerning both service sectors and general private business activity. The most celebrated case is deregulation of air transport, which entailed keeping safety regulation but deregulating the business side. This resulted in total reorganisation of the industry and was hailed as a success because it dramatically lowered air fares.
2 De-monopolisation – the administration sought to break up the 'natural' utilities monopolies and introduce competition and market discipline to telecommunications and energy markets. An Anti-Trust lawsuit by the Department of Justice against the monopoly AT&T (formerly the American Telephone & Telegraph Company) dating back to the early 1970s was settled in 1982, when the company agreed to break up its Bell telephone exchange business into seven regional companies (soon to be known as the 'Baby Bells'). This in turn led to liberalisation of the market for related products, such as telephone terminals.
3 Competitive tendering – early in Reagan's Presidency the federal government encouraged the states to expose more public services to the market through competitive tendering and increased use of private contractors, in what Osborne and Gabler (1992) called an 'American perestroika' (after Gorbachev's restructuring in the Soviet Union). Early studies of refuse collection in North America, compiled and compared by Savas, indicated improvements in both economy and equity: services were cheaper, of the same quality, and service provision was no longer subject to political favouritism (1987: 124ff).

The effect of deregulation in the USA under Reagan was perhaps greater abroad (as an ideological model) than at home (as hard reality). Tax cuts and deregulation were more significant than reduction in government expenditure, and even in the late 1980s the US was sometimes accused of engaging in something close to European style industrial policy by way of its government spending (for example, on defence) as well as tax, trade and environment policies (Wilson 1990: 59ff). Balanced budgets had to await the second Clinton administration, only to see a return to deficit spending (the biggest ever) under George W. Bush. By contrast, in Britain, the Thatcher government had both the political power and ideological 'purity' to see through consistent and radical reform, both in terms of regulation and public services, although even her Conservative governments found it more difficult to reduce government expenditure.[1]

The combination of pressure on the public purse, technological innovation, new economic ideas and the electoral victory of the right came together as dramatically in the UK as in the USA. When Margaret Thatcher took over the leadership of the Conservative party in 1975, after the party's electoral defeats of the previous year, she lost little time in turning the party toward a more radical form of politics that included calls for privatisation and liberalisation. However, as in the USA, there was no clear blueprint for reform. The state was far more heavily involved in the utilities than on the other side of the Atlantic, and previous Conservative governments had by and large chosen not to reverse nationalisation (the two main exceptions were steel and road haulage in the 1950s). Moreover, even if Thatcher had clear ideas, there was no consensus in the cabinet, let alone in the Conservative party or among its supporters in the Confederation of British Industry for radical large scale privatisation. As Chapter 5 will show in more detail, the first priority was simply to economise, or to reduce the cost of government. Privatisation only developed gradually, as a part of what became a two-pronged strategy to improve the efficiency of public services that also included New Public Management. In the UK, privatisation and liberalisation came to entail four elements: US-style liberalisation of regulated markets (or 'deregulation'); a broad shift away from British post-war corporatism; privatisation of state-owned industry, of the kind that most European states would embark on; and privatisation of public monopolies accompanied by efforts to establish competitive markets where none had so far existed.

> After her electoral victory in 1979, Thatcher's government embarked on a series of measures that amounted to US-style deregulation, and, considering the starting point, were considerably more radical. This included abolition of a series of capital market controls (such as control of foreign exchange, dividends, bank lending, and stock exchange brokerage), deregulation of labour markets, land and property market reform, and deregulation of a series of goods and services (such as price controls, shop opening hours, monopolies for trades like opticians and solicitors, and bus services). The cumulative result by the end of Thatcher's tenure in 1990 was deregulation in the very real sense of the word – the removal of regulations – in some sectors, and a fundamental change in the state's involvement in industry.
>
> This was part of the government's overall strategy to shift the British economy away from Keynesianism, corporatism and interventionist industrial policy, and to expose British

---

[1]General government expenditure stood at 43.0 percent in 1979, and dropped to a low of 37.9 percent in 1988, before rising again and peaking at 43.0 percent in 1993 (Office for National Statistics: 'General government expenditure as a percentage of gross domestic product, 1901 to 1998', available at www.statistics.gov.uk).

industry to full competition and the discipline of the free market. Radical changes to industrial relations law weakened the trade unions, and, combined with the government's reduction of state aid and rejection of industrial policy, this amounted to a broader overhaul of economic governance than seen so far in any Western European state.

The state's direct role in the economy, as an owner of companies and operator of public utilities, was to be reduced by means of privatisation. This started with British Petroleum, which crossed the threshold to more than 50 percent of shares held by private investors shortly after Thatcher won the 1979 election, and a series of others, such as British Aerospace, Cable & Wireless, the national Freight Corporation and Jaguar. The big watershed event was the privatisation of British Telecom in 1984, after which the privatisation of gas, electricity and water utilities followed over the next five years (Newbery 1999).

Liberalisation got off to a slower start in the UK. Although the government's original plan was to break up and privatise British Telecom, opposition from both the workforce and management forced the government to change its plans and privatise it intact (Lawson 1992). Competition was therefore only introduced more gradually, as alternative providers emerged.

Although both the Conservative and Labour governments that followed after Thatcher's fall in 1990 took a considerably less radical and ideological approach to economic policy and industrial governance, they did not, on the whole, deviate from the trajectory of privatisation and liberalisation that was developed in the 1980s. Although the Labour government that took office led by Tony Blair in 1997 would change public management in several respects (see Chapter 5), it by and large accepted the inheritance of the previous 18 years in terms of economic and industrial policy in general, and privatisation and liberalisation in particular (Richards and Smith 2002).

The consensual pattern – the Netherlands and Scandinavia

In contrast to developments in the USA and the UK, the drive toward liberalisation and privatisation in Scandinavia and the Netherlands was slower, less extensive and more driven by European integration. In contrast to the UK, where the Thatcher government broke trade union power and therefore could take full advantage of the power that the UK political system gives its single-party majority governments, the consensual democracies generally feature slower and less radical decision-making. Trade union power remains considerable, and the social democratic parties have been in power (albeit in coalition) for much of the last two decades. Across the political spectrum, policy-makers are also less receptive to ideological influence from the USA than their British colleagues. Liberalisation and privatisation initiatives and practical reforms have been led by economists and engineers in the civil service, rather than by elected politicians with a strong ideological commitment. Reforms have therefore tended not to go further than the 'technocrats' considered practical or necessary; yet in many cases this meant going much further than most politicians initially wanted. Although there are a few cases in which the initiatives originated at the state level, such as Norwegian electricity liberalisation, most of the privatisation and liberalisation initiatives in Europe (East and West) were placed on the agenda by EU proposals for liberalisation in the context of the Single Market. This holds also for the non-EU states that are members of the European Economic Area: Norway, Iceland and Liechtenstein. Although most of the big liberalisation programmes, including telecoms, electricity and now also rail and postal services, were developed within the framework of the Single Market, some of the concerns found in the UK were also reflected in the consensual countries. Telecoms liberalisation was motivated by the hope that it would lead to cheaper services and more rapid economic growth, informed by the US and UK examples, at the same time as the Commission launched its drive to extend the Single European Market to the utilities sectors.

The corporatist pattern – France and Germany

France and Germany have, broadly speaking, been far more sceptical towards the method of liberalisation and privatisation adopted by the US and the UK, and therefore also towards many of the Commission's initial proposals for liberalisation of utilities markets in the EU. Because of this opposition to US-style liberalisation, the EU Commission's initiatives were delayed and watered down considerably, especially in the electricity and gas sector. Nevertheless, once EU directives had been adopted, France and Germany were not noticeably slower than other member states when it came to transposition and implementation of the directives. In fact, when it came to establishing and operating truly independent regulatory agencies, the two countries were ahead of some of the consensual states. Successive French governments' approaches to liberalisation have been to favour liberalisation in terms of free competition in the market in order to achieve lower prices and better economic growth; but at the same time they aim to ensure that this competition is 'won' by strong, (partially) state-owned, French 'national champions'. An important lesson drawn in France was that the EU-driven liberalisations of the 1990s watered down the traditional French emphasis on the importance of *service public* – the principle that public services are guaranteed, partly through public delivery and partly by strong regulations, particularly in terms of quality and security of supply (Grard et al. 1996). In the last decade, France has therefore sought to re-establish the *service public* in the EU.

Liberalisation and the Single Market – the regulatory state in Europe

The role of the European Union in West European economic policy changed dramatically during the late 1980s, when two trends that were developing independently in Western Europe joined together in the Single Market project: the trend of privatisation and liberalisation that was developing in the Western European state in the 1980s met the trend of increasing supranational cooperation between these states. At the same time as the states were beginning to privatise and liberalise, and to replace industrial policy with competition policy, European integration received a new boost. To be sure, this was partly because the states found some common ground in the effort to establish a common market with free flow of goods, services, capital and labour, but the EU process was also being driven forward by the supranational organisations, developments in global politics and economics, and because some problematic issues such as the UK contribution to the EU budget were resolved. These two trends flowed together in the mid-1980s, and since the Single European Act they have reinforced each other. At the state level, governments were adopting more rule-based governance: indirect steering through regulation rather than direct intervention in the economy through industrial policy and state aid to industry (Majone 1994, 1997). At the same time, the EU's limited financial resources made regulation the most appropriate tool of governance (McGowan and Wallace 1996, Scharpf 1999). Hence the suggestion that the European Union has evolved into a 'regulatory state', and that in fact the EU's institutions fit much better within a world characterised by privatisation, liberalisation and regulation than the world of industrial policy that had characterised Western Europe thus far.

In one sense, therefore, the EU in the late 1980s was the ideal time and place for the regulatory state. The Commission is generally committed to a regulatory approach that is compatible with the Single Market rules and in particular its competition policy. By the 1990s, EU policy was generally seen as more free market oriented, a driver for liberalisation and even privatisation in Europe. This marked the end of industrial policy, and increasing use of competition policy to regulate and liberalise, rather than to protect, European markets. Even in areas where common policies were built and common standards exceeded those of some individual states, as has been the case in Environment and Health and Safety policy, the Commission's role has increasingly been that of a regulator. In the 1990s, the EU shifted the emphasis of the Single Market effort to the public sector, in what was called the 'public turn' of EU competition policy (Gerber 1998). By the end of the decade the foundations had been laid for liberalisation of a series of public services, from telecommunications and electricity to rail, gas and postal services. However, although the EU played (and continues to play) a considerable role as a driver of liberalisation, its role in privatisation has been far more limited. The EU has little or nothing to say about whether a company or utility is state owned, but much to say about discrimination and other measures that limit competition. The last section of this chapter turns to the dynamics of liberalisation in the utilities sectors in Europe, with a focus on telecommunications, energy and postal services.

Liberalising Public Utilities in Europe

Although the Single European Act did not immediately extend the Single Market to the utilities sector, the European commission and the more liberally oriented member states soon embarked upon several projects to extend the Single Market to these excluded sectors. As in the UK, the EU's attention turned first to telecommunications.

Between 1988 and 1998 the telecoms markets in the EU (and EEA and applicant) states were liberalised, at least on paper. Because the Commission used its power under Article 86 (or Article 90, as it was at the time) to break up national monopolies, it is often seen as the driving force behind European telecoms liberalisation (Sandholtz 1993, Héritier 1999). Under competition policy rules, Article 86 permits the Commission to issue directives without support from the Council of Ministers or Parliament. This was done for the first time ever in 1988. Up to this point, the Commission had focused on encouraging harmonisation of networks and equipment through the European standardisation institutions, to promote R&D cooperation and to build networks of actors that supported liberalisation. However, as it turned to liberalising the market for terminal equipment and value-added network services by issuing Article 90 Directives in 1988 and 1990 respectively, member state opposition came to the fore. Although both decisions were challenged, they were upheld by the European Court of Justice. In fact, as the liberalisation process got under way, or was discussed in most member states, opposition decreased. Germany and France remained committed to protecting their monopolies even as others such as Norway and Sweden began to liberalise in anticipation of EU-level liberalisation, but in the early 1990s even French and German utilities gradually began to reorient their focus toward the potential benefits from foreign markets (Bartle 1999). In the event, the Commission pushed for the full opening of telecoms markets, including voice telephony, in its 1993 Telecoms Review. In the meantime, it had begun to address related services such as cable services, satellite communications and mobile telephony, which were liberalised in a series of directives between 1994 and 1996. The last steps in the process of replacing the old monopoly network operator concept were laid down in a directive passed in 1997, and by 1998 telecommunications markets were formally fully opened. In practice, however, full liberalisation took considerably longer.

Even if the Commission may have been the driving force behind telecoms liberalisation, it accomplished this by a gradual process that involved building up support and accommodating a considerable degree of member state diversity (Thatcher 1997, Eyre and Sitter 1999). Although the Commission was prepared to use Article 90 to push through liberalisation in the face of some member state resistance, some analysts went so far as to argue that the Commission did little other than accommodate national preferences and industry interest (Davies 1994, Esser and Noppe 1996). At any rate, the Commission proved reluctant to use the same means for the much more controversial project of liberalising the energy sector. Although Competition Commissioner Karel van Miert threatened to invoke Article 90 in the struggle for electricity liberalisation in 1995, the Commission eventually accepted a compromise that permitted far more protection of national monopoly operators than in the telecommunications sector. One reason for this difference between telecommunications and energy, lay in the balance between firms that sought to enter the market and the incumbents who resisted liberalisation (Schmidt 1997, 1998). In the telecommunications case, an 'electronic alliance' of large corporate users, multinational companies and IT equipment suppliers proved an important ally in favour of liberalisation. In the energy case, the Commission's proposals for liberalisation met far stronger opposition, and the outcome has been much more ambiguous.

In the energy case, in the face of considerable resistance from all member states except the UK, the Commission opted for an incremental approach based on bargaining with the governments. The Commission's aim was to establish 'common carriage' across the EU, i.e. free access for energy users or distributors to the networks. The central questions concerned how much of the market should be opened and how and to what extent competition should be permitted in the supply of gas and electricity. The Commission's original proposal introduced the concept of regulated third party access to pipelines and transmission networks, with an EU-level regulatory authority (Stern 1998, Andersen 2001). However, the proposal met with immediate opposition from 11 of the 12 member states, and the Commission was obliged to re-submit a separate proposal for electricity and gas liberalisation. Over the following years the EU Commission worked on an alternative, watered down version of the original directive. A directive on electricity liberalisation was finally agreed in 1996. It represented a victory for the advocates of limited liberalisation, as it allowed for continued existence of the single buyer model and permitted states to impose 'public service obligations' on utilities. Liberalisation would only take place gradually. However, both the Commission and the liberalising states envisaged further liberalisation.

The negotiations for gas liberalisation got underway after the electricity compromise, in 1996–7. Negotiations were dogged by the same problems as in the electricity talks: they centred on qualitative and quantitative levels of market opening. The directive on gas liberalisation that was finally agreed in late

1997 was, like its counterpart in the electricity sector, very much a compromise between the Commission and the more liberal states on one hand, and the more protectionist and industrial policy-oriented states on the other. It opened up the old monopolised markets to competition, but the regulatory systems were to be decided at the national level. Exceptions could be invoked on the grounds of security of supply, public service obligations and environment policy. Nevertheless, the directive unleashed dynamic forces of liberalisation. A new gas directive was adopted in 2003, to address the shortcomings of the liberalisation process in the gas market. It mandated regulated access tariffs and independent regulators for the gas industry, and non-discriminatory third party access to be developed through legal unbundling of gas transport from trading services. By 2007, according to the Commission, only one of the member states had completed market opening in the gas sector: the UK. In the electricity sector, the UK was joined by Sweden, Finland, Norway and Denmark.

Liberalisation of postal services has progressed far more slowly than the other utilities because this has been a central monopoly (and source of income) of most European states and empires for more than half a millennium. In this sector, all European states come close to the French *service public* approach. Even in the UK, privatisation plans prompted considerable controversy over the public services that local post offices provide. The postal service is also generally strongly unionised in most EU states. Perhaps more importantly, this is a public utility that involves strong distributional conflicts on the geographical (centre vs. periphery) dimension. The principle that everybody should be able to send a letter to somebody else in the country for a fixed price irrespective of location has strong roots everywhere in Europe. Nevertheless, a degree of liberalisation has taken place. As in the telecoms sector, this began with the business side of the service. Delivery of large parcels to firms by private companies was the first acceptance of liberalisation of the sector. Other non-core activities followed, such as money transfers and small parcels. Almost two decades after the Commission's first proposal for postal liberalisation in 1988, the deadline for liberalisation of all postal services (including letters) has been set for 2010.

The experience with liberalisation and privatisation in the European Union and most of its member states has proven quite different from that of the USA and the UK. In the liberal states, privatisation and liberalisation were parallel and strongly interlinked projects. Liberalisation required privatisation, and vice versa. Both were also seen as integral parts of a deregulation programme. Elsewhere in Europe, at least in the first decade after the Single European Act, liberalisation was not taken to imply privatisation. To be sure, liberalisation involved opening up utilities markets to competition, and thus to private competitors that would challenge the public ex-monopoly. Yet both politicians and company executives expected that the former monopoly utilities would be able to operate as fully state-owned corporations in the new market. Although EU law requires liberalisation, and sometimes even company restructuring, there are no EU rules that require privatisation as such. This resulted in newly liberalised markets that were dominated by one large actor: the incumbent or former state monopoly. The need for regulation to protect small firms or new entrants to the market was therefore much more urgent than in the USA. Over time, however, it has turned out to be difficult to operate corporatised state-owned companies in the fierce competition that has begun to characterise liberalised markets. This may be because private shareholders are more profit-oriented than the state and therefore generate stronger pressure for adaptation by the firms, and possibly because state ownership sometimes involves priorities other than pure profit (Eliassen and From 2007). In any case, developments in the liberal, consensual and corporatist states alike, and in the EU as a whole, demonstrate an increasing need for more complex regulation of markets. Deregulation fostered re-regulation, because the rational action of market actors is to 'kill the market' – to seek to establish dominant positions. A well-functioning market for public services turns out to require more regulation than is required for monopoly operations. The next chapter therefore turns to developments in regulation and competition policy.

Further Reading

Hall, P.A. and Soskice, D. (eds) (2001) *Varieties of Capitalism: The Institutional Foundations of Comparative Advantage* (Oxford: Oxford University Press). An edited volume that includes comparative studies of various aspects of capitalism. The editors' essay on 'An Introduction to Varieties of Capitalism' (Chapter 1) provides a good discussion of the main differences between modern capitalist systems and the causes of these differences.

Scharpf, F.W. (1999) *Governing in Europe: Effective and Democratic?* (Oxford: Oxford University Press). A good discussion of the relationship between the European Union and its member states in terms of democracy, capitalism and welfare regimes. Chapter 2 on 'Negative and Positive Integration' explains why the Single European Market is particularly oriented towards liberalisation and removal of barriers to trade.

Osborne, D. and Gabler, T. (1992) *Reinventing Government* (New York: Addison-Wesley). A classic text on the case for market-oriented reforms of public services, with reference to the USA. Chapter 2 on 'Catalytic Government: Steering Rather than Rowing' sets out the case for a 'smaller but stronger' public sector in the USA. Chapter 3 on 'Competitive Government: Injecting Competition into Public Service Delivery' is relevant to the broader debate about competition in the public sector.

(Continued)

(Continued)

Bailey, S.J. (2002) *Public Sector Economics: Theory, Policy and Practice* (London: Palgrave). A good textbook on the economics of public policy, with particular focus on the UK. Chapter 13 on 'Nationalisation, Privatisation and Regulation' is particularly relevant.

There are a number of good journal articles on liberalisation in the EU in the *Journal of European Public Policy* and the *Journal of Common Market Studies*. One particularly pertinent example is Schmidt, S.K. (1998) 'Commission Activism: Subsuming Telecommunications and Electricity under European Competition Law', *Journal of European Public Policy*, 5:1, 169–84. This article explains why liberalisation has been easier in the telecommunications industry than in energy markets, looking at the role of the European Commission, the preferences of member state governments, and the role of firms and organised interests in the liberalisation processes.

FOUR

Regulation and Competition Policy

Regulation and competition policy have become constituent elements of modern capitalist economies. The questions of how to create markets and sustain competition have given rise to a series of rules and regulations that are sometimes said to amount to a country's 'economic constitution' – competition policy. The basic idea behind market regulation is summed up in Bruce Doern and Stephen Wilks' observation that 'neither competition nor the market is inevitable or natural', and that both must be sustained by regulation (1996: 1). Adam Smith famously remarked that 'it is not from the benevolence of the butcher, the brewer, or the baker, that we expect our dinner, but from their regard to their own interest' (1776: 20). The corollary is that 'people of the same trade seldom meet together, even for merriment and diversion, but the conversation ends in a conspiracy against the public, or in some contrivance to raise prices' (1776: 137). The common underlying assumption for most liberal democracies' approach to regulating markets has long been that competition is desirable, but that it is shaped and sustained by institutions. The disagreements about regulation have concerned how much is warranted, and of what kind? This is the normative question: What ought to be done? A second question turns the attention to who benefits from regulation, and asks: Who wants regulation? The third question, which is the main focus of this chapter, is how regulation and competition policy has been developed, and how (and whether) it is changing.

Why regulate? Regulation and market failures

The most widely accepted basis for government regulation and public services is the idea that market transactions may have some consequences that are not (and perhaps cannot be) mediated through the price mechanism – that there might be a degree of *market failure*. Even voluntary market transactions can have a detrimental effect on third parties. Under certain circumstances the market cannot be expected to work perfectly. In fact, even a minimal market requires a series of institutions, like property rights, law enforcement and courts. Beyond these minimal requirements, most liberal democracies have sought to address at least four major forms of market failure. These are situations in which voluntary market transactions lead to a level of production that is less than Pareto optimal, that is, one or more persons could in theory be made better off without any other individual becoming worse off.

First, the possibility of *negative externalities* is often thought to warrant government intervention in the form of regulation, or at the very least (re-)allocation of property rights. Although voluntary transactions ought to make both parties to the transaction better off, a transaction might harm a third party. The classical example is pollution. Unless property rights are adequately specified (so that ownership to clean air is established) or regulation governs pollution, the parties to a transaction may have no incentives to take into account the negative effect of their production of goods or services on the environment or third parties. All liberal democracies therefore have, for example, laws regulating pollution and protecting the environment (as well as 'common pool' resources, to which everybody has access).

Second, the distinction between *public* and *private goods* is often invoked to explain why market allocation might lead to *inadequate provision of public goods*. Public goods are indivisible (non-rival) and non-excludable. One person's consumption of, for example, clean air or a television broadcast does not reduce the scope for others' consumption. To the extent that it is difficult to exclude non-paying consumers from pure (or even mixed) public goods, the market might lead to sub-optimal provision because each individual has an incentive to 'free ride' (consume, but not contribute). Defence and policing are examples of classical public goods, clean air and avoiding climate change are also increasingly accepted as important public goods.

Third, a series of economic activities are characterised by decreasing returns to scale: the more is produced, the less the cost of each additional unit. This particularly applies to network services, such as rail transport or telephone lines. These have long been considered *natural monopolies* in many countries. Once a rail-line has been built, it is cheaper to add capacity than build a new rival line. Market competition will therefore tend to lead to monopolies, because the incumbent can always under-price a new entrant (and put the price back up once the challenger has withdrawn). Although the Pareto optimal level of production is the point at which the cost of supply equals the cost of producing one more unit, the monopolist may be tempted to produce somewhat less than this and charge a higher price, thus extracting profit (monopoly rent) that would be much more difficult to extract under full competition.

Fourth, as Adam Smith and successive economists have warned, left to themselves producers may well collude to *fix prices* above the market efficient level. Like a monopolist, a cartel may decide to produce less and sell at a higher price, thus extracting monopoly rent. In addition to measures against monopolists' or near monopolists' abuse of dominant positions in the market, competition policy is usually designed to restrict cooperation between supposedly competing producers (horizontal restraints on trade), as well as arrangements that limit competition between producers and retailers (vertical restraint).

A broader set of justifications for the state's provision of public services or regulation involve invoking the 'general public interest', for example, quality control dealing with information asymmetries, or providing cross-subsidies or access to services and security of supply, or regulating risk (Baldwin and Cave 1999, Hood et al. 2001). This implies a wider definition of market failure: it suggests that modern markets are so complex that, in a number of transactions, the consumer lacks the necessary information. Consequently, some potential transactions might not take place, or become more unnecessarily expensive. Regulation is therefore based on the desirability of reducing the costs to consumers and the risks to which they are exposed, as well as to meet social goals determined through the political process. These motives for regulation tend to be more controversial than the narrower types of market failure set out above. Critics of excessive regulation point to the danger that the cumulative effect of each interest group's demands on the state might be the expansion of the public sector as well as increasingly complex and costly regulation.

First, market transactions might not always feature the level of safety and quality control that would allow for a Pareto optimal amount of exchange. If there is uncertainty about product safety or quality, a risk premium may be detracted from the price. Over the last century, most liberal democracies have developed a series of measures to address this, such as product liability laws (which make producers liable for a product's faults, even if they are not a direct party to the final transaction between retailer and consumer), quality standards, obligatory safety measures, and increasingly, product information and even health warning labels (for example, on tobacco products).

Second, it is sometimes deemed politically desirable that a particular product should be available across the country, irrespective of location. Utilities are therefore subject to obligations to supply, for example, to deliver mail, install phone lines or operate train services even in cases where the specific operation runs at a loss. Even when privatised, they therefore engage in a certain amount of cross-subsidies between, for example, profitable and loss-making local post offices or bus routes are obliged to provide a certain level and quality of service.

Third, another variation on the same theme includes equitable distribution of costs or cross-subsidies. A number of European states at one point or another chose to subsidise certain public services, for example, gas, electricity or telephony, shifting costs from private to industrial consumers, or vice versa. Most states have also sought to establish a basic and equal price for local calls in a country, irrespective of location within the country.

Who wants regulation? The demand and supply of regulation

The classical normative question about regulation – what is to be done? – is often implicitly associated with a *pluralist* theory of the state. Pluralists see the state as an arena in which multiple interest groups compete on more or less equal terms (the term *pluralism* literally refers to this basic assumption about a *multitude* of interest groups). Organisations reflect the common interests of the individuals they represent. When a group organises and demands action on any given issue, there will be a tendency for another group to organise on the other side. In other words, politics is a game where competing interest groups struggle to influence public policy, and where the group with the most members and strongest preferences is more likely to win. The state may be thought of as a passive or neutral organisation that reflects the struggles between different interests; or as a more active 'broker' that has interests of its own or supports one side or the other (Dunleavy and O'Leary 1987). The central point here is that different political games, featuring actors with different interests, values and relative power, produce different outcomes. In liberal democracies these outcomes are legitimised by the process that gives rise to them: the democratic political decision-making process. However, this focus on who wants regulation and lobbies in favour of it has given rise to a number of theories that depart from the pluralist assumptions that more or less equal rival groups will compete to influence policy in a democratically legitimate way.

This change from the normative question of what kind of policies are required to correct market failures to the positive question of who benefits from the current set-up, radically altered some of the fundamental questions in public policy analysis. The new central question became who had developed the present policy regimes and in whose interest, in other words: Who wants regulation? Positive theories interpret regulation as a product of pressure from interest groups (demand) and the response of decision-makers (supply). Regulation is seen primarily as an exercise in rent-seeking or utility maximisation, and it is therefore not necessarily in the public interest. On the demand side, this raises questions about the relative power and influence of different organised interest groups, particularly business and labour. Not all pressure groups succeed, and Olson's (1965) 'logic of collective action' analysis suggests that industry and labour is generally in a stronger position than consumers. Developing the argument further, Stigler (1971) argued that regulation is demanded and 'acquired' by industry, and therefore operated in the interest of the 'target' industry. On the supply side, most of the focus has been on the consequences of elected politicians seeking re-election and financial support for campaigns and on the extent to which bureaucracies over-supply public services (Downs 1957, Tullock 1976).

Taking the individual actors' pursuit of his or her interest (by rational means) as a starting point in the explanation of which public services are provided, the assumption is that private actors, firms and organised interests treat regulation as yet another means for enrichment. Organised interests, whether in the form of capital or labour, will demand from the state the kind of economic policy that will benefit them the most. This may lead to political battles between different parts of an industry, for example, between the established firms that seek to protect their market shares and firms that hope to break in to the market. For example, Coen and Héritier (2000) found that incumbents in the European electricity and telecoms industries tend to favour regulation through competition policy because it treats firms more or less equally, while new entrants favour industry-specific regulators that are sensitive to special obstacles to competition. A good example is number portability – allowing mobile phone users to keep their phone number when changing operators.

This analysis builds on the assumption that organised interest groups primarily pursue benefits that come to them alone. They pursue private goods rather than public goods. Olson's *Logic of Collective Action* (1965) challenged the pluralist assumption that society consists of a number of cross-cutting interests, and that most people with common interests will organise politically. Olson argues that only groups that can offer their members benefits that are higher than the cost of membership, and that non-members will not be able to enjoy, will be able to organise successfully. Others will suffer from a free-rider problem, as potential members will seek to enjoy the benefits of collective action without taking part themselves. Consequently, groups will tend to pursue private goods; goods that can be distributed among the members. This means that all but the very largest groups in society will seek a larger share of the common 'pie' rather than pursue policies that contribute to increasing the size of the pie. In other words, interest groups tend to pursue redistribution of resources in their favour, rather than economic growth.

The flipside of the demand for public services is the question of supply: Who supplies public policy and regulation, and why? The two most influential answers centre on elected politicians and the bureaucracy that support them: politicians seek re-election and financial support for campaigns, while bureaucracies over-supply or at least try to shape public policy in their own interest (Downs 1956, Tullock 1976, Dunleavy 1991). The logic of electoral politics in modern liberal democracies is that in order to fund election campaigns, candidates or parties seek the support of large organised interests by enacting legislation that these trade unions of industry groups favour. This, in turn, may be counter-balanced by the disciplining effect of political parties, which must balance their quest for resources against their three overriding goals: the quest for votes, office and policy (Strom 1990). Moreover, civil servants may pursue their own interest and therefore over-supply regulation (Niskanen, 1971), an argument that we return to in Chapter 5. Equally problematically a government department or regulator may, over time, become closely involved with the industry that it charged with regulating – 'regulatory capture' by industry.

Consequently, the development of actual regulatory regimes may be as much the product of the demand and supply of regulation as debates about what kind of regulation is warranted by different kinds of market failures and what kind of public policy preferences should be prioritised. Olson's arguments about organised interests' demands led him to conclude that societies with strong interest groups were less prone to economic growth (1982), even though the democratic process as such is necessary for fully functioning market economies to develop and be sustained in the long run (Olson 1993, 2000). On the other hand, it has also been suggested that even if regulation is acquired by industry, political parties (which pursue votes) act in such a way that the interests of firms and consumers are balanced (Peltzman 1976). Focusing on the effect of several companies competing for regulation, Becker (1983) argues that politicians will supply regulation to the companies that can make best use of it. The Chicago School economists are therefore somewhat less concerned than Olson about the effects of regulation, because they argue that competition for regulation is likely to lead to the most effective regulation being adopted in the long run.

How has regulation developed? The evolution of regulation

Since the early 1990s, and particularly as the European Union and its member states began to develop new and complex regulatory regimes for the newly privatised and liberalised utilities sectors, a third question has dominated much of the literature on theories of regulation: How has regulation developed? This literature approaches regulation and competition policy as a matter of long-term development. Although regulatory reform is driven by the quest for efficient rules of the game, it is almost always designed to operate in a broader institutional context, to fit an existing set of policies, institutions and rules of the game (Quirk 1988, Bulmer 1993, Majone 1996, Kassim and Menon 1996, Lodge 1999, Ogus 2002). Regulation is the product not only of political games, but also of the social, economic and legal contest in which it operates. The second and third parts of this chapter therefore turn to the comparative study of competition policy and regulation, and explore variation in regulation across countries and sectors as well as the present challenges of the regulatory state in Europe.

The Comparative Study of Competition Policy and Regulation

The variation in capitalism found in Europe is also reflected in diversity in states' approaches to regulation and competition. Whereas many EU members states have moved toward increasing use of strict and legally enforceable competition law and independent sector regulators, others have long preferred corporatism or mixed models. Yet all states face a common set of issues related to the operation of competitive markets. The responses they adopt have varied, as has the extent to which anti-completive measures are interpreted as a problem, but a set of core questions are common to most competition policy regimes (Doern and Wilks 1996, Gerber 1998, Martin 1998).

Regulating for competition

Competition policy is essentially a 'negative' instrument in the sense that it lays down restrictions, in contrast to the 'positive' instruments such as subsidies and other government intervention in support of industry. Competition policy is centred on law and legal action, and directed against (private) restrictions on competition. In contrast to a range of industrial policy instruments that might or might not be designed to promote competition, competition policy is essentially concerned with ensuring that the actors in the economy do not excessively restrict competition. This means that competition policy focuses on five central questions (though not all are addressed by all regimes).

First, perhaps the oldest and most obvious challenge to free market competition is monopoly power. Although monopoly power is clearly advantageous to the firm that can use it to extract higher profits that would be possible under competition, it is problematic for the consumer that has to pay the higher price which constitutes the monopoly rent. Nevertheless, a number of states have chosen to grant monopoly rights or establish state-owned monopolies for a range of reasons. Some European telecommunications monopolies, for example, can be traced back to pre-industrial monopolies on postal communication that were designed to raise revenue. Others, such as the Nordic monopolies on the production, import and retail of alcohol, were instituted for health reasons. In the case of utilities networks, the logic of 'natural monopolies' was usually taken to suggest that because it would be wasteful to run two parallel networks and a monopoly was therefore almost unavoidable, the monopoly should be state-owned so that the profits go to the state.

Second, the most obvious challenge in a multi-firm sector is price-fixing or other efforts to restrict competition by the core firms in any given industry. The restriction of cartels has been a central challenge to free competition. Most capitalist economies include some restrictions on cartels, or at least their most obvious tool: price-fixing. However, a number of states have encouraged cartelisation of some industries as a tool of state policy, in order to create 'national champions' or groups of firms that dominate export or import markets or provide price stability for a certain commodity.

Third, the more complex version of the same problem is that firms may use (or more precisely, abuse) their power to impose restrictive practices on other actors in the market or otherwise seek to harm competitors. This is normally a question of market power, of a firm that has a strong or dominant position in the market using this to impose restrictions on its suppliers or retailers. However, it is of course also possible that smaller firms engage in restrictive practices that do not amount to a cartel, for example, when a producer grants exclusive retail privileges to an agent and thus limits competition in a given geographical area. Restrictive practices are usually divided into 'vertical' and 'horizontal' restrictions, where the former are restrictions up and down the supply chain and the latter across one level of the chain. Examples of vertical restraints that are permitted even under EU law include the exclusive links between oil companies and petrol stations, and in countries like the UK, between brewers of beer and pubs. Even in the absence of cartels or restraints, dominant positions might in themselves be considered problematic. Some (prohibition-based) competition policy regimes include rules that limit how large a share of the market a single firm is permitted to control; other (abuse-based) regimes only prohibit dominant positions if the firm in question abuses its dominant positions. Examples include selling goods at less than cost price in order to drive out a competitor.

Fourth, in increasing order of complexity and controversy, is the question of the effect on competition that a merger of two firms might have. If monopolies, cartels, dominant positions and restrictive practices are problematic, it follows that a merger of two companies might increase the danger of such behaviour. A number of states have therefore adopted rules that restrict mergers and acquisitions, in some cases based on form and in others based on effect. The European Union merger regime reflects the link between mergers and the competition concerns discussed above: its merger competence grew gradually out of its power to restrict abuse of dominant position in the 1970s, long before the formal Merger Control Regulation was adopted in 1989 (Weiler 1991, Gerber 1998).

Fifth and finally, an independent competition authority might be called upon to vet (or even restrict) state subsidies if these distort competition. Restrictions on state aid to industry is an integral part of the EU competition policy regime, but it has not been a standard element of most national regimes. In fact, with the exception of the German regime, most European competition policy systems have traditionally been subject to political control rather than run by a fully independent competition authority. Although most EU (and EEA) member states have adopted increasingly independent competition policy rules, and competition policy cases often involve close cooperation between the national and EU regulators (From 2001), several systems maintain an element of political discretion. Reduction in state aid has therefore been driven more by governments' policy choice and the limits set by common EU rules than by national competition law. We have added restrictions on state aid as a fifth point on the list here partly in order to include all the five central objectives of EU competition policy.

Comparative competition policy

The study of competition policy has been dominated by three academic disciplines, or main approaches: law, economics and public administration. Other approaches, such as organisational theory or strategy could be added to this, and have been. Although the comparative study of competition policy must inevitably include elements from the various disciplines, what follows is (in line with the general themes of this book) a more public policy oriented approach.

The normative questions are a more precise sub-group of the broader 'what should be done?' questions pertaining to regulation, discussed above. The answers fall into three broad categories. First, the classical libertarian approach rediscovered by the Chicago School and influential in the USA holds that Adam Smith's 'invisible hand' tends to result in reasonable competition and that regulation might well be counterproductive. These analyses concede that real existing competition is hardly perfect, but question whether it can or should be corrected by political interventions. The core of the Chicago School's argument is that markets are dynamic, and that the key concern should therefore not be the actual degree of competition but the possibility that a new entrant might enter the market. In other words, they adopt an 'as if' approach, where the central criterion is whether markets operate as if they were competitive rather than whether they actually are competitive. Consequently, abuse of dominant position by, for example, predatory pricing is not really a problem, as long as the mere threat of a competitor entering the market makes the dominant actor act as if there were actual competition. Markets need not be competitive, only contestable. In contrast, most competition policy regimes in Europe have been based on the assumption that markets are messy, complicated and imperfect. In the post-war era, most states adopted mixed regimes that relied more on informal tools of governance than on competition law, including, for example, widespread state ownership, such as the post-war German model and EU competition policy regime, which rely more on active intervention by independent competition authorities.

Turning to the question of positive analysis of comparative competition policy, or the study of how competition policy operates, comparative analysis usually involves looking at three different levels (Doern and Wilks 1996). At the *macro-level*, the question concerns the objective of competition policy. The most important independent variables are politicians, political games and (economic) ideology, as well as the political institutions that make up the rules of the game and shape the parameters of competition policy reform. Although the international dimension is sometimes identified as a separate level, we prefer to consider competition policy as a case of multi-level governance where rules and political games take place at several levels. The study of competition policy reform in, for example, Denmark would therefore involve analysis of both the Danish constitution and the EU rules that shaped Danish competition policy reform. Apart from the UK (which followed shortly afterwards), Denmark was the last of the old member states to adopt an EU-style 'prohibition' approach to competition policy in 1998 (Wise 2000). The central question is: Where does competition policy fit into the state's overall economic policy? Is it indeed an 'economic constitution' that overrides other policy areas, such as industrial policy, research and development, consumer protection and trade, or is competition policy to be balanced against other policy priorities? These questions are not only important as far as the state's overall economic policy is concerned, but are particularly pressing when it comes to sectors that are subject to special regulation, such as telecommunications, infrastructure, defence, culture and the media.

At the *meso-level*, the study of competition policy shifts the focus to institutional arrangements and practical rules and norms. Each competition policy regime involves different types of competition authorities, with different degrees of independence, legal or political chains of authority and accountability, variations in formal powers and the locus of discretion, as well as different relationships with other agents of the state such as sector regulators. Going beyond the formal rules and guidelines, study of competition authorities as organisations reveals that there is considerable variation also in terms of practice, and that norms and values vary considerably across organisations even if their formal structures become relatively similar. Despite considerable evidence of pressure for 'quiet harmonisation' of competition policy in the EU member states, comparative studies show that competition law is organised, operated and enforced in different ways by the European Commission and national authorities (Martin 1988). In terms of content, the changes in the German and UK systems in the 1990s were described as 'national tunes' that differ considerably with reference to the 'European melody' (Eyre and Lodge 2000). Key questions include: What kind of rules and organisations are appropriate, and how should exemptions be formulated? Should competition policy prohibit certain forms (for example, more than certain share of the market), or merely actual and proven abuse of market power? How should the 'relevant market' in any given case be defined, and economic models be applied by the competition authorities?

Legal studies of competition policy have naturally focused more on the actual operation of competition law at the *micro-level*, analysing how the law is interpreted and applied and focusing more on outcomes. At this level the focus may also shift to the impact of competition policy on markets in reality, or on how effective competition policy actually is. The impact of individual leaders of competition authorities and of the organisation's staff has been much studied, particularly in the case of the EU because competition policy has developed considerably over a relatively short period of time (Cini and McGowan 1998, From 2001). Several of the more operational questions about competition policy listed in the paragraph above are relevant at the micro-level as well. Perhaps the central question here, however, is: How effective are the different policy regimes? Are certain types of instruments counterproductive inasmuch as efforts to increase competition actually ends up constraining it, while less restrictive application of competition law might in some cases enhance competition? What is the causal relationship between competition policy and actual economic outcomes, and how to measure or evaluate this given the distance between policy and its effect?

Evidence about how a regulatory regime works, or whether a particular reform has had any impact, can be sought at all three levels. At the macro-level, the effect of reforms can be evaluated in terms of the real changes in competition policy rules. Here 'Europeanisation' would mean adaptation of the goals and structures of the national regime, to render it more in line with the EU rules. This has been well documented in a number of European cases (Martin 1998). At the meso-level, the focus would be on organisational change, and the evidence of Europeanisation might be sought in changes in the resources and organisation of the regulator or in the way the regulator operates in practice. At the micro-level, the central questions would concern the effect of competition policy, particularly whether rulings are increasingly similar across countries or even if the effects of rulings on market competition are more or less the same across Europe.

Competition policy and regulation in Europe

Competition policy is the cornerstone of the EU's Single Market. It is the single most important tool available to the Commission for enforcing the Single

Market rules, the policy area in which the Commission has the strongest and clearest powers, and it has justifiably been described as the EU's first supranational policy area (McGowan and Wilks 1995). Yet its evolution was gradual and uncertain for the first three decades. The strengthening of EU competition policy in the 1970s and 1980s was a gradual process, driven by cooperation between the Commission and the European Court of Justice, in a process that saw a gradual expansion of the remit of EU competition law and the 'metamorphosis' of the Commission's Directorate General for Competition (then known as DG IV) into something very much like an independent federal agency (Weiler 1991, McGowan and Wilks 1995). In its inception, in the 1950s, the EU system was designed not only to enforce common rules, but also to complete the free trade project and combat private agreements that might distort free trade. The system was influenced by the two main continental approaches to competition and industrial policy, as the French and German governments sought to project their own rules and norms onto the new supranational level. In the end, the EU system came closer to the German model. The EU regime was also indirectly influenced by US thinking on competition law, although some of the administrative procedures and the organisation of the Directorate General reflected French practices (Gerber 1998). This reflected the differences in the European states' traditions of industrial policy and competition law.

The roots of the EU system lie primarily in one of four main European traditions: the German 'ordo-liberal' system and social market economy, rather than the more *dirigiste* French approach, the mixed Scandinavian models or the UK's more pragmatic and less formal system (Doern and Wilks 1996). Although most post-war Western European competition policy regimes were based on abuse-control, developments in Germany and the USA came to exert heavy influence on European thinking about competition policy in the second half of the century. Gerber ascribes much of this to the German ordo-liberal approach providing a new intellectual framework for competition law, which drew on classical liberalism combined with the need to protect society from abuse of economic power. This notion of free market economic order based on a strong state provided a central force behind both the German approach to European integration and the formulation and development of EU competition law. Combined with the free market and competition-oriented Single European Act, this legal approach became the focus in the 1980s when the policies of Western European governments were 'increasingly called into question by economic changes, rival conceptions of competition law and the process of European integration' (Gerber 1998: 231).

Although the EU member states' approaches to regulation and competition were very different in the 1960s and 1970s, by 2000 a considerable degree of convergence at the macro-level was evident. France, which had featured a *dirigiste* economic and regulatory system that accorded a considerable direct role in economic affairs to the state and features only limited provisions for competition policy, was the first EU member state to substantially reform its competition law to bring it into closer line with the EU system in 1986 (Gerber 1998: 403ff). Its new system followed the ideas and structure of EU competition policy, including prohibiting arrangements that restrain or distort competition, prohibiting abuse of dominant positions and establishing merger controls. Italy, which until 1990 did not have a competition law, followed suit. The Scandinavian countries' systems for regulating competition date back to the inter-war period, during which they differed considerably, having started as ad hoc efforts to deal with monopolies or other specific problems. In the post-war era, they converged around a model in which price control was the core building bloc. Their move toward the EU model started in the 1980s with changes from price regulation toward regulation of competition, and was followed by shifts from the abuse approach toward the prohibition approach and close (at least in the Danish and Swedish cases) alignment with the EU regime in the 1990s. The UK system, a 'public interest' system based on evaluating the economic effect of firms' behaviour that involved a considerable amount of political and administrative discretion, underwent radical reform in 1998 when a new prohibitions-based system that was much more aligned with EU law was adopted (Wilks 1999).

Competition policy reforms in the EU member states indicate that Europeanisation has been a means to an end rather than an end in itself; that it has followed reforms rather than driven them. However, once the reform effort is under way, and if the envisaged reforms are inspired by the same logic as the EU regime, there are strong incentives to aligning the national regime to that of the EU. Reduction of the uncertainty and costs to industry that two systems with different rules and procedures entail has played a central role in arguments for alignment with the EU competition policy regime. At the macro-level, therefore, the EU member states have seen some convergence in competition policy. At the meso-level, however, considerable differences remain in the organisation, resources and operation of competition authorities and national regulators. As successive reports on economic developments in the EU show, considerable differences also remain at the micro-level, in terms both of how competition policy is carried out and broad member state approaches to economic policy, industrial policy and state aid (Howarth 2006).

This long-term trend of the development of a strong competition policy regime at the EU level and in most member states, but with a degree of heterogeneity, is continuing into the late 2000s. Despite the decentralisation of EU competition policy in 2003, when the Commission gave up exclusive powers to rule on restrictive practices and abuse of dominant position and shared this with national competition authorities, the Commission remains a strong actor in EU competition policy. To be sure, the 2003 reforms are sometimes seen as a reaction to the excessive centralisation of power with DG Competition, and therefore as a drive towards more decentralised competition policy. The Commission had been criticised for slow and unpredictable (un-transparent) decision-making in competition cases, a criticism that focused both on its competence and its workload (Gerber 2000). However, the 2003 reform seems to have strengthened the Commission's role rather than weakened it (Wilks 2005, 2007). It established DG Competition as the central actor in a network of regulators, the European Competition Network, that shares information, allocates cases and coordinates activities. In doing so it drew on a long tradition of strong cooperation between DG Competition and national competition authorities, and the ECN stands out as one of the strongest EU networks in terms of developing a common 'culture' of competition that involves common understanding of the goals of making the market work better, of the law, and of the role of economics in applying competition policy.

The Regulatory State and its Challenges

It is often said that we are living in the 'regulatory state' – that most European states have replaced direct interventionist industrial policy with indirect regulation (Majone 1994, McGowan and Wallace 1996, but for critical discussions see Moran 2002, Levi-Faur 2006, Lodge 2008). Whereas the old industrial policy regimes were characterised by protectionism, direct state intervention, active industrial policy, widespread state ownership and state aid to industry, the regulatory state relies more on indirect rule through rules and regulations. The state's central goals are no longer directly to support or protect industry, but rather to ensure that competition operates as it should. The regulatory state therefore involves a change in the central policy instruments of the state: a shift from industrial policy to competition policy. More or less independent competition authorities and regulatory agencies play increasingly important roles, and the role of government ministries of industry, energy and telecommunications play a more indirect role at arm's length from the industry than they did in Western Europe before 1980. Rules and legal authority are the principal tools that governments use to regulate industry, in contrast to the importance of direct state expenditure and ownership in the old industrial policy regimes.

The regulatory state in Europe came about as the confluence of three developments that were only partially related. First, there has been a considerable effort at the international level since the late 1970s to establish multilateral, rule-based free trade. This process has been partly driven by the free trade-oriented governments, but organisations such as the OECD and GATT have also provided arenas for development and exchange of ideas that have become a driving force behind the processes of globalisation in their own right. Second, the revival of European integration since the mid-1980s has led to a rule-based supranational regime in Europe that is rich in legal and regulatory authority but poor in financial resources. The EU adopted a regulatory approach partly by necessity, and partly because the regulatory models fit the EU's institutional set-up particularly well. Third, at the state level, most European governments have sought to modernise their public services, whether as a result of high costs and political change in Western Europe or of the collapse of communism east of the 'iron curtain'. The regulatory state has thus developed in the context for ever more multilateral free trade, a strong regulatory regime at the EU level, and privatisation and liberalisation at the state level.

The nation state in Europe has been changing in several different directions since the 1980s. Power has been delegated 'upwards' to the supranational EU, 'downwards' to local and regional government, as well as 'sideways' to more or less independent regulatory agencies and competition authorities, and some public services have been shifted to the market. In terms of regulation this has brought about double delegation – to the EU and to National Regulatory Agencies. Although the EU and the NRAs often pull in the same direction, toward more liberalised policy and more competition in the Single European Market, this is not always the case. Moreover, the focus on competition and a well-functioning market is usually clearer and stronger among competition authorities than the sector specific regulators. For example, a national energy regulator (or even the European Commission's Directorate General for Energy) may be more sensitive to specific problems in the electricity sector than the competition authority in the same state (or DG Competition). Questions about the relationship between general competition policy and sector-specific concerns remain even more important in sectors that are partially exempt from Single Market rules, such as financial services, the media and defence procurement. The motto proposed for the EU in the Constitutional Treaty – unity in diversity – may therefore apply almost as much to its regulatory regime as to the EU as a whole.

Two broad themes run through the debates about regulation in the EU. The first concerns the relationship between regulation at the EU level and the member state level. Should the EU's task primarily be to 'regulate the regulators', or should a stricter regulatory regime be developed at the EU level? Is EU-level regulation a task for the European Commission, or is there a case for establishing independent EU-level regulators? In reality the line between the Commission acting as a regulator and the establishment of a separate regulator at the EU level is blurred. DG Competition has long been the most independent of the Commission's directorate generals, often acting like an independent regulator. DG Competition has long investigated and taken positions on competition policy cases on its own, acting independently of the Commission as a whole, even if its final decisions must be approved by the College of Commissioners (by majority vote if necessary). However, in most of the sector-specific DGs, such as energy, telecoms or transport, the DGs are more comparable to the civil service in a member state than to NRAs. In most policy sectors, EU regulation has been a case of blending competition policy with the EU rules that regulate the NRAs and establish a framework for the member state regulatory regimes. European networks of regulators have emerged as an alternative to EU regulatory agencies, and the result has been networks for cooperation and coordination. However, these networks vary considerably both in terms of independence from national governments and how successful they are in enforcing compliance, with success being more likely in sectors that are not characterised by strong state interests (Kelemen and Tarrant 2007).

The second theme follows from this: most policy sectors involve a balance between the concerns of competition policy and sector regulation, and some areas are even excluded from common EU rules (and national competition policy rules) altogether. Although some politicians, like the Thatcher government, expected competition policy to provide a sufficient tool for regulating liberalised sectors, such as telecommunications and energy, the experience in both the UK and the rest of Europe has shown that sector-specific regulators for telecommunications (in some cases subsequently merged with the media regulators), energy and rail transport are necessary for regulation of the liberalised utilities markets (Newbery 1999, Lodge 2002). In the EU and its member states the balance has tended to tilt in favour of competition policy concerns in the telecommunications sector, where the Commission used competition policy to force through liberalisation and both national and EU sector regulators make much use of competition policy tools; whereas it has tended to tilt in favour of sector regulators in the energy and rail sectors. Other sectors have been more or less excluded from both the Single Market and competition policy, notably the media, the defence industry and financial services. Broad agreement on the justifications for exemptions from competition rules is largely confined to the media sector, where the logic of protecting cultural plurality remains. The basic concern in the defence sector is the protection of the states' defence capabilities, but in most cases the member states' reluctance to open defence markets to competition is driven by economic and industrial policy concerns: to protect national defence industry. Likewise, the protection of the financial services sector from the full force of EU merger rules reflects concerns that citizens' savings might be threatened by insufficiently vetted mergers or acquisitions, but has since been used to defend national firms from foreign take-overs.

From a late 2000s perspective, the regulatory state in Europe still looks robust. It is anchored in the WTO regime, the Single European Market and in public policy reforms at the national level. Nevertheless, changes at all three levels indicate some of the limits of the regulatory state. Internationally, Russia adopted a more assertive posture under President Valdimir Putin. International relations in Europe are increasingly characterised by geo-politics as much as multilateral trade rules (Correljé and van der Linde 2006). At the EU level, enlargement to 27 member states has rendered the EU a more heterogeneous organisation, and homogeneous integration can hardly be expected (Andersen and Sitter 2006). Some member states go further than particular directives require, whereas others take full advantage of the ambiguities, derogations and loopholes that are often built into EU directives as part of the negotiating process. At the state or policy level, the regulatory state has developed into a far more complex set of policy regimes than the term 'deregulation' might suggest (Levi-Faur 2006, Lodge 2008). Despite considerable macro-level convergence in the EU, variation remains both among states and between sectors. All public policy regimes tend to engender new problems and challenges, often of fairly predictable type (Hood 1991, 1998), and the regulatory state is no exception. The tasks assigned to national regulators are increasing in number, trade-offs and dilemmas between different priorities are becoming more pressing, and unanticipated developments are forcing regulators to adapt and change. Meanwhile, political and organised opposition to regulation, and the reactions of the target industry, adds to the challenges and new issues faced by both regulators and the makers of public policy. In addition to changes in macro-level frameworks, the last two decades have therefore also seen considerable focus on micro-level efficiency to complement macro-level change. The next four chapters duly turn to changes in the organisation of public management as part of the broader effort to modernise public services: looking in turn at changes in public management, eGovernment, organisational change and the tools of leadership and management.

Further Reading

Majone, G. (1996) *Regulating Europe* (London: Routledge). The classic text on regulation in the European Union. The first four chapters elaborate on the political economy of regulation and are particularly relevant. Chapter 2 on 'Theories of Regulation' provides a strong theoretical discussion.

Gerber, D.J. (1998) *Protecting Prometheus: Law and Competition in the Twentieth Century* (Oxford: Oxford University Press). An excellent history of competition policy in Europe, which covers both the policy debates and historical developments. Chapter 9 on 'Competition Law and European Integration' and Chapter 10 on '1986 and After' provide good discussions of developments in Europe.

(Continued)

(Continued)

Baldwin, R. and Cave, M. (1999) *Understanding Regulation* (Oxford: Oxford University Press). A good textbook on regulation, with a focus on the UK. Chapter 2 on 'Why Regulate' and Chapter 3 on 'Explaining Regulation' provide good introductions to regulation theory and the contemporary debates.

Newbery, D.M. (1999) *Privatization, Restructuring and Regulation of Network Utilities* (Cambridge: Massachusetts Institute of Technology Press). Covers regulation theory and the experience of utilities regulation in the UK. Chapter 5 on 'Introducing Competition into Network Utilities' provides a useful overview of the debate, and the individual chapters on electricity, telecoms and gas provide good coverage of selected utilities markets.

Jordana, J. and Levi-Faur, D. (eds) (2004) *The Politics of Regulation: Institutions and Regulatory Reforms for the Age of Governance* (Cheltenham: Edward Elgar). An edited collection that includes a number of strong essays on regulation in theory and practice. Chapter 6 by Martin Lodge on 'Accountability and Transparency in Regulation' provides a good discussion of the issues of accountability raised by various regulatory regimes.

FIVE

Modernising Public Administration: To the New Public Management and Beyond

If the first strategy for improving state capacity involves the state trying to do less, the second involves the state trying doing what it does better. Globalisation increased the demand for leaner, more efficient and more adaptable public administration; and at the same time digitalisation and the IT revolution opened up a whole new set of possibilities for modernising and re-engineering public services. As the political and academic critique of the public administration systems associated with the post-war welfare state became ever more intense during the 1970s and 1980s, most Western liberal democracies began to search for ways to improve public service delivery. Criticism of the excessive size of the welfare state prompted efforts to reduce costs – to improve *economy* in the public sector. Suggestions that public services had more scope for slack than private business because it did not face competitive pressures gave rise to measures to use public resources better – to improve *efficiency*. The charge that bureaucracies were more preoccupied with following procedure than with actual outcomes led to increased focus on evaluating the results of government programmes – a quest for increased *effectiveness*. In most states these three changes in governments' thinking about public policy came about gradually, but by the 1990s it had become commonplace to speak of a change from public *administration* to public *management*. In 1991 Christopher Hood (1991) coined the term *New Public Management* to label the broad set of changes that were taking place in the UK, and the term soon became a label for a broad set of programmes that sought to reorganise public sector organisations, to introduce elements of competition into public service provision, as well as to 'borrow' some private sector management techniques. It is this development and the subsequent reactions and reforms across the liberal democratic world that is the subject of this chapter.

From Old Public Administration to New Public Management

New Public Management (NPM) was not so much a single coherent agenda as a term coined to capture a set of changes which, when taken together, added up to a fundamental shift in public service delivery. The reforms drew on a coherent critique of public administration set out by the New Right, based largely on analyses that built on economic theory. In the 1980s and 1990s NPM-type reforms became synonymous with *modernisation* in many political programmes, but this was hardly the first time a broad set of modernising reforms swept the Western liberal democracies. The system that the new reformers were keen to replace was itself once hailed as the modern and rational system that would take public administration beyond the arbitrary, politicised and clientelist practices of nineteenth-century Europe. The system that most modern European states adopted in the half-century before the First World War or during the inter-war era, is best summed up in the work of the German sociologist Max Weber (1922/1947). Weber saw the system as the result of an effort to establish professional, hierarchical, legalistic and more or less politically neutral civil services across the European and the English-speaking democracies, and indeed the empires, of the time.

Weber's model of public administration

The fundamental principles behind the kind of systems that Weber analysed were the rule of law, equal and predictable treatment, and an impersonal, professional civil service. The rule of law and the belief that authority rests on a legal right to issue commands forms the basis of *rational legitimacy*. This rational legal authority stands in contrast to 'traditional legitimacy' (where authority is based on the sanctity of immemorial traditions) and 'charismatic legitimacy' (authority based on an exceptional person's characteristics). The modern (as it then was) public administration would be rationally organised, goal-oriented and efficient, operating according to an established set of rules and principles. The Weberian ideal-type's main characteristics can be summed up in five main points.

1 Hierarchical organisation and impersonal authority. Bureaucracies are organised hierarchically, and the higher echelons control and supervise the lower ranks. Authority is linked to the formal position of each civil servant (rather than his or her personal authority). Civil servants are appointed from above (rather than elected 'from below').
2 Fixed and formal competencies. The competencies of bureaucracies are laid down in formal rules, and discretionary power strictly regulated. Administrative law establishes procedures and the parameters of the use of sanctions (for example, fines). The civil service is clearly delineated from the private sector.
3 Specialised division of labour. Bureaucracies are specialised organisations, with well-defined division of labour. These specialised tasks require formal theoretical education,

which forms the basis for recruitment based on competence and formal qualifications. The result is highly specialised expertise within the organisation.

4   Written procedures. The civil service operates in accordance with well-established and transparent rules of procedure that require a written record of administrative decisions. The presence of written records facilitates appeals processes, whereby private actors may appeal against a decision up through the hierarchy of the organisation.

5   Full-time professional staff. Bureaucracies recruit full-time employees, based on competence. Civil services posts are subject to more or less fixed pay-scales (graded according to rank), promotion based on competence, and feature predictable, gradual and generally life-long careers.

The effect of this system is not merely a rational, legal, predictable and transparent regime, but also one in which civil servants enjoy a degree of independence from the political executive. This holds both operationally and in terms of protection against arbitrary dismissal. In the UK this is often summed up as the civil servant's ability to offer impartial advice 'without fear or favour'. Furthermore, Weber assumes that, in return for a safe and predictable life-long career, the civil servant assumes a duty of loyalty to the service (in contrast to the personal loyalty that characterises clientelistic systems). The system rests on a *civil service ethos*. It is this assumption about the motives and characteristics of the individual bureaucrat that was challenged and gave rise to a substantial critique of Weberian bureaucracy.

However, even as an ideal type, the Weberian model was far from universally accepted. Weber himself pointed to the practical difficulty of separating politics and administration. Mixed systems – for example, arrangements which retained elements of clientelism – remained in a number of states that aspired to the Weberian model (perhaps most notoriously in the south of Italy). Other regimes rejected the model outright. Fascist and communist authoritarian regimes in Europe politicised the civil service and rejected elements of the system of legal legitimacy. In 1989, as communism collapsed in the old Soviet bloc, the emerging liberal democracies therefore faced not only the triple challenge of a transition to democracy, independent nationhood and the free market, but also a transition from a politicised to a Weberian civil service (Goetz 2001). This came just as the established liberal democracies were beginning seriously to reform their public administrations, based on critiques of the Weberian model that were developed in the 1960s and 1970s.

Downs and the pluralist critique of Weber's model

Anthony Downs' analyses of bureaucracy and his critique of Weber's model may be characterised as *pluralist* inasmuch as it is based on a challenge of Weber's unified model (Dunleavy and O'Leary 1987, Dunleavy 1991). Downs' starting point in *Inside Bureaucracy* (1967) is a far more heterogeneous picture of the bureaucrat than the one presented by Weber. This, in turn, is derived from an analysis of the bureaucrat's motives. Although Downs counts loyalty to the service as a motivation, this is only one among several motivations. On the one hand, employees in the public sector are assumed to be motivated by a set of broader goals that includes, but is not limited to, a *civil service ethos*. These goals also include professional pride, loyalty to the immediate group, and even commitment to specific policies or programmes. On the other hand, however, civil servants also pursue their self-interest, and this implies more than offering complete loyalty to the service in return for a secure career. Self-interest may also include monetary income, power, prestige and a relatively low work-load. Different combinations and prioritisations of these goals allows for a plentitude of different types of civil servant, and thus for a pluralist model of bureaucracy (Dunleavy 1991: 148ff). For example, senior civil servants may face very different incentives from those who are situated on the lower rungs of the same organisation.

Because of these mixed motives, Downs (1967) suggests that not only is there a variety of civil servants, but the priorities of politicians and civil servants might not correspond completely. Types of bureaucrats range from *climbers*, who pursue their own career, power and income, to the more altruistic *statesmen* who focus on the pursuit of general welfare in accordance with civil service ethos. Between these categories are the *conservers*, who engage in the self-interested pursuit of a stable and predictable rise up the career ladder; the *zealots*, who are committed to specific programmes and therefore more open to radical change (if it enhances these programmes); and the *advocates*, whose loyalty is to their organisation and who promote everything under their own jurisdiction. In different ways, and apart from the *statesmen*, all Downs' types of bureaucrat stand in considerable contrast to the civil servant of the Weberian model. Consequently, it must be expected that civil servants do not act fully in accordance with the priorities laid down by the elected politicians (this holds whether the politicians' goals and priorities are self-serving or not).

Given the potential for discrepancies between the preferences of elected politicians and civil servants, political control of the bureaucracy becomes an open question. These differences in goals cause 'leakage' as policies (or instructions) may be distorted as they are passed down the hierarchy among bureaucrats with different perspectives or goals. All large organisations engage in some activities that are unrelated to their formal goals. Hence Downs' three laws of control: no-one can fully control a large organisation; the larger the organisation becomes, the weaker the central control at the top level; and the larger the organisation, the more difficult it is to coordinate among its subunits. On top of this, Downs' law of counter control holds that efforts to exercise control are bound to result in efforts by those at lower levels to evade or counteract control. In fact, efforts to control and monitor may result in an entirely new bureaucracy of 'controllers', with control problems of its own.

Finally, Weber's model assumed a certain degree of homogeneity across the civil service. However, by the 1950s, most civil services had come to control a far vaster set of policy areas than in Weber's day. Variation among the range of organisations involved in delivering public services was, and is, considerable. The central concerns that are catered for in Weber's model, including due process, judicial review, transparency, clear lines of political responsibility and accountability, and equal treatment, need not be equally important in all cases of public service delivery. For services such as education, concerns like local autonomy, academic focus, employee consultation and even a degree of room for local variation may be more important. For others, such as refuse disposal, efficiency and adaptability, or even low costs, might take priority.

The New Right critiques and economic man

Perhaps the most obvious consequence of the kind of control problems that Downs discussed is the potential for bureaucracies to expand beyond their optimal size. If some bureaucrats promote the expansion of their programmes or departments, and control is incomplete and information is limited, the result is excessive growth (Tullock 1965). William Niskanen (1971, 1973) used models and assumptions drawn from economics to develop this line of reasoning much further. His work, the classic among a broad body of theoretical and empirical writings that emerged in the 1960s and 1970s, used economic models to analyse politics. Niskanen and others concluded that the state has a tendency to grow too large – the New Right critique of the state, based on *public choice* analysis (see Dunleavy and O'Leary 1987, Dunleavy 1991, Shepsle and Bonchek 1997). If civil servants are assumed to be rational individuals that pursue their (fixed) preferences in a rational way, and if they have more and better information about performance in the public sector than the politicians that allocate tasks to them, then the public sector is bound to grow. In Niskanen's analysis, this holds whether the individual bureaucrats are motivated by higher pay, non-pecuniary benefits such as prestige or power, or whether they seek less selfishly to expand the activity of their department on the grounds that its activities are considered beneficial to society.

Niskanen's analysis borrows directly from economics and takes the comparison between a public agency and a private firm as the starting point. The central assumption is that both types of organisation are staffed by individuals and managers seeking to maximise their self-interest, and that this self-interest is fixed (it is external to the model, or exogenous). The central difference lies in the availability of information and the structure of incentives. Whereas shareholders or the board of a private company can gain considerable information from its net profit (and indirectly from share prices), the ministers or parliamentary committees that control a public agency have no equivalent transparent and readily available measure of performance. Information is far more asymmetric, in favour of the top civil servant, than is the case in most firms. Moreover, Niskanen assumes that most top-level bureaucrats seek to maximise budgets, not profit, even if they can identify or estimate the difference between operating costs and the overall benefit to society. Bigger budgets mean more room for manoeuvre and budgetary growth may be taken as a sign of political success. Further, big budgets may permit a more comfortable working environment and possibly other perks. Whereas the executive of a private firm may have similar incentives to seek a large operating budget, the private firm is more likely to face external competition from other firms and internal incentives to maximise profit in the form of performance-related pay. Thus, because of differences in the internal and external environment, bureaucracies are assumed to maximise size rather than profit.

The principal lesson drawn from Niskanen's work was that both information and incentives need to be well-designed if public agencies are to be controlled and not to expand excessively beyond the point of maximum benefit to society. Similar lessons about the need for smaller budgets and improved political control were also derived from two other works on public choice, again drawing on theories originally developed for the analysis of private sector firms: *principal–agent* theory and *transaction cost* theory.

Principal–agent theory established a powerful model for analysing the potential problems involved when one person or organisation, the *principal*, delegates tasks and power to another person or organisation, the *agent*. The potential problem derives from the extent to which the agent has different preferences from the principal, and therefore pursues different goals. This may be a matter of different goals (for example, bureaucrats' pursuit of bigger budgets), but it may also be a matter of different time-frames (civil servants and elected politicians respond differently to electoral cycles), difference in availability of information and its interpretation, different norms or differences in aversion to or acceptance of risk, all of which may cause differences between the principal and agent even if there is broad agreement on the common goal. Consequently, a large body of literature devoted to the question of how the principals can control agents and minimise 'agency drift' has developed. McCubbins et al. (1987) argue that bureaucrats can work out how far they can let a policy 'drift' away from the original instructions before new instructions are issued. In political systems where there are several principals with differing views that have to agree unanimously to a policy change (for example, the president and two legislative chambers in the USA; or three parties in a coalition government in Norway) the bureaucracy may let the policy drift toward the ideal point of one of the principals.

The central question that follows from taking a principal–agent approach to public service provision is how the principals (politicians) can establish mechanisms for controlling the agents (bureaucracy). Options include selecting appropriate agents, specifying instructions and operating procedures in advance, and reviewing the agents' activities afterwards. McCubbins and Schwartz (1984) distinguish between two forms of control: *police-patrol* systems by which the principals continuously supervise the agents, for example, in the form of a legislative committee overseeing an agency; and *fire-alarm* systems that rely on the users or recipients of a service complaining if it is unsatisfactory. In a review of this literature, Shepsle and Bonchek (1997: 368–9) suggest that, in a similar vein, systems that permit users to take service providers to court could be labelled *fire-fighting* systems. The key point is that this kind of analysis draws attention to the need for control and oversight, but also to the limits of control mechanisms (see Pollack 1996 and 1997, for a good discussion of how this can be used to analyse the EU political system).

Finally, drawing on Coase's (1937) classical *transaction costs* explanation of why some activities are organised in firms whilst others are left to the market, questions have been raised as to whether all public services ought to be delivered by departments or if some activities could be better left to market-like mechanisms (Wilson 1989, Horn 1995). It is the costs of carrying out transactions (such as negotiating agreement and supervising implementation) rather than the costs of actually producing goods or services that determines whether an activity should be organised in market-type contracts, trust-based networks or authority-based hierarchical organisations. Applied to the analysis of public service provision the question is whether the traditional integrated department is an appropriate organisational form for a range of different services. Therefore, by the mid-1970s, and increasingly throughout the 1980s, the New Right established a coherent and powerful critique of the Weberian model of bureaucracy, or old public administration. Where this coincided with a political shift to the right, the scene was set for a series of reforms that would soon earn the label New Public Management.

The New Public Management

The New Right critique of contemporary public administration found its way into political programmes in the 1980s, and set the scene for the emergence of a series of reform initiatives that subsequently attracted the label New Public Management (NPM). NPM was not so much a coherent reform programme, as a label attached to a certain type of reforms. The reforms in public service provision carried out by the governments of Ronald Reagan (President

1980–8) in the USA and Margaret Thatcher (Prime Minister 1979–90) in the UK in the 1980s are among the clearest examples of NPM reforms. However, similar types of reforms were carried out across much of Western Europe (as well as in Canada, New Zealand and Australia) and have been well documented in the academic literature (Pollitt and Bokhaert 2000, McLaughlin et al. 2002). The common theme is a focus on improving the economy, efficiency and effectiveness of public services: first there are efforts to control costs; then a focus on producing more services for a given budget; and finally a shift to focus on the effect of the services, i.e. better public service provision. Osborne and Gabler (1991) coined the phrase 'steering rather than rowing' to sum up their formula for 'reinventing government'.

The confluence of the new economic and political thinking, the much-debated crisis of the welfare state in the 1970s, and a wave of centre-right electoral victories in the late 1970s and early 1980s made a fertile environment for public sector reform. The OECD provided a forum for an analysis of public services across the western states and for a discussion of NPM-type remedies. Its Public Management (PUMA) reports linked developments in economic and political theory with specific and detailed analyses of its member states public sectors (or rather, sector-by-sector analysis). This coincided with the peak of public sector size and the combination of unemployment and inflation in most OECD states during the 1970s, and with various political reactions. In Scandinavia, new populist anti-tax parties emerged and the long-dominant social democratic parties lost some support. In the UK, Thatcher won the leadership of the Conservative party, and then the 1979 election. West Germany took a turn to the right in 1982 when Helmut Kohl assumed the chancellorship (Prime Minister). French economic policy turned right-wards the year after, even if the left kept the presidency. Most conservative or Christian democratic parties adopted more economically liberal positions. In the late 1980s and during the 1990s, most social democratic parties across Europe followed suit. By the mid-1990s many EU states were governed by centre-left prime ministers who led 'renewed' social democratic parties that accepted at least some of the principles behind the reforms that their centre-right rivals had put in place.

Because New Public Management is a label attached to a series of reforms that a range of OECD governments embarked on in the 1980s, and NPM was hardly a comprehensive reform programme, it has been defined in a number of ways. Some approaches use NPM to cover both effort to reduce the scope of the public sector and reforms within the public sector (Aucoin 1990, Lane 2000); others focus on the latter (Hood 1991, Dunleavy and Hood 1994). Some (Walsh 1995) see it as a systematic programme based on managerialism and indirect control; others see NPM reforms progressing through several phases (Ferlie et al. 1996). Some see it as a 'fad', or yet another trend in public management thought (Christensen and Lægreid 2002), at best ineffectual and at worst dangerous because of the reforms' unintended consequences. Others point to substantial effects across a range of states, albeit not always in a systematic way (Pollitt and Bokhaert 2000, Pollitt 2002). This chapter follows the lead taken by Hood (1991: 3) and uses NPM as 'a shorthand name for the set of broadly similar administrative doctrines which dominate the bureaucratic reform agenda in many of the OECD group of countries from the late 1970s'.

NPM is therefore best understood as one element in the quest for improved state capacity, alongside regional integration (discussed in Chapter 2), privatisation and liberalisation (Chapter 3) and new management tools (Chapters 7 and 8). Drawing on Hood's discussion of the doctrinal components of NPM, three broad elements can be defined (Dunleavy and Margetts 2000: 7, see also Pollitt 2003: 27ff).

First, NPM reforms include *reorganisation* of the public sector with a view to improving information and control. This includes definition of explicit standards and performance indicators, strong emphasis on controlling and measuring performance, and 'disaggregating' the public sector into more manageable units with the intention of separating policy-making and service delivery. Second, NPM reforms generally include efforts to increase *competition*, either within the public sector or through direct competition between public and private service providers. Third, NPM focuses on *incentives-based management* in the public sector. This means importing personnel management techniques from the private sector, such as moving away from rigid pay-scales to performance-related pay, and in some cases limiting trade union influence. It also means more discretionary power to managers, and clearer demarcation between political and operational accountability.

Reorganisation: Disaggregation and arm's-length control

The first of the three broad themes that make up the NPM is reorganisation of public bureaucracies. An important source of the problem identified in the New Right critique of bureaucracies was lack of information. The reorganisation of bureaucracies is one means for improving this. Breaking up large monolithic government departments that were directly involved in everything from designing policy to front-line delivery of services might permit more transparency and thus allow for greater control. The term 'disaggregation' (Dunleavy and Margetts 2000) refers to explicit efforts to divide up large bureaucracies and divide them into units responsible for different aspects of policy provision. To be sure, not all OECD states featured UK-type large policy departments (Sweden, for example, has a long tradition of more or less independent agencies), but most EU states sought to divide up and/or clarify the relationships between public organisations. This, in turn, should theoretically permit both greater autonomy for the separate agencies and clearer lines of control and accountability.

The term 'arms-length' neatly captures the idea that reorganisation of bureaucracies could be designed to keep the functions of deciding how much of a particular service should be provided, purchasing the service, actually providing the service, and controlling and evaluating service provision, separate from each other. This is sometimes labelled the 'purchaser–provider' split. However, given the importance of supervision and control, it is more useful to speak of separation between purchaser, provider and controller. All three, in turn, make up the bureaucratic (non-political) element of the public bureaucracy, while the top-level civil servants who are directly involved in policy-making (drawing up policy alternatives, giving policy advice) can be clearly separated from the other three roles. This runs hand-in-hand with the elaboration of explicit targets and standards for measuring and evaluating performance. If the aim is to enhance both control and accountability the specific tasks and general objectives assigned to each agency must be clearly specified (and normally also quantified).

Competition: Benchmarking, quasi-markets and competitive tendering

The second broad theme in the NPM centres on the effort to break up or limit some of the monopolistic characteristics of public sector bureaucracies by introducing an element of competition. Whether through direct competition between alternative service providers or by inducing internal competition among the sub-units in a single monopoly organisation, the economically inspired critiques of old public management suggest that rivalry is the key to more efficient public service provision. In some sectors, such as public utilities, the solution has been privatisation and liberalisation. Among the services that remained within the ambit of the public sector, some of the more radical reforms included compulsory competitive tendering. In the UK, the Thatcher government introduced laws that required local authorities to put a range of services, from refuse collection to catering, up for competitive tender.

Less radical solutions have been used for parts of the public sector where open competition is judged less feasible. On the less competitive end, the range of quasi-market mechanisms include benchmarking provisions for measuring and evaluating the performance and resource consumption of agencies that are engaged in similar activities (for example, hospitals performing similar operations, or battleships' use of ammunition relative to performance in exercises). Intermediary measures such as internal price mechanisms have been introduced, for example, in the National Health Service's 'internal market' under Thatcher. Less controversially, doctors and hospitals in many European states have been obliged to compete for patients (Mossialos and LeGrand 1999).

Incentives: Management and contracts

Third, and finally, many NPM-type reforms have sought to change the hierarchical and unitary models of employment in the public sector. This has generally been oriented to rewarding performance and to attracting people with private sector experience, although in some countries, particularly the UK, it also included efforts to reduce trade union influence. Tools for public management are discussed in more detail in Chapters 8 and 9. The central point here is that NPM is not only a matter of organisational change and introducing elements of competition into public service provision, but also a matter of internal reorganisation and new management techniques. At the senior level, this includes external recruitment, performance-related pay and more short-term contracts. The aims have been both a more competitive senior level bureaucracy and more professional and autonomous management. Further down the hierarchies it has meant adopting practices from private-sector human resource management, including combinations and permutations of more flexible labour contracts, more short-term and task-related contracts, performance-related pay and promotion, and less uniform and hierarchical career prospects.

A range of combinations and variations of the kind of measure set out here under the three broad strands of the NPM have been adopted (and sometimes later abandoned) across the OECD states. Although many of these reforms have been radical, the focus on UK examples carries with it the danger of exaggerating the changes to public service provision in Europe over the last two decades. Some of the measures associated with NPM and set out above, such as the introduction of independent agencies or the use of external regulators and control mechanisms within the public sector, are long-standing features of many European states. However, it is the combination of a series of reforms that pull more or less in the same direction, and the spread of similar reforms across most European states (albeit sometimes more in intent than in effect), that makes NPM a useful label for a general phenomenon. The reforms that fall under the three broad topics set out above are rooted in the New Right critique of old public administration, and were designed based on well-established assumptions about human behaviour and the effects of incentives and competition. As they were put into practice they in turn prompted a new series of critiques, and further reform. When and where this coincided with the centre-left's return to power – as in the UK after Labour won the 1997 election – the result has been further reform and new initiatives. This time an alternative label to NPM was sought both for political reasons and to label a new set of reforms. The next section duly turns to the concept used to analyse public service delivery beyond NPM – *the New Governance*.

Governance – Beyond New Public Management?

The term *governance* has come to replace New Public Management in much of the literature on public policy and administration. This is partly because public policy reforms in Europe have developed beyond the stage where NPM adequately describes current practices, and partly because both academics and politicians have sought to distinguish between the NPM-like agenda of centre-right government and the modernisation projects of the new centre-left. Some of the elements that help define governance as something distinct from NPM were first developed as adjustments to NPM; as incremental changes to reforms and systems that were still inspired by the core ideas and political agendas of NPM. Other elements of governance were developed in contrast to NPM and draw on very different ideals about motivation and control in the public sector. Governance is therefore partly a matter of some (centre-left) governments' quest to improve on NPM, and partly a matter of a quest for an alternative political project that could combine the focus on market mechanisms and public sector efficiency with the left's more traditional focus on civil society and commitment to the welfare state.

Although the term *governance* is hardly new (Weller (2000) traces its use back to King Henry IV in 1399), it has acquired a new meaning in recent political science literature (Pierre 2000). The central question is whether the state's capacity for carrying out public policy, i.e., its capacity for governance, can be strengthened by reliance on indirect (or 'soft') policy instruments. Whereas the old public administration relied heavily on direct state intervention and on reallocation of resources, and while the NPM relied primarily on legal regulations, contracts and incentives, the debate on governance suggests that public policy depends on recourse to a wider set of tools (Rhodes 2000). The roots of the term lie both in the literature on changing public administration in the (West) European states and in the literature that sought to analyse the EU as a system of governance without government (Rhodes 1996, 1997, Bulmer 1993, Kohler-Koch and Eising 1999, Sedelmeier 2001). The governance debate therefore includes three central themes: modernisation of public services beyond NPM; the relationship between government at several different levels – the global, regional, national and local or multi-level governance; and a more centre-left political narrative or project.

First, a central theme in both the practical and academic debate on governance is the notion that NPM reforms (like any reform in public policy) rarely worked exactly as planned. In the UK, it was the Conservative government of John Major (1990–7) that began to modify some of the stricter NPM-reforms introduced by his predecessor, Margaret Thatcher. For obvious political reasons, Thatcher's reforms started with those parts of the public services that could most easily be privatised or exposed to competition without much risk, such as telecommunications and local refuse disposal (Richards and Smith 2002). These were the subjects respectively of early privatisation and Competitive Compulsory Tendering (local authorities were legally obliged to put services out to tender). As the Major government proceeded to more contentious and difficult sectors, from rail transport to health and education, somewhat more complicated models were required than the simpler ones used in the 1980s. The Major government therefore continued the NPM-line of reforms, but also introduced a more complex set of targets and performance evaluation than the ones envisaged in the early NPM reforms. These new initiatives established a stronger focus on citizens' rights and more involvement of the voluntary sector (Flynn 1997). Some of the government's activities were shifted to the market (service provision) and the individual (decisions about choice of service provider).

The second central theme in the debates about governance is the changing relationship between the state and supranational organisations, primarily the EU. The EU system rests on a combination of regulation and coordination. Even when EU rules take the form of directives, or 'hard law', implementation depends on transposition by the member state governments. Where the EU relies on coordination, or 'soft law', the room for national variation is even greater. In both cases EU policy-making and implementation involves a wide set of actors on several levels. Hence the suggestion that policy outcomes depend more on bargaining and persuasion than on hierarchical rules, and that norms about appropriate decision-making are as important as formal rules and power (Jachtenfuchs 1995, Kohler-Koch 1996). In this literature on multi-level governance, the central actors not only negotiate about the means, but also about policy goals, and their preferences may develop and change during negotiations. In a system like the EU, with limited hierarchical power and a limited budget, 'steering' seems more important that 'commanding' (Sbragia 2000).

Third, the term governance was linked to the centre-left's modernisation project in a number of European states. Particularly in the UK, Tony Blair (Prime Minister 1997–2007) and New Labour, the term was used together with the notion of the 'Third Way' (Giddens 1998) to distinguish Labour's public policy from that of its predecessors. Newman (2001) therefore analyses governance both as a political 'narrative of change' and as a set of theoretical approaches to public policy that differ from those associated with NPM. Public policy in the UK since 1997 has combined some of the emphasis on competition and faith in market-mechanisms associated with NPM with faith in the role of the state and civil society that is associated with the centre-left across Europe (Smith 2004). Similar combinations of some NPM-like policy tools and a broader, more voluntarist and consensual approach to public policy reform formed the basis of public policy reform under a number of centre-left governments in both Western and Eastern Europe, including the Scandinavian states, the Netherlands, Portugal and the Central European states that would eventually join the EU in 2004.

In short, the term governance captures both a new political project (largely associated with the centre-left) in the 1990s and efforts to develop public policy beyond the NPM model, and all in the context of closer European integration. Although the term governance has been used in a wide range of academic literatures and has been defined in several different ways (see Rhodes (2000) and Sedelmeier (2001) for good reviews of the literature), it may be reduced to five or six characteristics (Stoker 1998). The following section draws on Stoker's definition, but expands it to include the implications of multi-level governance.

Governance involves a broader set of policy instruments than legislation

Governance 'embraces not only the actions of government, but also the wide range of institutions and practices involved in the process of governing' (Newman 2001: 4), and 'refers to a set of institutions and actors that are drawn from but also beyond government' (Stoker 1998: 18). The central element of governance is that it involves more than the traditional tools of government, such as hierarchical control, legislation and the exercise of formal authority. Whereas NPM draws on reorganisation, regulation, contracts and incentives, governance draws on a broader set of policy tools. At the EU-level this is clearly evident in the Open Method of Cooperation (Cram 2001); at the national level it involves governing through a range of bodies, such as independent agencies that are located beyond the central hierarchy, and on efforts to change behaviour, for example, through information campaigns. Kooiman (2000, 2003) distinguishes between forms of governance that range from hierarchical control through 'co-governance' involving combinations of private and public actors, to self-governance.

The central point is the idea that the state's capacity to achieve goals or get things done depends on more than formal powers (Fukuyama 2004). Whereas NPM reforms focus on designing incentive systems and introducing competition into the public services, but retaining a clear boundary between the (now smaller) state and the private sector, governance relies on a wider set of policy tools or techniques. Stoker's (2000) analysis of changing patterns of urban governance suggests that governments increasingly rely on techniques that go beyond NPM, such as:

(a) persuasion, to establish legitimacy and promote partnership
(b) communication, to facilitate learning and openness
(c) government spending, to encourage cooperation between public, private and voluntary actors
(d) monitoring, in order to spread 'best practice' and thus improve performance (in contrast to NPM: monitoring to promote competition).

Governance blurs the boundaries between the public, private and voluntary sector

A direct consequence of the effort to use more than merely the formal tools of government is that governance tends to blur the boundaries between the private, public and voluntary sector. NPM reforms began to open the boundary between the public and private sector by opening up public services for tender, and thus involving private companies directly in public service provision. However, as a range of models for competitive tendering (voluntary and compulsory) were adopted by different European governments and across various sectors, contracting out has come to involve everything from private to public to voluntary organisations, as well as various hybrid groups. In the Scandinavian states, the political compromise that allowed a degree of competitive tendering in public services was based on agreements that competitive tendering should not be the functional equivalent of privatisation; even NPM reforms have been 'filtered, edited and refined in a process of pragmatic adaptation' (Christensen 2004: 39).

The popularity of the Public-Private Partnership (PPP) model is perhaps the clearest indicator of the blurring of boundaries between the public and private sectors. Efforts to encourage private sector involvement in parts of public service provision, from building-maintenance at the low end through to full involvement in running schools or hospitals at the high end, fit neatly into the focus on using a wider set of tools than those associated with old hierarchical public administration. Pollitt (2003: Ch.3) lists a number of motives for PPPs, including drawing on private sector expertise, attracting finance, strengthening legitimacy by involving voluntary organisations, sharing power and shifting some risks over to non-state actors. Each aim also involves its corresponding problems, such as possible erosion of public sector expertise, high long-terms costs and the possibility that even if operational risk is transferred to the private sector the public sector is left with the financial risk. Pollitt's review of the research concludes that although PPPs often involve short-term benefits, estimates of long-term costs and benefits is more problematic.

Governance involves several levels of government and mutual power-dependence

The third core characteristic of governance is that it tends to involve coordination and cooperation between several levels of government. Although elsewhere in Europe this has not involved changes as radical as they have been in the UK, where the unitary state model has been eroded through devolution, all public service delivery in European states is shaped to some extent by membership of the EU (or the EEA). Even in sectors that are not at the core of the Single Market, and where policy competence remains at the national level, such as health, employment and education, the EU's Open Method of Coordination affects policy outcomes. The central point in terms of public administration is two-fold: the relationship between the various levels has changed, and policy-making and implementation involves a broader set of actors. EU rules affect the relative power of the state capitals and local government, because Single Market rules and obligations constrain the central administrations' freedom of manoeuvre. Individuals, firms and private service providers have recourse to a set of rights and a legal process above and beyond the control of national governments. In short, national public administration takes place in a more complex environment.

Governance involves a holistic approach to governing: 'Joined-up government'

Fourth, the debate on governance has reactivated the old goal of coordination across government departments by invoking the term 'joined-up government' (Hood 2005). A central goal in the NPM strategies was to improve efficiency by reorganising government bodies and separating the purchasing, provision and control of public services. Consequently, the challenges of coordination between the vast numbers of governing bodies and more or less independent agencies or service providers has, if anything, only increased. 'Holistic government' has become the by-word for efforts to increase coordination across Europe at both national and local level (Bogdanor 2005). In the UK, dedicated task forces were established to address issues that were too broad to be addressed by a single department, such as gender equality and social exclusion, and operated across the insulated 'silos' through which public services were delivered (Richards and Smith 2004). In the 1990s, new and cheaper computer systems made cooperation and coordination between different public bodies much easier, and the digital revolution at the turn of the century gave rise to ICT-aided strategies for implementing public sector reform in all European countries.

Furthermore, although governance may involve decentralisation and less direct exercise of hierarchical authority, the need for centralised control and coordination is more pronounced under this kind of system than old public administration or NPM. Weberian bureaucracies rely on hierarchical control and clear lines of authority and accountability. NPM-type systems are based on the notion that control can be established through well-defined contractual relationships and regulatory bodies. Policy coordination is not supposed to be a problem if the public service system is adequately designed, tasks clearly specified and assigned, and appropriate incentive systems in place. Perhaps the most common response of Western governments to the practical problems of coordination between agencies of varying independence has been to strengthen the powers of the prime minister and other members of the core executive, such as the leaders of coalition parties and/or the minister of finance. In the UK, the role of the cabinet office (or the core executive) strengthened under the Thatcher, Major and Blair governments, as did the relative power of the Chancellor (finance minister) to control the spending of other government departments (Rhodes and Dunleavy 1995, Seldon 2001, Seldon and Kavanagh 2005). Holistic governance thus comes with a strengthened focus on central coordination.

Governance relies on autonomous networks as much as on hierarchical organisations

The fifth general characteristic of governance is a shift from hierarchical authority and command to power-dependence and negotiations. Agencies involved in public service delivery negotiate and cooperate not only with the central government departments, but also horizontally in networks of more or less interdependent actors. Whereas the relationship between actors in the NPM model is based on contracts and clearly specified goals, governance involves actors whose power derives from their expertise, resources, skills and participation in a network. The literature on policy networks and policy communities (see Richardson and Jordan 1979, Rhodes and Marsh 1992) drew attention to the way that stable relationships developed between government and non-government actors in many policy sectors, and this brought about policy-making by bargaining and negotiation rather than the top-down command systems associated with Weberian bureaucracy. New IT tools and communications systems make a much wider range of networks and policy teams possible, both within and across policy sectors across the public–private divide. ICT-based systems are increasingly used to enhance management and leadership in non-hierarchical organisations because they allow rapid flow of information between teams and leaders (outside the hierarchical command chain), for example, through the establishment of virtual project forums. However, this focus on the importance of *shaping* policy runs the danger of under-estimating the importance of *power*

(Kassim 1994), and the shifts of power within the 'core executive' (Rhodes and Dunleavy 1995).

Governance is oriented toward flexible regulatory systems for regulation inside government

The sixth, and final, theme in the academic and political debates on governance is the emphasis on flexibility and innovation. Privatisation, liberalisation and NPM reforms turned out to require a considerable amount of new regulation, and can therefore hardly be described as processes of deregulation (Levi-Faur 2006). Where 'league-tables' setting out the performance of, for example, schools had been established, the question soon became what to do with the information. In the English education sector the schools regulator established differentiated regulatory regimes for successful and poorly performing schools with 'light touch' inspections for the former and more thorough inspections for the latter. At the same time, resources were set aside for allowing middle-of-the-range schools that performed some tasks particularly well to spread information about 'best practice'. Similar measures were developed for local government (Stewart 2003). In other words, the relatively rigid and sometimes overlapping inspection regimes that developed with NPM have been developed further. Because NPM and governance reforms have been accompanied by a proliferation of inspectorates and control mechanisms, the new question is how to develop lighter and more flexible regulatory regimes (Hood et al. 2000, James 2000), while maintaining or enhancing accountability and transparency (Stirton and Lodge 2001).

Beyond NPM?

Both New Public Management and governance are labels that are applied to a series of connected developments rather than a clearly defined and coherent set of reforms. The one blurs into the other, but as more and more elements of NPM are developed along the lines of the six governance themes set out above, the overall result is a system that differs considerably from the NPM model. The academic literature on governance therefore reflects both policy developments and political developments, both through changes in how public services are delivered and in how governments justify and present public sector reforms. In parallel with this, an effort has been made to re-examine the assumptions behind the theoretical foundations of NPM. The assumption of the rational individual that seeks to maximise utility and pursues a fixed set of interests, and which informs much of the debate on NPM, has recently been questioned both in economics and political science literature. LeGrand's (2003) discussion of motivation and agency in public policy is perhaps the clearest case in point. While retaining the assumptions of rational choice,

LeGrand draws on empirical studies to challenge the assumption of egoism and makes allowances for altruistic motivations (and points out that both ego-ists and altruists may have 'collectivist' preferences). His model fits neatly into the governance debate as he calls for 'robust incentives', that is, for incentive structures that take into account both egoistic and altruistic motivation and are robust enough to handle both. Combined with a focus on empowering the individual citizen (or user), in line with both NPM and governance theories, this reasoning leads to governance-like systems that LeGrand argues are more robust than the pure NPM-inspired systems that are devised based only on assumptions of rational pursuit of self-interest. In other words, some of the lit-erature on governance and public sector reforms is linked to a set of assump-tions about actors that differ from the assumptions behind NPM in important respects. Ultimately, however, neither NPM nor governance sets out a clear programme for public sector reform. Both sum up, analyse, and usually recom-mend, a series of policy reforms that are based on a coherent set of assump-tions about motivation and agency in public policy; but governance covers a somewhat broader set of initiatives, is sometimes less coherent, and its claims are less bombastic. The result has been an approach to public sector reform that is more fluid, and that embraces continued reassessment and adjustment of public service delivery.

Further Reading

Dunleavy, P. (1991) *Democracy, Bureaucracy and Public Choice: Economic Explanations in Political Science* (London: Harvester Wheatsheaf). Provides a 'public choice' analysis that is highly critical of some of the New Right's impor-tant arguments about democracy and bureaucracy. Chapter 6 on 'Existing Models of Bureaucracy' and Chapter 7 on 'The Bureau-Shaping Model' are particularly relevant.

Ferlie, E., Ashburner, L., Fitzgerald, L. and Pettigrew, A. (1996) *The New Public Management in Action* (Oxford: Oxford University Press). A good introduction to New Public Management in theory and practice, which draws primarily on the UK experience. Chapter 1 on 'Characterizing the "New Public Management"' is a very useful starting point.

Pollitt, C. and Bokhaert, G. (2004) *Public Management Reform* (Oxford: Oxford University Press). A good comparative study of public management reform in general and New Public Management in particular, which draws on the expe-rience of a range of states and includes 13 short appendices on different national (and the EU) regimes. Chapter 4 on 'Trajectories of Modernization and Reform' provides a useful overview of patterns of change.

Pierre, J. (ed.) (2000) *Debating Governance: Authority, Steering, and Democracy* (Oxford: Oxford University Press). A collection of essays on governance that

(Continued)

(Continued)

address a broad debate on public policy from national and international perspectives. Chapter 4 by R.A.W. Rhodes on 'Governance and Public Administration' provides a good introduction to the different debates on governance.

LeGrand, J. (2003) *Motivation, Agency and Public Policy: Of Knights & Knaves, Pawns & Queens* (Oxford: Oxford University Press). An excellent short book on public policy that combines elements of NPM and governance, and includes five policy chapters. Chapter 4 on 'A Theory of Public Service Motivation' argues the case for designing policy regimes that take both egotistical and altruistic motivations into account.

SIX

Modernising Government – eGovernment

This chapter turns to one of the key aspects of globalisation introduced in the Introduction, namely the role of technological change and particularly the digitalisation process in the Information and Communications Technology (ICT) industry and the consequence for both private and public sector. The digital revolution has led to new options for designing public sector and service delivery, and *e*Government has become the label for the set of developments and possibilities linked to these processes. For most governments, *e*Government has become the cornerstone of modernisation strategy, even if the implications are rarely fully set out or even understood. The literature on *e*Government is rather limited and more oriented towards specific examples of digital solutions in the public sector and IT aspects of the new services, rather than to studies of the organisational possibilities for public services and organisation that this development has brought about (Heeks 2006; OECD 2003). In reality the digital revolution has, however, turned out to entail much more radical reorganisation of public sector organisations, management tools and service delivery systems than was realised when most such projects were embarked on. The consequences of public service delivery have been radical, even if this has not been fully accounted for in the literature. The strategies for introducing *e*Government are often of the 'soft' variety, centring on voluntary measures such as best practice, agenda-setting and learning. Although this reflects the difficulty of legislating on such issues, it also renders implementation more difficult. Finally, *e*Government constitutes a tool for revitalising democracy through increased possibilities for citizen participation, but at the same time it represents new challenges in terms of democratic control and privacy. This chapter discusses first the digital revolution and the impact of this technological shift on both business and government. It also introduces the concept of *e*Government as a parallel to *e*Business and discusses how public sector organisations can reach different levels of *e*Government maturity. This is followed by a more detailed discussion of the impact of digital solutions on the organisation of public services. Finally, *e*Government and democracy are discussed both in terms of the potentiality of increased citizen involvement and the challenges of a development of a digital divide both inside individual countries and between different countries in the world.

The Digital Revolution and the Information Society

The 'digital revolution' and the proliferation of the 'information society' set the scene for changes in the ways government provide public services, which in turn has affected some of the services themselves. The first of these concepts refers to the increased use of digital technology, and some of its consequences in terms of linking together agencies or activities that have long been separate. The second concept refers to the broader impact the digital revolution has had on society.

The digital revolution

The introduction of digital technology has totally changed the functioning of modern society all over the world, both in the public and private sector. First of all, this revolution has created a global information-based economy. This new economy favours intangible things like ideas, information and relationships, and the focus therefore shifts from production to knowledge of ideas, competences, networks and communication strategies. This has immense implication for the private and public sector alike. The strategies of global firms like General Electric and IBM have shifted from a focus on development and production to a 'virtual' strategy where the core competence is to know how, where and when to develop and produce. In the public sector, the corresponding development is one where the whole system of administration changes from a hierarchical, stable and static system of administration and public service delivery to a much more flexible, efficient and customer-oriented service delivery and administrative solutions. A modern digital public sector generates a system of information-sharing and transparency, which involves citizens more directly. The public services share information across departments, ministries and levels of governments. This makes the public sector more efficient, and gives citizens easy access to information and a possibility to participate (Markellos et al. 2007, Rocheleau 2005).

These technological developments have created intensely interlinked network economies that feature global links between economies, markets, payments, information, services and products. This, in turn, favours organisations that are based on information and knowledge, and the rapid development of mediating technologies. The new logic is that the more plentiful things become, the more valuable they become. This has substantial implications for all aspects of the public sector, in terms of both organisation and function. This is what we will address in this chapter. First, however, some discussion of the more general background for this digital revolution and the creation of the information society is warranted. Recent developments are sometimes branded the *second digital revolution*. For instance, the website *digitaldivide.org* points out that there has been a change from European and North American countries setting the pace, to a more global stage. Today the rural areas of the emerging market countries of Asia, which have become the new battleground for various technological platforms, are taking the lead. The result of this is that IT and telecommunications companies will be forced to be innovatative in ways that drive growth in both developing and advanced countries.

The information society

The actors in this new economy are the consumers, or subscribers to this new intangible world of ideas and information. IT-related industries, communication industries and telecommunication industries (ICT) are the backbone of the information society. Other important actors include network industries that can exploit the new digital logic, such as electricity providers, banks, insurance, travel, airline industries, as well as educational institutions. The production industries are rapidly shifting their focus and operation to become more knowledge-, information- and communications-oriented.

The information society has brought about many types of jobs that were previously unknown in industrial society. Firms and governments have developed new markets and new strategies that, in turn, have given rise to the terms *e*Commerce, *e*Business, and *e*Government. This has arguably increased life quality (more convenience, better services, better access to different types of services), job quality (convenience, increased job flexibility, teleporting, hi-tech work environments), and improved education through more flexible digital solutions like *e*Learning and blended learning concepts. However, it has also generated a 'digital divide', both inside countries (for example, rural and urban areas, elderly vs. e-literate young,) and between countries, such as between the US and some North European and Asian countries as they become advanced digital information societies while African countries lag behind (International Telecommunication Union 2006).

The creation of an information society has also established an emerging *e*Economy; a new global business environment in which global commerce is conducted. *e*Commerce is the exchange of information electronically within the context of the rapidly emerging *e*Economy, among *e*Enterprises and consumers, and within and with the public sector. *e*Enterprise is a business enterprise with the capability to exchange value (money, goods, services and information) electronically. The same distinction in the *e*Economy is found in the public sector, with *e*Government and *e*Government Organisation.

The consequences of the digital revolution for the new economy is that information is less expensive (often free) and easier to access. Consumers expect inexpensive or free services, and both the willingness to pay and the ability to charge are limited in internet-based solutions. Consumers have access to more information in a global market, they are more selective about information (they click increasingly rarely on ads and banners), and are more price-sensitive if they are forced to pay. The marginal costs of production are minuscule compared to development costs. This new economy has fundamental implications and effects on the public sector and public service delivery, and these effects are comparable to those found in the private sector.

Concepts and Strategies

The digital revolution and the emergence of the information society have begun to change the way governments provide public services and interact with both public and private actors. These changes are captured by the term '*e*Government', which was coined to describe the changes brought about as public services are increasingly delivered digitally and electronically. It refers not only to governments' interaction with business, but also to its interaction with citizens and with other public bodies. As new strategies have been developed in order to allow governments to take advantage of the digital revolution, the pace and extent to which governments make use of *e*Government concepts has come to vary considerably.

What is eGovernment?

Governments and public organisations in Western societies have been using computers for their administrative work since the early 1970s, but the last three decades have witnessed an enormous growth in the spread of digital devices, which have come to take many different forms and to offer many functions. Today, computers are linked into networks locally, regionally, nationally and internationally through the World Wide Web. Further, digital tools have progressed way beyond their original use, which was mainly for text handling, and are now used for an ever increasing variety of tasks including all kinds of data processing for both administration and service delivery, with all types of interactive connectivity. This is the development of *e*Government. The use of computing technology has radically transformed the logic and functioning of the public sector in all societies. A definition of *e*Government could therefore run as follows: public services delivered electronically through a network, either locally or over the internet. This includes the digital service delivery and network aspects, both locally and globally, of *e*Government. Moreover, technological change is creating completely new structures and linkages internally and across public organisations, with the result that it has the capacity to transform the way many of these organisations work.

*e*Government not only represents a tool that permits more efficient implementation of existing strategies, it also affects strategy. Bellamy (2003: 114) argues that the new information and communication capabilities associated with ICT should be allowed to shape strategy. Re-engineering of business processes has a parallel in public service and public organisations, and this means that processes should be integrated horizontally across department boundaries as well as vertically between supply, production, distribution and consumption. These dramatic potential effects of *e*Government have made it very popular among both politicians and the public at large because it could perhaps restore the legitimacy of political institutions by increasing their accessibility, responsiveness and comprehensibility. Over the last five to ten years most countries have drawn up some kind of e-strategy for both the private and the public sector. The latest report from the UN shows that 94 percent of all member states are online (UN 2005). In Europe the EU launched its *e*Europe strategy with strong emphasis on public services, and each member state has its own e-strategy. The UN, the EU, UNESCO and several ICT firms have conducted surveys and written reports benchmarking the *e*Government efforts in different countries (see, for example, OECD 2003). Even among the Western countries there are still substantial digital differences between the front-runners in the US and the Nordic countries, and the other Western countries; in other words, the results and real effects for the citizens of *e*Government initiatives are mixed.

The concept of *e*Government contains several different elements. Most literature makes a distinction between Government to Business (G2B), Government to Citizens (G2C) and Government to Government (G2G). Government to Citizens (G2C) is sometimes also discussed in the other direction, as C2G, where citizens interact or form partnerships with the government. In this book the terms G2C and C2G represent the same element in the concept of *e*Government.

G2B – 'Government to Business' – often represents the driver for the development of *e*Government. Businesses are normally more developed with regard to the exploitation of digital communications and tools, and they demand the same readiness for this new world of electronic interaction both from government and local administration. *E*-readiness has become an important criterion for businesses in decisions about location. *Governments and local administration are also* *increasingly channelling procurement through the internet. This then requires suppliers to operate as eBusinesses*. The main reason for this is cost-saving, but it also makes it easier to link procurement to stock-keeping, logistics systems in general, and it serves to make procurement transparent and to avoid corruption and other forms of mismanagement of public funds. In addition to *e*-procurement, provision of licenses and permits, tax returns, tax and duty payment, public loans, and the communication of public regulation are areas for G2B. In some cases the interaction between government and businesses is completely digital, in other cases it is mainly internet presentation and eventually transactions carried out through G2B. For businesses, some transactions with public institutions can be entirely digital.

G2C – 'Government to Citizen' – is a growing sector in most countries, including developing countries despite availability of computers and network solutions being more limited among individual citizens. Even in the most advanced digital countries there will always be a residual group of citizens either without access to communication tools or unable to use these tools. In the less advanced countries, the local or national government could, for example, use a system of publicly available terminals in shops, libraries, banks etc.; use bank cards or other cards with chips for public services as well; or use mobile phones as terminals. We find several examples for each of these solutions around the world, although one will never find 100 percent digital solutions for public services. On the other hand, a nearly fully digital solution could allow the government to spend much more resources on the percentage of the population unable to use digital solution. These digital solutions could cover nearly all forms of relations between citizens and the public sector, such as filing taxes, renewing driver licenses, paying fees, sending in applications, and communicating with public officials. Such digital solutions also reinforce the notion that citizens are consumers, and make it easier to increase the quality and the availability of services. Services can be supplied whenever required, and without the user having to attend an office in person. This also opens up the possibility that a singe portal is set up for supplying several public services, and even for a mix of public, semi-private and private services.

G2G – 'Government to Government' – represents the internal digitalisation of public bureaucracy. This is often a by-product of G2B or G2C, developed because existing back office solutions do not support the new digital services. The cost, complexity and sometimes also unwillingness to implement these G2G restructuring processes often represent the main hindrance for implementation of G2B and G2C solutions. The G2G tasks will be to make information exchanges run more smoothly. Examples include new computers, networks, capacity increases, organisational change, intranet development, cooperation among departments, new billing and accounting systems, and digitalisation of archives. In many countries the driving force for this development is, however, not only the need created by new G2B and G2C solutions, but also the fact that it makes public administration more efficient and effective and can (in the longer run) create substantial savings in the public expenditure.

An important consequence of the digitalisation of public services both in G2B and G2C is the transformation of the services themselves, which the new technology makes possible. One example is the one-stop-shop; a single point of access for several different services. This makes it possible to integrate services, standardise information and the paperwork required for many public services. At the same time it opens up for a redefinition of services, for organisational change, and for the reassignment of responsibilities and competencies. A central point is the shift in focus, from the more traditional focus on service providers and delivery systems, to the needs of the user. In some cases help could be provided automatically, through Custom Resource Management systems where the government can 'remember' the user from one time to another.

Levels of eGovernment maturity

The internet has become the cornerstone of all public and private sector network activities, both towards the general public and towards other firms or public actors. However, both in the private and public sector, there is considerable evidence of several different levels of internet service maturity; in other words, how advanced are the different firms and organisations in using the internet. Most studies identify four levels of maturity: *publish, interact, transact* and *integrate*. Some studies of public sector *e*Government maturity have, however, divided the first level into two, and go on to suggest that for some of the least developed countries even the first level normally, acquired by national governments or local counties and municipalities, is too advanced and that it is therefore important to register the movement from the lowest to the next lowest level of 'publish' (UN 2005).

The *publish* stage implies that information from the organisation is made available through the internet. This includes all types of public documents, and covers many if not most of the different sectors where the ministry, agency or local authority is involved. There are, however, no interactions with users. They simply navigate the website to find the information they require. One of the problems facing the public institutions at this level of usage is the lack of procedures and capacity for updates and revisions of the content posted. Most public institutions in the Western world are at least at this level. The UN report (2005) indicates, however, that some developing countries are at what they label 'emergent presence', where the information available is more limited and basic, and where the information is static and with the fewest options for citizens.

The next level of internet maturity for public organisations is *interact*, where the online services of the government enter into an interactive mode with many new services for citizens. This level introduces several possibilities for two-way communication between users and the government. It implies downloading forms, computer applications for filling in forms via the internet, sending applications and simple payments for different types of services. In many countries and regions there is close cooperation between local banks and municipalities to facilitate both identification and payment procedures. Users can perhaps also set up an individual account with the public organisation. The application could also maintain context information for each user to provide a customised view of the website for the different groups. This level could typically include the use of more sophisticated web-pages that are created dynamically. Several public organisations, including many local and regional authorities, operate at this level.

The highest levels of internet maturity are *transact* and *integrate*, where the website and its associated services are no longer simply an extension of the organisation, but constitute a virtual organisation itself; the medium becomes intrinsic to the way of doing business. Transact implies that users not only interact with the application, but that they can carry out transactions which achieve a specific goal. At this level, non-financial transactions are included (for example, submitting a tax return) as well as more complex financial transactions (for example, paying tax or receiving a refund). Internet solutions at this level need to be sophisticated and stable enough to guarantee security, reliability and data integrity with a high degree of confidence. Even in the most advanced countries there is considerable variation among different public institutions as to the extent to which they operate at this level. Moreover, at this level the organisations may re-structure themselves around the new virtual organisation. This can be characterised by an integration of G2B, G2C and G2G interaction and could involve the rather sophisticated involvement of business and citizens in the operation, evaluation and eventual future development of the organisation's tasks. Very few public institutions are at this level and in most cases, at least for G2C, it is impossible to operate solutions exclusively at this very sophisticated level. Some citizens will always be unable to participate in such advanced interactions with an institution, which is a problem because in most cases public services have to be universally available.

Technology and Organisation

The development of new strategies for public use of digital and electronic tools in public service delivery has taken place in parallel with other important changes in the public sector. This has prompted a debate as to whether *e*Government should be seen as a new paradigm in itself, or as a development that complements other changes in the public sector. However, even if eGovernment is seen primarily as a development that fits New Public Management very well, these two developments are not closely linked and technological changes in itself are also driving new developments in public management.

Understanding the strategic implication of technology

It has been argued that eGovernment is remarkably consistent with, or even a consequence of, the current forms of managerialism in the public sector (Bellamy and Taylor 1998). It is perhaps more the case that eGovernment has reinforced changes to new forms of management that were already occurring (Hughes 2003). Certainly, in an electronically networked age the structures and formal procedures of nineteenth-century bureaucracy are hardly relevant, and it is clear that new forms of administration and service solutions had to emerge eventually. The digital revolution created a promising tool for setting up these new structures. In some cases the result was only a computerisation of old structures, archives and processes; in other cases it lead to a re-engineering of important parts of public services at both local and national level. In the first case, the point of departure was the technology and not the need for administrative reform. In the second case, the point of departure was the tasks to be fulfilled and changes needed in functions, management, networks and delivery systems, as well as how new technology could assist in creating these solutions. This logic goes for New Public Management solutions as well as for other theoretical and analytical approaches to management reform in the public sector. There exists, however, more description and analysis of the first type of logic than the more public administration-rooted questions of how reforms could be implemented through new types of digital network-based solutions.

The new technologies for service management were first brought into use in the private sector, which then lead to a demand for better public service management too. The same tendency held for new technology and organisational structures, and we will return, in Chapter 8, to the new trends and tendencies that new technology prompted in terms of flexible non-hierarchical organisational structure, with team and project organisation. On the one hand, the management reforms in public sector have been driven by technology. On the other hand, they also stemmed from a need for more efficient use of resources and to find new ways to increase the quality of public services that came from NPM and other paradigms for management development in the public sector. Some even argue that eGovernment is itself a new paradigm that builds on New Public Management but goes far beyond it. Traunmüller and Wimmer (2004: 5) describe the relationship as follows: 'New Public Management focuses on primarily better ways of managing process, in eGovernment the processes themselves are reengineered'. On the other hand, *e*Government fits the New Public Management agenda well as it focuses on service delivery to customers, can facilitate a mix of public and private service delivery, and emphasises efficient production processes (Hughes 2003). One very important aspect is that *e*Government can facilitate public management reform by providing the requisite information system. The networking aspects are also of considerable importance, both in assisting strategy development (*e*Government as decision support system) and in the execution of public management reform (as an implementation tool).

Mobile or fixed-line and eGovernment solutions and use

Today a majority of internet traffic is carried out within fixed line networks, mainly because of the capacity and availability of traditional telephone lines. This also holds true for both B2B and B2C *e*Government. For several reasons this is going to change rapidly both in developed and developing countries. In developed countries, other networks like cable, electricity, radio link, satellite and mobile technology (both second and third generation – 2G and 3G) will take a rapidly increased proportion of the internet traffic because of availability, capacity and partly price. In developing countries, mobile networks are less expensive mainly due to the fact that most of the developing world has inadequately developed fixed line networks and the cost of rolling out cables is very high. The development of mobile networks makes it easier for such countries to take part in the new economy and reap the benefits of the internet and ICT for both *e*Commerce and *e*Government services. In addition the possibility for pre-paid services and customer identification is an additional advantage in countries where bank- and payment services are underdeveloped. Some of the advantages for less developed countries are also directly applicable to remote regions and not-so-developed countries in Europe, especially in Eastern Europe. In these countries a rapidly growing part of digital services, both private and public, will be carried out through mobile solutions.

This will particularly be the case with the introduction of 3G or UMTS mobile technology when the capacity and speed of the connection is increased substantially. Users can surf the internet with reasonable speed, read email anywhere, and carry out *e*Commerce and *e*Government tasks at anytime. Communication with citizens can be simplified by developing portals specifically designed for mobile users. These portals can be accessible with the touch of a key on mobile phones and they can offer public services to everyone, everywhere, whenever desired. In addition, because UMTS users are continuously online, information can be sent at whatever time is relevant for different groups of users. There are several aspects of 3G which are of importance for national and local government. In particular, distress calls can be positioned, law enforcement and fire brigades get more accurate and up-to-date information, and public preparedness for crises can be increased. *Bluetooth* technology can be used to transmit between devices over short distances. For example, a physician can transmit a prescription to a patient's phone and the patient can pay with the phone. The availability of services can be announced to users when they are in the vicinity.

Why is *e*Government possible both in advanced and not so advanced countries? First of all it is 'fun': citizens, parents and teachers are willing to participate because they are already exposed to the digital technology in the private sector both at work and at home, through TV, mobile phones, bank terminals etc. Most people have access to one or more of these terminals at home and/or at work, and they are used to using the technology. The internet is increasingly accessible in most countries through telephone, mobile, cable, TV and other sources, and most countries are undertaking significant investment in ICT equipment, the cost of which is falling rapidly. Thus, systems and programmes for *e*Government are increasingly available even if they were not installed or acquired for this purpose. Technology is driving the extension of *e*Government.

Redefining Public Service

Over the last two decades, technology has contributed considerably to change in the organisational structure and management of the public sector. Officials soon had their own computers, with access to both the internet and intranet. Along with this came more flexible systems that allowed for new ways of electronic communication such as email, document imaging and data exchange. Internally, a practical result of these new technologies was that all licensed officials could have access electronically to the cases they were working with, they were no longer tied up with paper copies and physical archives. Relevant information has become easily available, something that should result in less bureaucracy and more efficiency for the clients (Hughes 2003). However, these changes to public service delivery have been controversial, and led to implementation problems in the short term and to a 'digital divide' in the longer term.

A tool for improving public service

With the growth of the World Wide Web, wider use of plastic debit and credit cards, online shopping, third generation mobile phones (3G), and digital interactive TV, policy-makers have started to explore how they could use these new technologies to serve citizens better. The ambition of *e*Government is strongly driven by the hope that it will help to restore the legitimacy of political institutions through increased accessibility, responsiveness and comprehensibility, and even participation. However, new technology is not without challenges and drawbacks. First of all it creates new dividing lines, and this *digital divide* separates those who have access to technology and those who do not. Another challenge is the issue of trust: whether citizens trust that their personal data are safe with the use of new technology (this point is taken up in the next section). Finally, to be able to benefit from technology the government needs effective policies for how to disseminate technology, design information management and operate regulatory regimes (Bellamy 2003). These challenges aside, the politically most interesting aspect of *e*Government is the potential for substantially improving public services in terms of some of the most important aspects of service quality: availability, accessibility, price, popularity and customer focus.

This new technology also made it possible for private individuals to access huge amounts of information and to communicate electronically without having to leave their homes. This raises the possibility of a 24·7·365 community where time and space are close to irrelevant just as long as the technology is adequate. People can sit in their own living room, or anywhere with the required infrastructure, whenever they want and go online, for example, to fill out forms, mail questions or report changes in personal information, such a new address: in many situations, people no longer have to be physically present at any office any longer.

The result of these new digital services characteristics is the ability to fundamentally reorganise public services and to use resources for servicing different types of clients. There is not an exact or common guide on how to re-engineer the public sector, but the common theme is that all strategies focus on how to make use of new technology to improve public services (Hughes 2003, Bellamy 2003). The main goal with any re-engineering process is to improve public services: 80 percent of the clients could be serviced with five percent of the resources, and this implies higher efficiency and the opportunity to reallocate more resources to more demanding and less resourceful citizens. Public employees can allocate more time to core activities, and resources can also be re-allocated to other services.

Implementation problems

The actual implementation of *e*Government in local or national administrations faces several problems that have restricted both the use and the success of these actions. Heeks (2006) made this his main focus in his book about *e*Government. First of all, the digital administrative systems involved in the reorganisation must be compatible, and the new structure must fit the different logics in the underlying computer systems. A large proportion of the failures in implementing *e*Government solutions are linked to an inability to integrate the previous different systems of computers, data-archives, communication and other digital systems developed over several years and by several different ICT firms on various types of ICT platforms.

Back-office activities must be streamlined, integrated and improved, and this is often met with resistance from employees and bosses alike, usually because there is a lot of prestige and power built into existing administrative solutions. There are also substantial costs involved in reorganising and eventually digitalising huge public archives and registration systems like patients' records – and these high costs are often in themselves prohibitive. Employees often resist change because of consequences in terms of job security or changes they don't like in the content of their job. Large, digitally-assisted administrative reorganisations often involve a substantial reduction in manual or simple jobs, but eventually to an increase in more advanced and complicated positions.

The digital divide

One important challenge of the global development of *e*Government is the huge inequalities in the ability to employ digital solutions to different types of public service delivery both between nations and within nations. To a large extent, the same divide is also present with regard to *e*Business, but it is perhaps more challenging for basic public services. The most serious access divide exists across the world between the developed and developing countries. The world in general improved its *e*Government readiness from an index value of 0.4130 in 2004 to 0.4267 in 2005 (UN 2005). A particular concern, however, is the countries of South and Central Asia and Africa, which together house one-third of humanity. Africa, as a whole, has a mean *e*Government readiness estimated at two-thirds of the world average and just 30 percent of that of North America. As a region, Europe followed North America, while South-Central Asia and Africa brought up the rear. Many of the 32 least *e*-ready countries showed little relative progress in 2005 compared to other countries. Despite steady improvements in the regional means, the data show a huge disparity in access to information society parameters. Collectively, Northern America and Europe were around 140–330 percent more *e*-ready than Africa (the least *e*-ready region in the world) in 2005: North America 0.8744, Europe 0.6012 and Africa 0.2642 (UN 2005) These inequalities constitute a huge challenge both for the world community and for the ICT industry: how to counteract the digital divide between countries, not to mention local and regional administrations in Africa and Central Asia, and at the same time develop more cost-efficient digital instruments, such as computers and mobile phones, for governments to use? Neither the international community, nor national governments or industry can bridge this gap and the solution probably lies in combined efforts of all these actors on a scale not seen so far in the world of digital development (www.digitaldivide.org 2003).

There are also substantial differences within Europe and inside each of the EU member states. Some states in Europe are not far above the level of the most advanced states in Africa, and parts of the migrant population in the inner cites of all Western nations are also at a very low level of digitalisation. Cuervo and Menendez (2006) summarised the multiple dimensions of the digital divide with two factors: the first is related to ICT infrastructure and use; the second to costs and the availability of online public services. Their analysis shows that France, although on top in terms of economic development, is part of the less developed group together with the southern European countries. Moreover, it reveals the weakness of Belgium and Luxemburg in not providing cheap access to the internet and online public services. This study also confirms the well-known north–south divide in Europe. The results, therefore, reinforce the fact that digital disparities mirror (to some important extent) social and economic imbalances across countries. The problems confronting European countries are, however, much more solvable with a substantial effort from national and local governments than the challenges confronting Africa. The European Union has this as one of the top priorities in the *e*Europe programme, which is part of the Lisbon agenda, and *e*Europe is an ambitious strategy to bring all EU countries to a leading position in digital solutions, both regarding *e*Business and *e*Government.

The *e*Europe plan was launched at the Seville European Council in June 2002 and the aim of this plan is concerned with both public and private environment. It focuses upon the development of modern public services and a favourable environment for private investments, new jobs and the boost of productivity. This should be possible through widespread availability of broadband access at competitive prices and a secure information infrastructure. Taking things a step further, the i2010 (European Information society in 2010) was launched by the EU in June 2005. The i2010 addresses the main challenges and the developments in the information society and the media sector up to 2010. It argues for an open and competitive digital economy, and for the inclusion of ICT to improve the quality of life. The priorities of the i2010 is first to create a Single European Information Space, second to invest in the innovation and research in ICT, and finally to improve the public services and life quality through the use of ICT (Europe's Information Society 2007).

eGovernment and Democracy

One of the most promising aspects of *e*Government seen from a democratic perspective is the way it can empower citizens and increase citizen participation in all aspects of public sector activities. This involves three major developments. First, the new technology can vitalise traditional political life by introducing television and internet presentations of all types of meetings of public officials, including regular internet meetings with politicians and 'question and answer' sessions on the internet. Second, the technology enables direct citizen involvement and participation in the production of services, leading to immediate feedback and questions, and to possible adjustment of the services, not just the citizens giving response in opinion polls. Regular user panels can continuously improve services, and political administration can interact directly with citizens. Finally, new technology leads to greater transparency and facilitates access to information for the citizen, which is vital for democracies to function well. All kinds of laws and other types of decisions can be accessed immediately by citizens.

As already noted, a strong democracy needs well-informed and active citizens, and internet democracy and *e*-democracy are terms that suggest democratic processes are facilitated by ICT. And indeed, ICT enables relevant information to be made more easily accessible and understandable. In particular, it can bring information regarding current public policies, laws and regulation directly to the people by the posting of such information on official internet web pages. Further, online debates or discussion forums enable public officials to make use of this information in policy-making (OECD 2003).

E-democracy can emerge through a top-down or a bottom-up process, or as a combination of both. A top-down approach is likely to be seen in the first – the publish – stage of *e*Government maturity. This stage is characterised by providing official websites with links to various departments and current archived information. The information flows from government to citizens; it is a top-down approach. However, a top-down approach alone is not sufficient to strengthen democracy unless it is combined with equal access and opportunities to empower citizens in the decision-making process. Thus, there is a need to allow citizens to influence policy formulation through a bottom-up approach: citizens move from merely being consumers of policy; they are also able to be producers. The OECD (2003) specifies two levels in this regard – consultation and active participation – which can also be termed *e*-consultation and *e*-participation.

E-consultation occurs when governments need information about citizens' views on various issues, and usually takes the form of a discussion forum. In this way governments may get an idea of how likely and why citizens are to agree (or not) to new policy initiatives. *E*-participation is an extension of consultation, but here governments acknowledge a central role for the public in proposing policy options and shaping policy dialogue. One mechanism could be to enable citizens to initiate referenda online. Thus the promise of *e*-participation is numerous; better policy quality, greater chance of trust and acceptance of new policy, and better balance of power in lobby organisation. However, to date, few countries have included e-participation in their decision-making process (OECD 2003, Loudres et al. 2006, Rho 2007).

One demonstration of e-democracy at all levels is the European Commission's web page. First, simple features, such as information on policies, regulation and laws and new updates on audio visual, are provided. Second, the discussion forum, Discuss Europe, with designated questions is published. Third, White Papers are posted in order to get contributions or feedback from individuals and business. The outcome of a public consultation is given in a report (European Commission 2006) and it is also posted on the web. It appears that they use their website to collect and analyse reactions, as an input to the European Union policy-making process.

Privacy and security

Linked to the question of the consequences of eGovernment for democracy are problems associated with the threat to privacy of the electronic information and problems of security both at the personal and at the municipal and governmental level (Belanger and Hiller 2006). The new technologies give unlimited possibilities for improving public service delivery, but at the same time they provide unlimited possibilities for surveillance and control, as well as exposure of identities and activities of people at sites and portals totally outside the control of the individual. Every time the plastic payment card is used, or a user has entered into, for example, a railway station, searched the internet, made a mobile phone call, or sent an email, her or his activities are registered and could be tracked or traced by the authorities. At the same time the use of bank cards and the pin-code linked to it in a cash machine could lead to identity theft. The security of even highly secret military programmes and information is not guaranteed.

This problem is a major concern for most governments, but effective solutions are limited by both the technology itself and by the temptation to use the technology for more and more advanced and comprehensive information and communication purposes. Most nation states already have laws and regulations for the use of information, privacy, security etc., and governments try to adjust these protective measures to rapidly developing digital technology. Governments are both concerned about the privacy and security risks and at the same time eager to use these new technologies to control citizens and to combat crime. The war against terror has particularly highlighted some of these serious contradictions in the attitude of many governments (Baylis and Smith 2005: 630–1).

Another aspect is the ownership of all the information collected about individuals and companies and how and to what extent it is legal to sell this information, merge it with other types of information or to post it on different types of platforms. Information about individuals has become a commodity, and a large proportion of this information is collected by the government and often then put at the disposal of private firms. This can be used for mailing, screening and eventually excluding different groups of customers from certain types of services. The newest types of internet posting of videos at special sites make it particularly difficult to protect individuals from exposing globally very intimate details and activities placed totally outside their control on such a website. This also relates to another issue in the digital world: copyright protection and the use and misuse of the information on the web, not only regarding personal indiscrete videos, but films, songs and books. How do we find ways of protecting the owners of the rights to this material from digital theft?

The Future of Public Management in the Information Age

*e*Government has become popular with politicians and citizen alike, and it may be becoming ever more popular as a solution for all sorts of public sector problems than developments so far suggest. Politicians are increasingly interested in *e*Government because they see in it a new way of addressing more challenges than they have traditional resources to meet; at the same time as they find these solutions to be popular among the voters. They like these solutions because they employ technological tools already used by citizens for both entertainment and work. Most countries have ambitious *e*Government plans and initiatives and there is much political consensus about the introduction of *e*Government in many European municipalities, where increasing numbers are investing in the development of e-strategies for public service delivery. More than 60 percent of such municipalities want to perform transactions with public administrations on the internet, as do 80 percent of firms, 75 percent preferring to use a local portal, i.e. the municipal or city they live in. There is a strong wish for permanent (24·7·365) access to services, for reduced costs, and for easier access to information. All this is very well, but in the future these solutions have to deliver; to show that the benefits are greater than the costs. At the same time politicians have to be willing to pay the short-term cost for both ICT infrastructure and the back-office reorganisation needed to reap the gains from these new digital solutions to public sector service delivery. Management philosophies, and management and leadership tools, also have to be adapted to the new possibilities offered by digitalisation. Last, but not least, new visions and strategies for public services have to be developed to take advantage of the digital possibilities in a fundamentally new way. The digital age is still at the beginning of a process of transforming the public sector in all societies in the world.

Further Reading

Heeks, R. (2006) *Implementing and Managing eGovernment: An International Text* (London: Sage). Provides an extensive coverage of issues facing managers, practitioners and consultants in dealing with managing and implementing *e*Government. Providing key points at the beginning of each chapter, activities aimed at both students and practitioners at the end of the chapters makes this book very helpful for students and practitioners. Chapter 5, 'Core Management Issues for *e*Government', is a good summary of management issues that arise in relation to *e*Government.

OECD (Organisation for Economic Co-operation and Development) (2003) *Promise and Problems of E-Democracy: Challenges of Online Citizen Engagement* (Paris: OECD Publications). A report that mainly deals with how to use technology in order to enhance citizens' engagement and the future possibilities of the internet in relation to democracy and public policy-making. The number of case studies which are presented provides a useful illustration of the theoretical foundations and findings explored in the report.

UN (United Nations) Department of Economic and Social Affairs (2005) *UN Global E-government Readiness Report 2005, From E-government to E-inclusion* (United Nations Publications). Available from URL: < http://www.unpan.org/egovernment5.asp>. This survey (also undertaken in 2003 and 2004) assesses *e*-readiness of governments in 191 member states in order to provide basic social services. Moreover, the government's ability to promote *e*-participation is also assessed. Together with best practices examples, the wide-ranging statistics make this survey a valuable tool when attempting comparative analysis and evaluating member states' progress in the field of *e*Government.

Rocheleau, B. (2005) *Public Management Information Systems* (Hershey: Idea Group Publishing). Explores the challenges facing managers in the public sector in managing information systems, and in particular, implementation problems which are touched upon in this chapter. Chapter 8, 'Information Management and Ethical Issues in Government', provides useful insights to emerging ethical issues and new dilemmas caused by new technology.

SEVEN

Organisational Design and Institutional Governance

The central themes in this book are strategies for reducing the scope of the state and for making public management more effective. While Chapters 5 and 6 addressed changes at the macro-level and the broad impact of technology on public service delivery, this and the following chapter turn to changes at the meso- and micro-levels inside the public organisation. In particular, this chapter explores different ways of organising public service delivery; and Chapter 8 addresses management and leadership inside public sector organisations. This chapter is not intended to provide a complete and detailed account of all public service organisations in Europe, but to present the major patterns and examples that are particularly pertinent to understanding the mechanisms involved in institutional governance.

The central question here, then, is how public sector organisations are structured with respect to independence, decentralised power, and user choice. First, public sector modernisation programmes have to address questions as to whether organisations should be owned, financed and controlled by the central government and administration – or by semi-private or private entities. Second, because a large share of public services has historically been tightly controlled by the state, modernisation has often involved a degree of decentralisation and the devolvement of power to local and regional government, although it is not known whether this improved the autonomy of local government and local service providers. Third, the New Public Management debate involved considerable emphasis on the individual's freedom of choice. Reforms of public service delivery have, therefore, needed to address the question of how much user choice is desirable in any given sector. The focus in this chapter is on the services that have remained under the auspices of the public sector, either through direct public provision or by contracting out to private or semi-private providers. This includes education, health and some local government services, such as refuse disposal and care for the elderly. The first two concerns, the organisation of schools and hospitals, have been salient political issues across Europe in the last two decades and involve the core of the public sector. Policies concerning refuse disposal and care for the elderly are typically the responsibility of local government, and provide examples of services that involve relatively straightforward tasks (refuse collection) and of those that are much more uncertain and controversial (putting 'granny out to tender'). The second section considers the three aspects of institutional governance – independence, decentralisation and user choice.

The third part of the chapter explores variations in institutional structures and government strategies: a) decentralisation without much competition; b) reforms in public service provision that lead to some competition, and c) reforms that generate fully fledged competition between public service providers. It is, however, important to underline once more that this chapter is not intended to provide a complete and detailed account of all public service organisations in Europe, but to present the major patterns and examples that are particularly pertinent to understanding the mechanisms involved in institutional governance. The final section turns to new questions about control and accountability that the different types of public management reforms have raised. Direct control through ownership was considerably easier, both politically and administratively, than the complex control instruments that have been developed to cope with modernised public service provision and market-like conditions. Deregulation and competition turns out to involve a considerable amount of re-regulation, which may lead to problems in terms of efficiency as well as control in the longer term.

Institutional Governance, Decentralisation and User Choice

All modern models of public management, from Weberian bureaucracy to New Public Management and New Governance, involve institutional governance – questions about how public service provision is organised in order to secure an optimal mix of government direction, efficiency and user satisfaction. The Weberian model (discussed in Chapter 5) leant towards central government control: hierarchical organisations with clear rules and written procedures, and a system that assumed well-informed and relatively altruistic public sector officials and accorded relatively little importance to user choice. LeGrand (2003) uses the analogy of chess-pieces to illustrate the point: public officials were altruistic 'knights' and the users were powerless 'pawns'. In contrast, the New Public Management models recommend a higher level of user choice, and are based on a more sceptical view of public sector employees' competences and motives. In LeGrand's terms, the users must be 'queens' (powerful players), whereas public officials might well be 'knaves' (i.e. self-interested). The New Governance reforms, and LeGrand's own models, are based on a combination of the two models: an effort to take into account the desirability of some user choice in certain sectors, and design institutional mechanisms that are robust enough to cope with both 'knaves' and 'knights' in the public sector.

Public service provision involves a raft of organisations, from central policy departments to public or private front-line service providers. We therefore examine how these organisations are designed and related to each other and to the central state apparatus by addressing the three central questions about institutional governance – independence, decentralisation and user choice.

Institutional governance – three questions about independence

Public sector modernisation programmes have to address questions about how and the extent to which organisations that provide public services should be owned, financed and controlled by central government and administration. In Western Europe the degree of central government control has historically been high, at least until the 1980s. At the same time, most public services have been fully funded by the state, or operated on the basis of very marginal individual contributions. As for ownership, there is a broad common pattern of public ownership, whether by the state or by local and regional government. One major exception has long been the insurance systems organised and operated by labour unions and similar professional organisations, and even here the state has provided the financial backbone of these operations (Esping-Andersen 1990). France, and to some extent pre-Thatcher Britain, provide the clearest cases of centralised hierarchical control and ownership; whereas the German federal republic is, by its very nature, a more decentralised system of strong regional government. The Nordic and Dutch models historically feature a high degree of local self-government, but with relatively strict rules and regulations that make them comprehensive and egalitarian welfare states (Pierson and Castle 2000, Hermerijck et al. 2006).

Most of the countries discussed above have based their welfare state on the general idea of universal service obligation – that individuals have rights to minimum services, which should be provided or regulated by the public sector, but without precise prescriptions as to ownership, finance and control. In contrast, the French *service public* model is based on the notion that public services should be provided by state institutions, fully financed by the central state budget and operated under strict control by national political and administrative authorities (Grard et al. 1996, Boyen 1997). The French public service model, however, has come under considerable pressure from the EU's liberalisation programmes in many different sectors, because the EU initiatives tend to be based on the universal service obligation logic. This accounts for some of the controversies in French public sector reform, and explains the French government's recent attempts to reinforce the principles of *service public.*

As far as *ownership* of public service providers is concerned, the post-war norm in Western Europe has been that the state, regional or local government owns the institutions that provide public services directly. However, since the early 1980s, all European governments have experimented with new forms of ownership, including privatisation and semi-privatisation as well as a range of new and innovative forms of public ownership in the shape of trusts, independent agencies, public corporations etc. Many of these arrangements are 'new' in terms of political rhetoric rather than form; the Scandinavian states, in particular, have a long tradition of semi-public institutions that operate at an arm's-length from the central administration. Today a wide range of public and semi-public bodies, with a variety of legal forms, can be found across Western Europe: in the UK the term Non-Department Public Bodies (NDPB) has been coined to capture this multitude of quasi-government and quasi-non-government ('quago' and 'quango') organisations.

The most important aspect of innovation lies in the elaboration of explicit contractual relationships between the central political institutions and new fully or semi-independent bodies (Lane 2000). Even if, in some cases, there may have been little change in organisational form, the relationship between organisations can have changed dramatically. Moreover, whereas before 1980 almost all non-state actors involved in public service delivery were non-profit organisations (often from the voluntary sector), there is now a much wider range of private and for-profit organisations involved. Consequently the distinction between private and public ownership has become blurred, while the importance of developing other forms of control in order to secure price and quality has increased. This has proven to be a great challenge, and the control mechanisms are now far more complex than the direct control that was and is exercised through state ownership.

The central questions about *finance* are who pays and who is allowed to charge users? Historically, public services were based on the notion that the state paid the service providers and the citizens got the service more or less free of charge at the point of use. This held for everything, from health and education to road use and refuse collection. On the other hand, with public services in which the individual transaction is easy to identify and the usage varies considerably from individual to individual, such as post, energy and telecommunications, the tradition has been payment for use at cost-based or subsidised rates. Today, the picture has become far more complicated. First, prices have become more market-based. Second, even for services that were previously provided and paid for by the government, elements of cost-based user charges have been introduced (in particular for private or semi-private providers). Third, there has been an increasing tendency to involve private actors in public–private partnerships in a range of sectors, such as health, and even road construction. This, in turn, has led to arrangements where private actors are licensed to charge for services that would previously have been considered public services. Motorway charges are a case in point, either in the form of private companies building roads and charging for road use, or through various kinds of public–private partnerships (that raise private finance to fund public projects; Pollitt 2003: Ch.3). Even if there is no logical direct link between finance and individual user choice, the question of whether users should be allowed to choose between alternative providers and to determine the amount of services they consume is often linked to the question of user charges. Vouchers are sometimes seen as the key to user choice, for example, by allowing parents to spend an education 'voucher' in a school of their choice, be it state or public. In effect, however, many countries have operated a system of free choice concerning schools that even includes subsidies for those who opt for private schools, without a formal voucher system (the funds 'follow the student').

These developments toward less direct state ownership and a greater variety of forms of finance have increased the need for more effective *control* systems for public services. The central concerns are quality, cost, security, availability and equality of access. Historically, control has been exercised by central government departments as part of hierarchical government structures. However, changes in ownership and finance have warranted a much wider set of control mechanisms. These include formal rules and regulations, explicit contracts, systems for evaluation and customer feedback, self-regulation and a variety of incentive systems. For example, an important element of Thatcherism was that collective control (and accountability) implemented through the democratic process would be replaced by individual control exercised through competition and market mechanisms (Walsh 1995). Individual user choice was thus seen as a major component in the new control system. However, experience has shown that asymmetrical information – it may be difficult for an individual to gather sufficient information about which school or hospital is the best – has made this control mechanism somewhat less effective than originally anticipated. The most effective of these new control mechanisms has been the legal rules and regulations that limit the discretionary power of service providers and which give users instruments for legal redress. Consequently, similar rules and regulations have spread to public service providers. Even when public organisations merely set voluntary targets (such as the British 'Charter Mark' system) this has generated an increased focus on rules, regulations and targets as instruments for governance. However, once again, the danger is that the proliferation of rules and targets might, over time, reduce the efficiency of service provision; particularly to the extent that the capacity to comply is more or less fixed, both for individuals and organisations.

Decentralised governance – three questions about autonomy

All EU states have gone through a process of decentralisation, whether as part of New Public Management or as a part of a broader pattern away from the centralised welfare states of the post-war era. There is, however, considerable variety in Europe, in terms of their point of departure in the 1980s as well as in their present situation (Batley and Stoker 1991, Denters and Rose 2005). Historically, France has been the most centralised system, with a very low degree of decentralisation. On the other hand, in the Scandinavian states, particularly Norway and Denmark, a tradition of local governance dating back to the early nineteenth century has brought about a system of decentralised service provision in areas like social services, primary health care and technical services. A tradition of local self-government was thus established, and this provided a basis for decentralisation of public services in the second half of the twentieth century. Education and hospitals were historically part of the central administration, but during the twentieth century this was decentralised: Primary education was placed under the control of the municipalities; secondary education was devolved to the counties, as were hospitals (except university hospitals, which, like higher education, remained administered from the centre). In Germany many public services, including health care and education, were historically the responsibility of the regions (*Länder*). Postwar Britain was a centralised state in terms of public service provision, with the exception of some local services, until Thatcher's market-oriented reforms and the devolution introduced by Labour after 1997 dramatically altered the system. However, the trend toward decentralisation is not completely unambiguous. In Norway, after the turn of the twenty-first century, hospitals were taken out of county control and made part of the state system in the form of fully state-owned corporations.

The autonomy of local government involves a balance between local government's freedom to make choices and thus develop local variation, and the central government's concern of equality of service provision across the national territory. The central government's tasks also include quality control; and many politicians at least want the option to intervene in very specific local matters. The most powerful engine for decentralisation has been the shift in budgetary practice from detailed budgets that control individual items of local expenditure to framework budgets that give the municipalities a lump-sum budget they can use at their own discretion. This has been a very forceful development in all Scandinavian countries (and to some extent in the Netherlands), and has provided the corner-stone of local democracy and self-government in these countries. However, the main challenge to this freedom stems from the tendency of the national politicians to assign to the local authorities many more tasks and services than the lump sum transfers were designed for. Moreover, there are several cases of national politicians demanding actions on specific matters, such as drug abuse or policing, without considering local priorities and budgetary constraints. In France, as most decisions are made at the national level, the question is far less pressing. Nevertheless, after more than two decades of 'decentralisation', local autonomy has increased somewhat: the central government defines rules and procedures, and is now less involved in direct intervention (Borraz and Le Galès 2005). In Germany the question of decentralisation has also been less politically salient than elsewhere, but for the opposite reason: regional government has been strong and the subsidiarity principle (things should be done at the lowest possible level) has long been well-established (Gabriel and Eisenmann 2005).

Decentralisation comes in two forms. The first increases the power of local government; the second increases the power of the local institution, such as a school, hospital etc. This is an important difference with severe implications for budgets, efficiency, quality control and equality. Broadly speaking, the social democratic parties tend to favour decentralisation to local government, which often implies more control over the service providers; whereas the centre-right parties tend to favour decentralisation of power to the organisations that deliver public services rather than local government. The British experience illustrates this well: after a decade of Conservative rule in the 1980s, Britain seems 'out of step' with the rest of Western Europe in its focus on reducing the discretionary power of local government and forcing through systems of compulsory competitive tendering (Stoker 1991); after the 1997 election, however, Labour's programme of devolution and decentralisation brought Britain more in line with the trend in Europe (Wilson 2005). Nevertheless, there was no question of a return to the old system of local government control of monopoly public services. Although the system of compulsory competitive tendering was abandoned, it was replaced by a 'best practice' system that involves targets, inspections and sanctions and is oriented toward competition in local service delivery (Stewart 2003).

As the British case suggests, delegation within the public sector may generate as much autonomy as decentralisation between levels of government. In the primary education sector, local authority control of public service delivery has decreased, with more power going to local schools and school boards (in terms of management), the Department of Education (in terms of the curriculum), and to the independent regulatory agency OFSTED (in terms of setting standards and evaluating performance). Somewhat less controversially, the balance between local autonomy and equality is less problematic in other sectors, such as higher education. Whether universities are state-owned or private, and whether education is fully funded by the state or not, the tendency in Western Europe has been for considerable autonomy for institutions of higher education compared to other public services. This is perhaps the clearest case of equal provision for all users being far less important than a considerable degree of local autonomy, both for its own sake and because variation between institutions may be a policy goal in itself.

User choice – three questions about choice

The question of whether the collective or the individual can best determine how much any given individual should consume was a central question in welfare politics long before the recent wave of modernisation, New Public Management (NPM), and Governance. It has, however, been given new importance in the public policy debate, with the advocates of NPM invoking the importance of individual choice and even many critics of NPM advocating 'empowerment' of the citizen vis-à-vis local or central government. LeGrand (2003: Ch.5) identifies three major types of argument that long predate the current debate: a) the 'welfarist' approach focuses on the individual's well-being, but holds that in certain conditions the individual may not be the one best placed to make the optimal choice; b) the 'liberal' approach emphasises the desirability of the individual making their own decision, even if this might not have optimal consequences, therefore placing individual choice centre stage; while c) the 'communitarian' approach, places the welfare of society above the individual. However, most actual public service regimes are based on a mixture of all three approaches. For example, even if individual choice is permitted in the choice of a doctor, the choice of medical treatment in any given case may be left to the medical profession, and in the case of epidemics there may be provisions for compulsory vaccination or treatment. Across the public services, the question of individual versus collective choice has three central dimensions.

First, there is the core question of whether choice should lie with the individual or be made on behalf of the individual, and in the case of the latter, by whom or by what organisation? Across Western Europe, the classical model for welfare services has been close to what LeGrand labels 'welfarist'. Individuals are assigned schools, hospital places, doctors, care assistants etc. by the welfare providers; and services are provided on the basis of need and equal access, subject to little or no payment. In the event of shortages, queuing or prioritising may be used (e.g. for hospital treatment, or care of the elderly).

However, over the last two or three decades, a degree of user choice has been introduced in most European states; based partly on the (market-like) notion that user choice is good and that competition for users generates efficiency, and partly on the notion that the individuals should be empowered. Variations in the end degree of user choice depend on a number of factors, the most important being whether private operators compete for the users, what kind of private operators are permitted to compete, and whether user choice is fully free or restricted.

Second, if user choice is introduced, this often gives rise to the question of whether the individual should pay part or the full cost of the services. Historically, public services in the post-war era have been free of charge in most sectors. The introduction of user choice (whether full or partial) makes the cost structure of welfare services more visible, and thus makes it easier to charge a full or partial fee for these services. To the extent that this permits individuals to vary the amount they consume or the quality of the service (for example, requesting a single room in hospital), a degree of variable payment is logical. Moreover, in the last two decades, user choice has often been introduced as part of a drive towards cost containment in the welfare sector, particularly in the health and care sectors (Mossialos and LeGrand 1999). If user choice is open for competition from private profit-oriented suppliers, this may well lead to different cost and payment structures for private and public suppliers. This is, of course, familiar from the education sector, for example, in the UK, but it has now become common in the health sectors of many European states: private hospitals, medical centres or health insurers may offer faster and more luxurious service at a premium price.

Third, if user choice and payment is introduced to public services it is likely to raise another question: if a service provider (usually a school, hospital or care institution) is over-subscribed, should it be allowed to select 'customers'? The answer in the health sector is usually negative: providers are not permitted to choose the most profitable patients, but are obliged to operate some sort of queuing system. Hospitals may be allowed to focus on the most profitable types of procedures (and many do precisely that), but they are rarely, if ever, allowed to discriminate between patients. Schools, on the other hand, are sometimes permitted to choose the best or most promising students, though this is often subject to geographical restrictions ('catchment areas'). There is a potential grey area in the health care sector, which may arise when private suppliers also operate as part of the public system (for example, private doctors working part-time in the public health system) or public actors also operating part-time in the private market (for example, doctors or hospitals that also offer private services). In such cases, patients who face a queue for free public service may be offered the same service, by the very same doctor or institution, on a private basis at an earlier date. Private health insurance systems increasingly take advantage of such systems, for example, offering companies insurance that reduces the time an employee has to be on sick-leave.

Organisational Design and Competition in Public Services

There has been little or no consensus, either across party lines or across countries, as to the answers and implications of the questions concerning independence, decentralisation and user choice discussed earlier. The common trend in Europe has been a move away from the post-war hierarchical models of public service provision, but this has taken place at a very different pace and in various directions. Some governments have focused more on establishing independent service providers, others have emphasised decentralisation and autonomy, whereas others again have prioritised user choice. These different strategies have been shaped both by political ideology and institutional constraints. Single-party government in unitary states, such as the UK and France have had the opportunity for more radical reforms, although in practice, historical traditions and union resistance has made change much more difficult in France. In contrast, the federal system has made reform more difficult in Germany, because a number of actors at different levels can veto or delay it; and even the consensual democracies in Scandinavia and the Netherlands have generally sought cross-party consensus on serious welfare reforms. Although the result has been considerable diversity, a common theme has been the gradual introduction of more competition into public service delivery, from refuse collection to the management of schools and hospitals. The rest of this section explores these patterns of variation, starting with reforms that have brought about little real competition, and proceeding through systems with limited competition, to fully fledged competition in public service delivery.

Public service modernisation with little or no competition

A substantial part of the public sector modernisation programmes in Europe in the last 20 years has not been concerned with competition, but rather with reorganisation, decentralisation and delegation – both in terms of delegation from the central administration to local offices and agencies, and in terms of delegation within the local organisation. For example, the central tax authorities may delegate some tasks to regional offices, which in turn delegate tasks to their local branches. This kind of decentralisation and delegation breaks down or circumvents traditional hierarchical structures, often generating 'flatter' systems that organise tasks around teams or projects (we will return to this subject in Chapter 8).

Decentralisation has also been pursued for its own sake, even in the more centralised states. France embarked on a project of decentralisation in 1982 which, even if limited, was radical in the French context. Since 1997, decentralisation has been a central aspect of Labour's reforms of UK governance, including devolution to Scotland and Wales as well as a degree of local autonomy and choice in public service delivery. This has brought the British model much closer to that of the consensual states, although it remains a long way from the German federal model.

A whole range of services are fundamentally unsuited to competition because they are an integral part of the system of liberal democratic government. Service such as courts, the military, the police, taxation, customs and excise, and to some extent prison services, are unlikely candidates for privatisation or competition, because they are central to the execution of state power. In these cases, legal procedures and the requirements of equality before the law severely constrain the potential for efficiency gains through competition. Efficiency improvement at the cost of legal certainty or security is hardly going to be acceptable for any mainstream political party. Nevertheless, all these services have been subject to reforms, often in terms of reorganisation and delegation. Degrees of decentralisation vary widely: for example, the British police has long been extremely decentralised, whereas the Norwegian police was directly controlled (even operationally) by the ministry of justice until the mid-1990s. Denmark and Sweden have long had central police agencies with relatively high autonomy, but this system was abandoned in Norway after 1945 in an effort to establish direct political control over an organisation that had operated as a 'state within the state' during the inter-war years.

In a number of other cases, legal or de facto monopolies have been established for practical reasons rather than because they are central to the execution of state power. Historically, this has included telecommunications, electricity and gas, rail transport, water and postal services. Today most of the utilities and transport services are being part-privatised and liberalised. However, some services (for example, local bus routes) function as de facto monopolies because it is impractical to operate a parallel competing service system. This holds even for some private services: cable television is often in practice a matter of local (even city bloc-by-bloc) monopolies, even in national capitals. The same logic applies to primary education and elderly care in some regions or city districts, particularly in remote towns or villages. Moreover, competing service providers may cooperate: for example, recent reforms to the English school system encourage schools in the same local area to establish networks for mutual support and cooperation that in effect limit competition.

Purchaser–provider arrangements with restricted competition

The central premise for competition in the public sector is the separation of different functions of public service provision – in particular the separation between purchaser and provider. The state remains the purchaser of public services, but a range of actors may compete to provide the services. Competition between providers ranges from a limited number of public operators competing with each other, to full market-like competition that involves private suppliers. The degree of competition, however, is not linked directly to centralisation and decentralisation: in Denmark and Sweden, regional and local government have introduced a degree of competition in health care; in Norway and the UK, centralisation has been combined with increased competition.

Despite the expected gains in efficiency from the introduction of competition, purchaser–provider arrangements (and public–private partnerships) have often been problematic in practice. First, such mixed models may suffer from the problems of both the market and monopolies. Public service concerns, and the difficulties some users may have in exercising informed choice, sometimes undermine the degree of real and effective competition, with the consequence that the full potential benefit of competition may not be realised. Second, at the same time, the public purchasers – often regional and local government – may lose some expertise and control over the increasingly fragmented set of service providers. Third, even if competition works according to plan, in a new market the winners of auctions or tendering processes may turn out to be the providers that under-estimated costs and over-estimated potential profits – the so-called 'winner's curse'. Fourth, many public service providers operate in both protected and competitive markets, and it is difficult to ascertain the extent to which such operators cross-subsidise their competitive activities from protected profits. Fifth and finally, in the health and welfare sectors – from hospitals to kindergartens – it is more difficult to ascertain real savings and profits (compared to, for example, the telecoms sector). On the one hand, the service providers – or their employees – may be in a position to extract profits, on the other hand improved efficiency may lead to quality improvement that is difficult to quantify. In either case, gains from efficiency in service provision resulting from the introduction of limited competition are usually difficult to measure and assess.

The most obvious factors threatening to restrict competition can perhaps be categorised as physical or practical. From a physical point of view, for example, only a limited number of networks for mobile telephony can be established because of a scarcity of band-with. In reality, of course, the number of licenses issued by a government is likely to be well below the physical limit.

The point, however, is that both physical scarcity and the economics of networks mean that competition cannot be unlimited. The same kind of logic applies to most networks from a practical viewpoint; competition between operators may be feasible in, for example, public transport, but the physical networks generally remain monopolies. By a similar logic of scarce capacity and economy of scale, competition is unrealistic in services that require heavy investment or advanced expertise, such as advanced cancer or heart disease hospitals.

More controversially, some governments only permit private actors on an exceptional basis in certain sectors. For example, although the UK has a long tradition of private schools, and Denmark and Sweden increasingly allow private operators, in Norway practically the only private schools allowed are either religious or justified because they operate 'alternative' pedagogies. In the same vein, although private health providers are making inroads into the hospital sector in much of Europe, in Scandinavia most non-profit private hospitals have religious roots.

Even in cases where full competition is legally envisaged and physically possible, actual competition may turn out to be more limited. In cases where the local government controls the tendering processes, political and ideological preferences may affect the scope for real competition. The actual operation of a public tender may depend on the openness of the process and how local government manages bids and competition. Moreover, particularly in small states or local authorities, the number of competent service providers might be limited in practice.

Purchaser–provider splits with effective competition

Although the New Public Management theories suggest that the best way to run public services efficiently and effectively is perfect competition, in practice is has proven very difficult to establish and sustain fully competitive arrangements for delivering public services. Successful and lasting competition has largely been limited to technical local government services, such as refuse collection, street cleaning and snow clearance, the construction and maintenance of public buildings, and some local transport services. In other areas, especially related to the core welfare services such as general care, health and education, the result has been closer to restricted competition of the type discussed above. The other option has been to run parallel public and private systems, for example, in cases where the public kindergarten system is supplemented by privately owned and operated day-care providers. The last possibility is, of course, full privatisation and liberalisation, as has taken place across Europe in telecommunications, most of Europe in electricity, and in the UK also for rail transport and water supply.

In the UK, under the Thatcher government, competitive tendering was introduced in the form of *Compulsory Competitive Tendering*, i.e. local governments were obliged to put certain services out to tender whether they wanted to or not. Elsewhere in Western Europe, the norm has been voluntary competitive tendering, i.e. local governments are permitted to put certain services out to tender but are not obliged to do so. The result has been a variety of patterns of competition across local authorities. In Denmark, for example, the public fire brigade is operated either as a normal publicly owned municipal service or, after competitive tendering, by a single private company – Group 4 Falck. In the case of Falck, the lower costs of the private operator is due to three factors that are found in many case studies of competitive tendering: a) the company does only what it is paid for, and does not provide the other free services that a public fire brigade typically provides such as rescuing cats from high trees; b) their pension systems are 'leaner'; and c) the profit motive generates incentives for running a surplus and thus puts pressure on costs, whereas a public fire service that runs a deficit may actually get a larger budget the subsequent year.

The overall picture is one of a great variety of experiments in liberalisation and modernisation of public service delivery, ranging from limited competition to fully competitive arrangements. However, upon closer inspection, the patterns of reform seem to involve more modernisation in the form of different elements of competition inside public services and within the publicly owned service providers, rather than fully liberalised competitive arrangements. Second, in many of the cases in which competitive tendering has been introduced, some elements have subsequently been modified or reversed. The effective re-nationalisation of the British rail-track network is a case in point. In other cases, much of the initially envisaged freedom of competition has been limited through the introduction of new rules and regulations that blur the clear-cut price-based tendering processes by introducing other selection criteria. For example, to the extent that refuse collection must include separation of different kinds of garbage, competition may be limited to highly specialised operators. Clear and transparent rules, and the presence of an impartial adjudicating body, are prerequisites for sustainable competitive arrangements for public service delivery.

Control, Transparency and Accountability

The fundamental change in thinking about public management in the 1980s and 1990s was that by 2000 the state was generally no longer seen as the impartial arbitrator and guardian of the public interest. Whereas the post-war welfare state was based on the assumption that the state should exercise impartial and efficient control over public service provision, the introduction of competition and liberalisation has brought with it new ideas proposing that it is the political state which must be controlled. The independent judiciary, and increasingly also independent agencies, are the new tools of impartial control in the 'regulatory state' (Majone 1997, James 2000). Their power to monitor and control the private actors, former monopoly incumbents and other public actors has increased dramatically across Europe. Although there is a considerable debate as to whether this is a matter of 'Americanisation' of European public administration, there is little doubt that some of the central ideas and models for independent regulatory agencies can be traced to the US experience. Even though EU directives do not specify the shape and form of regulatory agencies, but merely state that certain functions must be carried out, there are surprisingly many similarities across sectors and countries, both within and beyond the EU. These new independent agencies raise questions about control, transparency and accountability that have turned out to be problematic and politically controversial in most European states, even those that have well-functioning agencies in place. The agencies are rarely permitted to be fully independent, either because of government decree and action or by parliamentary legislation. For example, in a number of cases governments have intervened when the independent regulators set interconnection charges too low for the tastes of the incumbent telecoms operators. As for accountability, a central question is to whom the agencies are accountable – to the market actors, the government, or even to the EU? Or, in the time honoured phrase – who controls the controllers?

Perhaps the biggest question about control is related to the costs of compliance. This relates both to the individual actions taken by the regulator and to the overall cumulative effects of regulation. Although in some cases costly regulation for an incumbent operator may benefit new competitors, the overall cost of regulation is likely to hit both incumbents and their competitors over time. The EU telecoms review, and the subsequent 2003 regulatory package, represented an effort on the part of the Commission to address the cost of a growing set of complex regulations in the member states. In the UK, the Blair government's Better Regulation Task-Force was established with a mandate to review complex public regulation. Similar problems have been raised about regulation within the public sector, in particular with regard to education and health care. Compliance costs are the most obvious issue and have prompted criticism that doctors and teachers spend a disproportionate time 'filling in forms' rather than performing their professional duties. In the UK, the experience of the education regulator OFSTED has demonstrated the need to consider how the 'league tables' of school performance are put to use. The assumption that parental choice and competition would prompt better schools was not realised, and systems have been put in place to reward (and lighten the regulatory burden on) well-performing schools and to assist (and ultimately close down) under-performing schools. An important reason that the cost of compliance in the public sector has generated so much controversy is that organisations like schools and hospitals hardly have the administrative capacity necessary to process the control requirements. These organisations were developed under direct state control and are ill-adapted to the regulatory state, even where control requirements are not particularly excessive. The other side of the coin is the increasing burden that more complex regulation and monitoring requirements place on the regulatory authorities. In the UK, OFSTED continually reassesses and changes its control system and the way it interacts with schools.

The central idea behind the regulatory model was that it would improve transparency, and thus enhance consumer choice. Regulatory agencies and regimes would disseminate information about the price and quality of services offered by the competing market actors or suppliers of public services, and this would strengthen both the private and corporate consumers. The *e*Citizen would be 'enabled' or 'empowered'; a fully informed rational citizen would chose the most suitable mobile phone tariffs, the best local hospital or doctor, and the best school for their children. Even though agencies in all sectors and countries have put considerable effort into increasing transparency, it is far from clear that most citizens are sufficiently informed to make optimal choices about mobile phone contracts or electricity providers, let alone schools and hospitals. At least, this is what the limited rates of change between providers indicate. The principal reason for this in the telecoms case is that the competing companies tend to offer complex packages that are not easily compared; and this is often deliberately done by the companies. The electricity sector offers a clear contrast: it is more difficult to package the simple product of electricity in very different ways. In education and health care it is not only more difficult to assess that value and quality of services, but the very process of measuring and evaluating (and publishing the results) has generally proven controversial wherever it has been attempted.

Finally, the agency model was intended to increase accountability by establishing clear demarcation lines and lines of responsibility. However, this model of accountability includes some problems linked to its central operating principles. Accountability is strong at the time the 'buyer' (state or local government) contracts or renews a contract for a service, but it is much weaker in the intervening period. The reason is that all instruments of accountability are set out in the contract, and the public procurer cannot intervene during the operation of the contract as long as the formal conditions of the contract are fulfilled. This places heavy demands not only on qualified negotiators with strong powers of anticipation, but also on the stability of the environment. A relationship based on trust or administrative authority requires less in the form of foresight or stable and predictable environments. This is, of course, hardly new, having been a built-in feature of the Swedish model of public administration for two centuries, where politicians can control the independent agencies only by law and annual budgets. Sweden has thus long stood in sharp contrast to most other West European systems in which the relevant minister has had the power of instruction. In principle, this model should also alter the role of the individual somewhat: from citizen to consumer. As consumer, the individual would not only hold the government accountable on election day, but also hold suppliers to account by choosing between alternative suppliers or inter-active participation through IT-based systems. However, this partial shift from democratic to market accountability has been limited by three factors: voters still blame politicians for the quality of public services; there is insufficient choice to make switching suppliers a sufficiently strong tool of accountability; all of which is further weakened by insufficient information and lack of trans-parency. It is possible that more use of *e*Government may go some way to ameliorate this problem.

In summary then, the principal message of this chapter is that the liberali-sation and modernisation of public services has found expression via many dif-ferent forms of organisation and delivery of public services. Even within relatively similar models and types of organisation, there is further room for diversity due to different types of leadership and management styles. Although some organisational forms tend to foster certain management styles, for exam-ple, traditional public administration is associated with hierarchical command systems, whereas non-hierarchical semi-private service providers tend to have management-by-teams, there is almost unlimited room for variation in permu-tations and combinations. The next chapter addresses the more modern non-hierarchical forms of management, because this kind of organisational arrangement is often brought about by liberalisation and modernisation processes.

Further Reading

Hughes, O.E. (2003) *Public Management & Administration: An Introduction* (London: Palgrave). A good comparative introduction to public management that elaborates on many of the themes addressed in this chapter and draws on the experience of several countries. Chapter 4 on 'Public Management' provides a good starting point.

Denters, B. and Rose, L.E. (eds) (2005) *Comparing Local Governance: Trends and Developments* (London: Palgrave). Provides a broad and up-to-date overview of developments in local governance, with country-specific chapters on a number of modern liberal democracies. The editors' concluding chapter, 'Towards Local Governance?', provides a good comparative assessment of current trends.

(Continued)

(Continued)

Walsh, K. (1995) *Public Service and Market Mechanisms: Competition, Contracting and the New Public Management* (London: Macmillan). A thorough account of the use of various mechanisms to introduce competition into public service provision that draws primarily on the British and American experience. Chapter 5 on 'Contract and Competition' provides a good discussion of the increased use of contracts in public services.

Pollitt, C. (2003) *The Essential Public Manager* (Maidenhead: Open University Press). A very readable assessment of public service reform, which at times employs a conversational style and draws examples and anecdotes from the UK over the last two decades. Chapter 4 on 'Politicians, Accountability, Citizens and Participation' provides a good discussion of the relationships between public managers and other actors, from politicians to citizens.

EIGHT

Tools of Management and Leadership

With Inger-Margrete Svendsen

This chapter discusses the potential and scope for, as well as the limits to, introducing techniques and practices from private sector management to public leadership.[1] The limits of private leadership tools are linked primarily to the greater difficulties involved in identifying the overall goals of public organisations, the need to maintain legal obligations and procedures, and the somewhat greater concern for protection of employee rights and privileges. Public sector management and leadership takes place in a different framework than private sector management: in particular, there are three major differences that render public management more challenging:

1 the objectives and goals of the organisation;
2 the role of rules and regulations;
3 the special effects of having politicians as the top executives.

Public sector organisations almost always face multiple and complex objectives. These are not always explicit, sometimes involve trade-offs, and may even be contradictory in the aims they try to pursue; in contrast to the private sector where profit is the main goal of any business. At the same time, rules and regulations are not only the framework that shapes the activities, but often constitute the tool itself (i.e. applying rules and procedures may well be more important than outcomes). Finally, politics often introduces a more short-term

---

[1]We would like to express our thanks to Lene Bråtesveen for her assistance in our work with this chapter.

perspective on the activities of the institution, and political rule involves dependency on re-election and therefore on the voters.

There are also a number of other differences between public and private management that might constrain leadership in a public organisation. First of all, the relationship between the political and administrative level is different compared to the management and the board of a company. Then there are differences in the allocation of tasks, the (sometimes conflicting) relationships between the parties involved, and in the sheer heterogeneity of actors recruited to political positions. In the public sector, the ultimate owners are often found on both sides of the table: as voters/taxpayers and as consumers of public services. Furthermore, the decision-making process is longer and more complicated. The organisational culture may involve other norms and values, such as making the correct or appropriate decisions according to rules and regulations, stability and order. In addition, the products are often different: public services are often free of charge at the point of use, plus there is usually less flexibility in human resources policy and personnel recruitment. These differences may have decreased over the last decade or two, but they still make for a different operational environment for leadership in the public sector.

Concepts and Theories of Management and Leadership

What, then, is management and leadership? There is a large variety of different theories and definitions that emphasise different aspects of leadership and management: situational leadership, transformational leadership, knowledge management, super leadership, self-management, value-based management, charismatic management, to mention just some of the more significant ones. The history of management has to some extend been a history of reductionistic attempts to establish some common approaches, definitions and functional models, but at best with limited success to create a comprehensive unified approach or model. The reason is that management and leadership constitute rather complex processes where context, regime and communication are coming together into very complex patterns. The point of departure for theories and models of management is also several very different scientific traditions, including psychology, political science, sociology, organisational studies, anthropology, decision studies and other academic fields. Thus, there is no single, established definition available that identifies the most relevant aspects or dimensions of the concept, nor does one scientific tradition dominate this field of study or of consultancy (Bass 1990, Yukl 2006). Consequently, and because this is a single chapter that deals with management and leadership on micro-level in a broader volume on Public Management, we focus on a few selected important issues.

Most definitions of leadership emphasise the ability of an individual to influence and motivate others towards reaching a shared goal. The term 'others' may refer to an individual, a group or an organisation (Bass 1960, Hemphill and Coons 1957). Leadership, therefore, is a process that involves interaction between individuals (Yalom 1995). Schein defines leadership in this vein, but puts it in a slightly different light: 'leadership is the ability to step outside the culture, to start evolutionary change-processes that are more adaptive' (Schein 1993: 2). Thus, most definitions of leadership reflect the assumption that it involves a process whereby intentional influence is exerted by one person over other people to guide, structure and facilitate activities and relationships in a group or an organisation (Yukl 2006). Our conclusion is that leadership is best understood by the use of concepts such as goal, process and influence.

The concepts of management and leadership are used interchangeably in many textbooks, as we do partly in this chapter. One simple distinction is that management is to carry out activities, which is closely related to planning, organising and controlling; whereas leadership is to influence, motivate and produce change (Kotter 1990). Sometimes we find that leadership is used for the more micro-oriented and individual direction and the motivation of employees. Accordingly the major distinction is between administration, culture and relations (Colbjørnsen 2004). These constitute the tasks which all organisations have to fulfil. All organisations are created for a purpose, and the core issues in administration are therefore to formulate goals, find the resources to reach these goals and to manage the use of resources. These activities are in turn closely related to the overall strategy of the organisation. Culture is the informal environment inside the organisation in which the administration of the organisation and the development of these relations is carried out. 'Relations' involve motivating the employees to reach the goals of the organisation.

In this chapter, we will focus on two important aspects of management and leadership: *organising* and *interacting*, with theoretical background from organisational studies and psychology respectively. The main questions are how the work of the organisation is organised for efficient and flexible management, and how the relations inside the organisation are developed and nourished. The first question is closely related to the theme of the previous chapter on the organisational effects of New Public Management inside public organisations. This chapter focuses mainly on one important aspect of organisational development linked to the leadership function in the organisation: the rapidly increasing use of *non-hierarchical organisational* forms in the public sector, and, most importantly, *team organisation*. Finally, regarding interaction, we will focus on communication – in particular with relation to management in non-hierarchical organisations and management coaching.

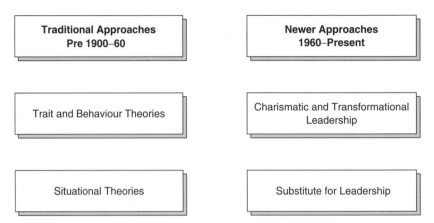

Traditional Approaches Pre 1900–60		Newer Approaches 1960–Present
Trait and Behaviour Theories		Charismatic and Transformational Leadership
Situational Theories		Substitute for Leadership

Figure 8.1   Four main types of approaches to management and leadership

Leadership theories and models

The literature on leadership is vast, and consists of various approaches from interdisciplinary fields. The role of leadership has been of great interest for centuries since it appears to be a crucial part of entities' effectiveness and, latterly, the ability of an organisation to adapt to a changing environment. Grouped according to traditional and newer approaches to leadership, Figure 8.1 sets out some of the theories that have attracted most attention from researchers in their quest to analyse leadership. The traditional approaches go back many years and take a somewhat narrow view of the variables involved in explaining the effect of leadership. Newer approaches acknowledge the complexity of variables involved and consequently cut across concepts such as charisma, influence, communication and empowerment. A large part of this chapter is dedicated to coaching, self-management and the role of communication, which are linked to newer approaches such as *substitutes for leadership* and *transformational leadership*. However, as both the traditional and newer approaches are important to understand a leader's role and leadership effectiveness, the evolution of leadership theories deserves some attention.

'Trait and Behaviour Theories' (pre 1900–60), on the left of Figure 8.1, assumed that leadership depends on personal traits and behaviour. This implies that all other variables are of less importance. Trait theory attempted to identify which traits distinguish leaders from non-leaders in order to select the 'true' leaders. Some of the traits found to have an effect include attractiveness, above-average height and intelligence (Bass 1990). The search for the 'great man' has preoccupied academics and philosophers for centuries. One example is Carlyle, who in 1841 in his book on heroes claims that the history of the world is a biography of Great Men (Carlyle 1841). However, inadequate measurement and failure to identify traits changed researchers' attention towards exploring the behaviour of leaders. By the 1940s behavioural theories emerged. Well-known research programmes from this era include the Michigan Studies and Ohio States Studies, which were able to identify patterns in leaders' behaviour that were correlated with performance (Bass 1990, Likert 1961). Findings from behavioural studies were inconsistent and therefore led to a new proposition: there might not be one best way to perform leadership, and leadership behaviour may vary from one situation to another. This paved the way for 'Situational Theories' of leadership.

Situational theories (bottom left corner in Figure 8.1) aim at identifying situations that require different leadership styles. Important contributions to situational theories include House and Mitchell's (1974) Path Goal Theory, and Hersey and Blanchard's (1988) Situational Leadership model. Fidler's work on situational leadership started in the 1960s, and his main thesis states that a work group's effectiveness depends on the match between the demand of the situation and leadership styles. Leadership styles were identified as either task-oriented or relationship-oriented. Different situations were assessed through an analysis of the relationship between leader and member, the task structure and leader's task expertise and leader's power granted through the hierarchy. For example, when the situation was characterised by a good leader–member relationship, high task structure and strong positional power, the most effective leadership style would be a task-oriented leadership (Fiedler 1967). Hersey and Blanchard (1988) argue in similar vein, and in addition assess the importance of level of expertise and motivation of the employees (readiness). Their Situational Leadership model suggests that leadership styles should match the readiness of the followers. Even though situational leadership has a intuitive appeal, empirical results are not strong (Graff 1983). Additional variables needed to be explored to give a more comprehensive picture of leadership and effectiveness. Later models recognised this complexity.

Newer approaches to leadership theories are those of 'Charismatic and Transformational Leadership' (on the right in Figure 8.1). Charismatic leadership assumes that leaders have a form of interpersonal attraction that inspires people, and that their charismatic behaviour has a profound effect on their followers. This is similar to trait and behaviour theories, but the new variable of interest is how leaders influence others. Characteristics found in a charismatic leader are strong confidence, an extraordinary ability to communicate goals and visions, but also a need for power – a need which is reinforced by their own sense of morality. While non-charismatic leaders are able to make changes incrementally by directing employees towards established goals, charismatic leaders are able to transform their followers and enforce radical change programmes. So who are these super humans? Research suggests the charismatic leaders can be either 'dark-side' or 'bright-side' leaders. Dark-side leaders emphasise personal power (focus on themselves) – Hitler and Bin Laden are often mentioned as examples here. Bright-side leaders, such as Nelson Mandela, Gandhi or Martin Luther King Jr., emphasis social power that empowers their followers. Needless to say, charismatic leadership can have a negative effect on their followers (House 1977, Conger and Kanugo 1988).

A related perspective is transformational leadership. This perspective has many similarities with charismatic leadership, but is much boarder since charisma is only one of the characteristics a leader possesses. Moreover, transformational leadership is about leading through empowering followers, and thereby differs from charismatic leadership where followers place their trust in the leader's expertise and have a passive role in a change process (Yukl 2006). Both Bass and Burns identified transformational leadership as a leadership style that lifts motivation of followers to a self-sacrificing behaviour. Bass further contrasts the transformational dimension of leadership with a transactional dimension. Transactional leadership is essential for the completion of tasks, but is performed without necessarily being inspired by a leader. It is the day-to-day operations, and an effective result that is the predefined performance parameter. Transformational leadership, on the other hand, goes beyond agreed performance and is a crucial component for successful change programmes because it has the potential to minimise resistance to change. Bass stresses that both leadership styles are important to achieve success. Moreover, it is possible to develop transformational leadership skills through training, which clearly departs from traditional trait theories (Bass 1985, 1990, Burns 1978).

The last approach we will look at is substitutes for leadership, which claims that leadership is sometimes irrelevant. Important variables here are the characteristics of individuals, the task and the organisation. For example, in a situation where tasks are routine and employees are highly experienced, individuals may require little instruction, thus reducing the need for directive or supportive leadership. Moreover, in cases where employees are highly professionally orientated and there is a need for independence, individuals may not want social support from the leader (Kerr and Jermier 1978). Research from this approach has shown mixed results, but, given the emerging importance of teams and self-management, the concept of leadership substitutes is likely to be important.

In summary, the development of leadership theories demonstrates incremental adjustment to the understanding of what leadership is, of what variables modify effectiveness, and of how an organisation's ability to transform itself can be enhanced. In addition, behavioural and situational theories continue to play a role, but are placed in a broader and more complex framework interacting with variables such as communication, empowerment and power. And finally, theoretical foundations can be used to analyse teams, coaching and self-management. The remainder of the chapter deals with this. For example, transformational leadership may be applicable to self-management since motivating and leading through empowerment are important components of successful self-management. Moreover, substitutes for leadership may also be applicable to team activities since teams often specify their own goals and standards and eliminate the need for a leader to map out ways of achieving goals. On the other hand some element of influence is needed in every type of organisation – leadership is essentially about power and communication.

Power and communication within leadership

In our definition of leadership, one key component is influence, and in order to fully understand how leaders are able to influence others, it is necessary to explore the concept of power. Power can best be explained as the ability to modify the behaviour of others without their consent. Accordingly, a leader with power is able to make one or more persons do something they would otherwise not have done in order to achieve their own preferred outcome (Dahl 1957, Pfeffer 1981). Sources of power can stem from the manager's position in the organisational hierarchy (positional power) or from the person's characteristics (personal power; Bass 1960). Consequently, a good leader can rely on personal power in order to obtain commitment and compliance from the other members of the organisation. Moreover, power and influence is a prerequisite to move towards an organisation's goals.

The ability to make oneself understood, explain and convince is a requirement for gaining power so that, in this sense, power and communication become two characteristics of leadership. In other words, the communicative process is an important aspect of the leadership role: *how* the message is given, and how this contributes to relationship *quality* become central points. A second aspect is co-creating, where actors are mutually interpreting and acting in a communicative context and become each others presuppositions. Thus, a leader who wants to gain power is dependent upon legitimacy for the task, and legitimacy is derived from trust. Thereby trust is not created as a result of a leader's position in the hierarchy, but because of the leader's ability to communicate, which enhances the possibility of a constructive interplay. In the same way, distrust can be a result of destructive interplay patterns.

Major cultural differences exist in the way power is exercised. In some cultures it is possible (and even seen as a virtue) to exercise power through positional power where instructions and sanctions are used as tools of governance. In countries with longstanding democratic traditions, rule by instruction and punishment is substituted by (at least as an intention) participation and dialogue in the decision-making processes. Democratic values create pressure for cooperation and dialogue as central aspects of exercising leadership, so that communicative consciousness and competence become critical skills in the act of leadership. In other words, to have influence, a leader must have acquired trust from subordinates in order to use their power in a constructive and ethically justifiable way. The colleagues give the leader trust, thus enabling the leader to exercise power. It is therefore anticipated that through the development of our knowledge-based economy this trend will increase.

Tasks of Public Management

Organisations have aims and goals that are the task of management to accomplish. This represents the basic function of all organisations from large corporations to a single interest organisation. Thus, the evaluation of the performance of an organisation has to be based primarily on to what extent and on how it is able to accomplish its goals. The complexity of the goals in most public sector organisations makes this a difficult task, whereas in business, profit is the overriding goal and all other goals have to be subordinated to it. In public organisations, however, there are usually several goals, often running into double figures, and there may be no clear hierarchy of these goals. In addition, the goals are often unclear and contradictory due to the fact that such organisations are typically governed by politicians who have several constituencies with differing interests. The first role of public managers, therefore, will often be to make priorities and to select a rather restricted number of the goals that the politicians can then try to attain.

As we have already seen, one of the central tasks of a leader is tied to reaching set objectives. An interesting question here is: Who defines the goals? Traditionally it has been the leader who clarifies goals and who formulates subsequent expectations to colleagues. This we see in models both of transformational and of visionary leadership. In other approaches the emphasis is on the group itself, or on joint definition of the goals in cooperation with the leader. This is evident in supra-leadership and directions emphasising the self-leadership approach where motivational leadership is central in order to reach goals instead of other means, such as sanctions and punishment.

If we return to the idea of distinguishing between administration, culture and relations as the three tasks of management in an organisation, *administration* has three different aspects. Performance management takes the point of departure in the main strategy and goals of the organisation and breaks them down into separate goals for the different divisions, sections and units, and into goals for performance for the individual employee. The second element is to communicate these expectations and follow up with performance monitoring and incentives to correct and reward the activities of the individual. The third aspect is the more bureaucratic performing management through rules and regulations. Control is through inspection and quality management systems.

A second aspect of management is the development, reformulation and adjustment of management *culture*. Culture is the dominating values, norms or understanding of reality that the members of the organisation have developed (Colbjørnsen 2004, Bang 1999, Schein 1993). Culture can be divided into two dimensions: underlying perceptions (which can be unconscious); and adapted values which are openly expressed. Adapted values do not reflect the culture if they are not in accordance with underlying perceptions. For example, if an organisation purports to have open communication, but the underlying understanding is that disagreement is harmful and should be avoided, the adapted value does not correctly reflect the culture. It can be difficult to penetrate the surface of such covert views to reveal underlying thoughts and perceptions.

Leadership and management are based on a relationship between various human beings and, as such, *relations* forms one of the most difficult aspects of management and leadership in an organisation. Indeed, interpersonal relations is a pillar of all execution of management functions, and the relationship between managers and employees at different levels, and among employees themselves, are, in modern organisations, the core element in goal attainment and in organisational change and development. Relations are also very closely linked to communications in organisations, which we will return to later. The time when relational leadership really matters is when an organisation has to undergo substantial change. To some extent, all management and leadership is about orchestrating change; comprehending, initiating, executing and evaluating change processes in the organisation.

Management and leadership at different levels

Management and leadership can, however, be exercised at different levels. Most of the literature has focused mainly on the lower and middle level of management in different types of organisations. In the last decades, there has been increased interest and focus on top management and on politicians as top managers: they are often occupied with strategic ideological and long-term perspectives in the organisation. This implies that the politicians develop the normative and value foundations for the organisation. The politicians and the top management direct the work in the institution and are in charge of the organisational, operational and leadership issues and make decisions on products, position and the broad future direction of the institution in the public sector like in private companies. Some aspects of this, like setting out the vision for the organisation, are also usually reserved for the top manager in cooperation with the board or the owners.

A division manager will be occupied with the operative management through administration, planning and finding and managing the resources needed for the implementation of the strategic plans of the organisation inside his or her division.

The unit manager will take the main responsibility for directing and motivating employees, and supervising and controlling the production process in the unit.

We can therefore distinguish at least four different levels of management and leadership.

- *Ideological Management*   This includes the formulation of the business idea, the vision and the mission of the organisation, the ambitions and leadership philosophy of the organisation in question. This is the responsibility of the top management and the owners of the agency or institution, often politicians.
- *Strategic Management*   This is the level of formulating the organisation's strategy, setting goals, and investigating the consequences of different strategies. It also includes making a final action-plan for the organisation, mainly done by the administration, but ultimately sanctioned by the politicians.
- *Administrative Management*   This is where the resources needed to reach the goals are assessed, found, managed and used. At this level the focus is also on the organisation and on personnel policy and development.
- *Operative Management*   This refers to the daily task of making the organisation work in accordance with its principles, objectives and plans, and involves both communication and motivation of the employees.

At all these levels, however, management and leadership can be performed inside very different organisational structures, from very hierarchal bureaucracies to modern knowledge-based organisations with a very flat structure.

Leadership in Teams

Recent years have witnessed a growing interest globally for more flexible and non-hierarchical forms of organisation. Such ideas have been around for several decades as an organisational form for tasks with a limited time frame and a formalised structure – namely projects, as can be seen in the increasing number of standard textbooks on project management (i.e. Mantel et al. 2005). Recently, however, a growing trend in organisations is to give more responsibility for important activities to more flexible organisational forms – namely teams. In many cases, the teams are empowered to make decisions collectively that were formerly made by individual managers (Yukl 2006).

Thus, in recent years the focus is on flexible organisations as a more normal and standard way of organising goal attainment in organisations through groups, teams and networks etc. There is a large variety of labels for these new forms of organisation, such as, teams, self-governed teams, project teams, management teams, units, groups, competence teams, network groups, networks etc. All imply fewer organisational levels, more flexibility in tasks and activities, limited duration and more management through coordination than instruction – both inside the team and in relation to the top management.

A *team* is a small group of persons where the members have a shared responsibility for reaching goals, with authority to make decisions inside their area of responsibility and with a continuous interaction among the group members. This can be distinguished from *groups* which are a small number of people, often with different qualifications, who exchange information and competence to assist each other's individual work. A *network* is a group of people exchanging ideas, information and knowledge for mutual benefit across organisational boarders.

With regard to teams, Yukl (2006) describes five different ways of leadership, depending on the different functions of the team. According to his work, teams differ in relation to: degree of autonomy; how long the existence of the team has been planned; stability of participation; differences in background of team members; and on the type of leadership authority. Yukl describes a Functional Operating Team, a Top Executive Team, and a Self-Managed Team, where the leader's authority is strong, and a Self-Defining Team and a more Autonomous Team where the role of the leader is weaker.

The earlier work of Katzenbach and Smith (1993) emphasises that individuals in a team have complementary skills, are committed to a common purpose, goals and approach, for which they hold themselves mutually accountable. A well-functioning team is characterised by members working together for a common goal, taking responsibility for the end product, having freedom of action, but also a common understanding and mutual trust, being able to listen and to adjust their own opinions accordingly, and to accept disagreement. A well-functioning team is also able to develop the team and its individual members in addition to reaching the goals the team has been set by their superiors.

Why teams?

Team organisation has become popular for several reasons. First of all, the complexity of tasks confronting many organisations today has rendered the traditional hierarchical organisational form unsuitable for problem-solving and goal-attainment. The pace of change in both organisational environments and inside organisations points in the same direction – rapid change increases the need for flexible and adaptable organisations. Teams represent an adaptable organisational form that makes it possible to produce high quality, effectiveness and efficiency in an organisation even when solving complex problems. Moreover, it adds a strong element of mutual learning. The team is well suited to engage and take advantage of different knowledge- and skill-bases and personal competencies in the organisation, and therefore permits more flexible use of employees. This organisational form also makes members more responsible, and ready to make decisions on behalf of the organisation.

On the other hand, to use team-organisation and teamwork requires more resources than other organisational structures. The use of teams therefore requires the competence of several different persons to attain a goal, and needs mutual competencies to be exploited when dealing with the team's tasks. If one person can do the work alone as well as or better than the team, then there is obviously no need for team organisation for this particular task – and there will always be tasks in an organisation that should not be organised as teamwork. Teams, therefore, should be used when tasks cannot be carried out in an optimal way by one person alone; where both the effectiveness and the quality is increased when the competence of two or more persons are utilised.

Teams should also be employed to increase motivation among employees, and to train them to ensure that several persons have the competencies needed for certain tasks in the organisation. This reduces the kind of organisational vulnerability that may arise when certain competencies are confined to one person. Team organisation is also facilitated by digitalisation and the new technological options created for disseminating decisions and competencies throughout the organisation. To exploit the advantages of more flexible organisational forms, the organisation needs, however, to create and develop the new structure of the agency or institution in a proper manner.

How to work with teams

The literature on teams also addresses the challenges of establishing teams, how to work with teams, and how to manage a team organisation. With regard to establishing teams, several studies illustrate the challenges of establishing well-functioning teams in an organisation. Primarily, it is imperative to make a firm commitment to the shift in the organisational logic towards a full or partly team-based organisation, and to build motivation and enthusiasm for this way of working. At the same time, most organisations also need to create a common understanding of what a team organisation is meant to be and how it is supposed to function. The point of departure for a team organisation and work in teams is the visions and goals of the organisation. Teams could be a more efficient way of meeting the challenges of the organisation if the ability to compose teams with the relevant mix of competences is fulfilled, and this includes a competence development in the different teams in parallel with the accomplishments of their designated tasks.

There are two main processes at work in a team. The first involves completion of the task at hand, the process of which is shaped by the degree of complexity and interdependence between participants. The second development is amongst the team participants themselves, and concerns the communicative quality and the communicative consciousness amongst the participants. This is a fundamental dimension that affects the degree to which the participants interact in order to solve their tasks. This dimension also has importance in conjunction with satisfaction and motivation. The team processes could also be decisive in relation to how much the participants identify with the team, and it is therefore possible that this dimension could affect the degree of loyalty the participants show towards decisions and acts determined by the team.

There are several signs that a team might be working effectively; in the sense that they reach the goals the team has set. First, the goal is shared, owned by all, and understood by all participants. Furthermore, the members' values are made explicit, and the members share the same values. It is also decisive that the team knows what to do, that the tasks are clear and that there are feedback routines during the process and after the work has been completed. Feedback has both a motivational and a disciplinary effect, apart from the fact that learning is possible. Consequently, open and honest communication is an important dimension in order to succeed as a team (Thomson 1967).

A recurring issue in the literature on team organisation is the ideal size of a team. Recent studies indicate that the ideal size is smaller than previously assumed; probably around five to seven members. There are also discussions in the literature on how to compose a team and the necessity of an element of volunteer recruitment as well as some form of management control and sanctioning of the team composition. The next step will normally be to agree with the management on the mandate, responsibility and authority of the team, as well as the mutual expectations from both the management and the team members as to what to expect from the team. These are among the most difficult issues in team organisation.

Management of institutions with strong emphasis on non-hierarchical organisational structures such as teams, is often more challenging than management in more hierarchical bureaucracies. Some of the recurring problems working with a team-based organisation include how to monitor the teams, correct mistakes and evaluate the results. An additional aspect is the role of the team leader. To lead a team is about two main processes. The first is to collect information and make it available to the team members in order to find solutions to their tasks. The second is to administer the human and material resources. The results of team activities should be threefold: the fulfilment of the tasks given to the teams; the learning process in the team itself; and the learning process among the individuals.

Teams and their members are normally confined to an organisation. However, sometimes there is a need to include competencies from outside the organisation in order to manage the task the team has been given. The solution could be a network that is linked to the team within the organisation that gave the team the necessary external information and competence.

Composition of teams

The main idea of the optimal composition of teams is that complementary skills increase productivity and enhance learning through cooperation. Differences in skills between team members can be of a professional nature, experience-based or based on personality. Previous research has attempted to find the key to the ideal mix of skills, but has met with limited success, because of the complex personality and group process variables that may influence a team's dynamics. The main conclusion is that if the differences between the team members are too great, this could impede group processes and, in the worst-case scenario, lock in conflicts. Belbin (1981) argues that in a well-functioning team, each team member has different roles and responsibilities. From various studies of teams, he has categorised behaviour into nine different roles. As the roles are complementary, no one role is more important than another, but their uses depend on the context the team finds itself in, the goals of the team, and what phase of problem-solving the team is in. The different roles can be divided in two main dimensions: the first runs along the extrovert–introvert axis, which is recurrent in most teams and is a personality tool. The other axis is goal-oriented–refinement. Belbin's system is often used to compose teams and, even more frequently, to assess the necessity for development for the members of already existing teams.

Management of Non-Hierarchical Organisations: Communication and Coaching

In both hierarchical and non-hierarchical organisations communication will be one of the basic skills of a leader. In leading non-hierarchical organisations, the communication process and its consequences are an important prerequisite for success. We have already cited different definitions of communication and interaction, and now we will introduce a new concept: *action*. This involves three sequences through which both the receiver and the sender of a message create meaning: a) intended meaning; b) action/language use; c) effect.

Action (including verbal and non-verbal action) builds on intentions and leads to an effect. Therefore interplay must be understood based on these three sequences:

1 I have an intention, something I wish to acquire.
2 Thus I act from this intention.
3 Thereafter my actions will have an effect on those who are influenced by my acts.

As sender of a message it is I who take responsibility for my intentions and my actions. It is I as sender who bears responsibility for how my intentions are conveyed to others, through the *manner* in which I communicate and by *what*

Figure 8.2   Intention, action and effect

I chose to be my message. Sometimes unforeseen effects, or effects other than those intended by the acting person, occur.

Communication when signifying dialogue is characterised by creating something beyond itself in interplay with others. We build a purpose or perspective that can be different from that which we brought into the conversation. In this way communication gives us the possibility of creating something together; creating more than what one person brought into the talk at the beginning. This perspective is relevant for leadership and for the benefit of organising teams. There is also another aspect here. When the effect we get in interplay with others is of a different character than expected, it would in some cases lead to us being positively surprised. We release more constructiveness than we thought we would. We obtain something free. We get into, or perpetuate, what we might call 'a good circle'.

At other times the effect is surprising, but in a negative way. We arose effects in those with whom we are connecting but in a negative or complicating way. My intentions could be the very best but if I release effects/reactions in others that are unwanted, I am in relations where my behaviour (language or other acts) has to be adjusted. In this way I can create effects more according to my intentions. I thus get the possibility of looking at my acts in a meta-perspective or a learning perspective. I can than raise questions such as: could I have done this in a different way? What would my colleagues wish I should have done instead?

The more authority a person has, the more important it is that this person listens to others. Auto correction – the willingness to adapt your own intentions and actions based on effects – creates confidence and authority. Moreover, leadership theory and flexibility is shown in practice. Suppleness in the relationship between leader and colleague or in other relations can be created through this self-reflectiveness. Here we are all challenged in communication and this is the most demanding factor in all interactions between people, especially between a leader and a colleague. Maybe because this can be an uncomfortable realisation, literature on leadership has a tendency to treat communication in a more technical and operational way. This is a continual process of reflection putting personal responsibility and ethical acts into a communication and leadership perspective. Through reflections on our actions, we can relate ethically to ourselves and to others; be ethically conscious of the life we live and of the necessary self-discipline our neo-liberal society has created as a cultural frame around our lives.

Coaching

Coaching is developed from and is closely linked to cognitive psychology and was developed first in the field of sport. Over time it has gradually been extended to management. The basic idea is that the coach and the coachee, the person being coached, together create a continuous communication process where the focus is on the development of the coachee. The focus in the communication process is on goals and results, and on how to fulfil these goals. The idea is to succeed by making the coachee more conscious about her or his situation and strengths. The aim is to get results and to increase individual capacity for growth and development.

Coaching is one of several communication skills that can be useful in circumstances where dialogue and management through others is a prerequisite for leadership performance. The development of projects, teams and other forms of self-managed organisational forms has not reduced the need for management and leadership, but it has warranted other forms of governance models within organisations. Even the most independent team or other non-hierarchical forms of organisational entities need to have a vision and a goal induced by the management. They also need resources, monitoring, reward and response systems, as well as final acceptance of the product or process delivered. All this requires management at different levels. Self-managed groups operate within a framework established by the formal and informal borders and by the limits of room for manoeuvre set by superiors. The different systems for reporting and control also creates room for management and leadership.

There are several different ways of managing non-hierarchical organisations, including counselling, mentoring, ICT-based virtual management inspection, and coaching as a management technique. Coaching has recently become very popular in management situations – in addition to professional executive coaching – as a way of developing leadership skills. A few years ago the coachee was normally a higher-level manager whereas today coaching is used at all levels in the organisation and for groups as well as for individuals. The professional coach is often a person with a management and/or behavioural science background who has some kind of coaching training – there are several educational programmes for certifying coaches. The coach could either be employed in the organisation or hired from outside for a particular task.

Why has coaching become so popular? The philosophical base for coaching is very positive and the results are often fast and brought about by the coachees themselves. Coaching is built on the assumption that human beings possess the answers to how their goals could be realised, but help is needed to understand this and in particular to move from words to action. The coach therefore puts questions to the coachee, which helps a person realise their potential and then challenges them to reach this potential. Thus, the coach is some kind of a professional discussion partner trained both to ask good questions and to challenge and support people in their own development to be more conscious about their own potential. The coach can work with the coachee on both office and private tasks. However, the coach is not a therapist or an advisor or mentor – focus is firmly on the present and future, and not on the past.

A coaching manager, therefore, is a manager who employs some of the coaching techniques to carry out part of his or her management function. The challenge is to stimulate the subordinates to take responsibility, to develop good working methods and to focus on doing the right things. The coaching method is also well suited for emancipating and developing the potential of the employees. Coaching is also exclusively oriented towards the future. When applying a coaching in management, it is important to know the specific situations when this technique is useful and then be able to employ different types of leadership techniques according to different types of management situations.

There are several different ways professional coaching can be used in an organisation. It is common to distinguish between four different types. *Individual coaching* entails a one-to-one relationship between a coach and a coachee. This is the most commonly used form for individual development. The coaching situation lasts six months to a year, or more. Another form is *individual group coaching* where the group one belongs to is used as a forum for coaching one individual. *Group coaching* is when the coach is coaching a group of individuals. And finally *team coaching* is when the focus is not only on the individuals in the group, but also on the overall functioning of the team.

Coaching can also be used in different areas for different types of challenges or goals for the individual or the group. Often it is related to the job and to the specific goals the individual or the group would like to achieve. In a working relationship, the goals could be future career, professional qualifications, accessibility, cooperation, responses, team deadlines, information, meeting procedures etc. These goals could often be limited and rather concrete, like the list here, or they could be more principal and fundamental like attitudes and more basic behaviour. In addition to job and carrier, recent years have witnessed a rapid growth in the application of the coaching method to family issues, relationships with friends, personal development in general and even health and habits like drinking and smoking. In general, to have a coach has been seen as a new way of realising goals and setting personal development in motion.

Coaching techniques

The main source of control a leader uses in coaching is questions, but where the questions themselves are of such a nature that the coachees themselves have to find the answers. Questions should stimulate commitment and responsibility for own development and task delivery. Coaching is also a way of directing the individuals involved and of inviting them to a dialogue. Questions are oriented to defining goals and objectives and planning how the coachee can attain them. This process could also entail identifying and working with different obstacles that hinder such attainment. Obstacles can be mental or practical. In an asymmetric relationship, as between leader and colleague, it would be appropriate that the conversation be practical and target-oriented since a coach is not a personal psychologist at the workplace. However, sometimes it is necessary to debate personal qualities, but it is important that leaders consciously consider what is wise to discuss in a work context.

Research on the effects of executive coaching on personal development and leadership effectiveness is limited, but the evidence so far seems to be favourable (Yukl 2006: 406) also for public sector managers (Olivero et al. 1997). There has, however, been an explosion in the use of coaching and coaching techniques in most Western countries and there are several studies under way which will analysis the effects of this new management-training tool in more detail.

Self-Leadership and Some Concluding Remarks

Supra-leadership and self-leadership are two sides of the same coin, in the sense that supra-leadership can be defined as the process of influencing oneself whereas self-leadership is the process of influencing others (Manz and Sims 1980, Manz 1992). Consequently, a precondition for successful supra-leadership is that a manager is able to lead her/himself. The development of the knowledge-based society requires a form of leadership that entails focus on goals and targets rather than on detailed governance. This might explain why supra-leadership has become a central concept within leadership literature.

The concept of self-leadership means that employees are responsible for their own progress. Managers become more akin to partners, in order to discuss topics such as motivation, goal-setting and rewards. More importantly, supra-leadership is about making oneself responsible for tasks that traditionally were a manager's. The traditional way of governing was, and to a certain extent still is, focused on allocation of tasks and goals. Motivation was tied to external compensation. Evaluation has traditionally been a process characterised by critique, and externally driven expectations. Through self-leadership, responsibility in planning, problem-solving, decision-making and evaluation is delegated to the individual. Thus, as employees, and not the manager, define their own goals, monitor progress and carry out self-evaluation, more is demanded of mental strategies from the manager.

In order to master these processes, successful leadership requires the leader to open up for dialogue in order to master leading oneself. This requires continuous dialogues on goals, progress and resources with fellow workers to take full advantage of their inner motivational driving forces. To realise the intentions behind self-leadership requires development and work on inner cognitive maps and models, giving rewards and power to continue bringing the individual towards goal attainment. The implication for a leader would be to develop a set of behavioural activities that helps colleagues to lead themselves. In this way, we could say that leadership deviates from goal- and result-orientation, towards the leader being a coordinator, motivator and supporter. From this perspective, it is possible to imagine the communicative competences of a leader becoming more important than ever. We suggest that in the future there will be more emphasis on these more flexible forms of leadership, supra-leadership and self-leadership, than we have discussed here because of the rapid change towards a knowledge and information economy.

This final chapter has centred on individual public sector management and the leadership tools and capabilities that are available to managers in modern public organisations. There is a large literature on management and leadership in general, and much of it has a private sector focus. We have drawn on this in order to show how, and to what extent, these strategies and techniques can be used in the public sector. The chapter has focused mainly on new forms of leadership, such as coaching, team management, motivational leadership and self-management. The central point concerns the importance of adapting an organisation's incentives and reward systems to broader changes in governance systems, and to more specific changes in the internal functioning of an organisation. Management or leadership is a matter of realising an organisation's goal through the people involved in the organisation. Or to be more precise: it is the process by which an organised group is moved toward reaching its goals. A corollary of this is that leadership is also a tool for change. Leadership is, on the other hand, an instrument that consists of a set of more specific tools for conducting the leadership tasks.

Because all organisations operate in context – in the case of public sector organisations the most important context might be modernisation programmes – an important aspect of management is to understand the relevant external conditions and the demands that are subsequently placed on the organisation, and to operate accordingly. This has, in fact, been an underlying dimension in this chapter and in the volume as a whole.

Further Reading

Yukl, G. (2006) *Leadership in Organizations* (Upper Saddle River: Pearson Prentice Hall). This is a well-known textbook dedicated to leadership in organisations and leadership effectiveness. Chapter 11, 'Leadership in Teams and Decision Group', is of particular interest as it discusses self-managed works teams and the leadership role in those.

Van Wart, M. (2005) *Dynamics of Leadership in Public Service* (New York: M.E. Sharpe). A readable textbook aimed at leadership and management in the public sector. Chapter 11, 'Leadership Theories: Charismatic and Transformational Approaches', is a useful supplement to this chapter.

Schein, E.H. (2004) *Organizational Culture and Leadership*, third edition (San Francisco: Jossey-Bass). Another classical textbook in leadership with an emphasis on organisational culture. Highly useful to both students and managers in order to understand the complex interplay between leadership and culture and how this affects team dynamics. Part 1, 'Organizational Culture and Leadership Defined', gives a thorough introduction to these topics.

Pettinger, R. (2002) *Introduction to Management*, third edition (New York: Palgrave). A comprehensive introductory textbook that covers all from basic management concepts and theories to organisational behaviour and strategy. Of particular relevance to this book is Chapter 14, 'Communication', as it discusses effective communication in greater length.

Conclusion:
Public Service Delivery in the
'Knowledge Society'

The central theme in this book has been the liberalisation and modernisation of the public sector and public service delivery. These developments have been analysed within a framework set by globalisation and digitalisation at the macro-level; and the implications at the micro-level for public sector organisation and leadership have been investigated. Globalisation and the process of European integration set the scene for the privatisation, liberalisation and modernisation processes that have been discussed in the core chapters of the book. The programme to make the state smaller – privatisation and liberalisation – gave rise to new challenges for the regulatory state and prompted changes in regulation and competition policy. The effort to make the state more efficient – New Public Management and Governance – led to further reorganisation of the part of the state apparatus that is involved in public service delivery and the functioning of its different organisation and units. This, in turn, is prompting many public sector organisations to explore a wide variety of forms of non-hierarchical management and leadership techniques.

The current and future developments in public management are being shaped by the 'knowledge society' – public service delivery takes place in a context that is increasingly characterised by widely accessible information, demanding and empowered users, and complex tasks that require knowledgeable employees. The boundaries of the national public sector have become less clear, both in terms of the delineation between the public and private organisations and in terms of the nation state, the European Union and the broader international environment. The public management reforms of the early 1980s were shaped by clear political economy models and strong assumptions about cause and effect in public policy. The 1990s not only showed that public service delivery is a far more complex matter, globalisation and digitalisation increased the complexity of public service provision even further. The digital revolution has created a new economy that is often labelled the 'information economy' because it generates an almost unlimited amount of information that is readily available for citizens, managers and politicians. The big challenge is how to take advantage of this information for making decisions and executing tasks in organisations. The principal effect of this in terms of management is a shift from leadership by instruction and direction to more non-hierarchical forms of leadership, where employees are developing and using the information available for carrying out the tasks independently. The knowledge society encompasses this aspect as well as the wider importance of knowledge as a basis for decision-making at almost all levels in society.

The present wave of globalisation and the European Union's response to this have established a radically new framework for the public sector in general, and for public service delivery in particular. Globalisation encompasses both a political process of trade liberalisation and the industry-driven developments towards more global companies in many important sectors. The last two decades have seen the gradual development of a consensus among mainstream politicians that free trade increases economic growth. However, it also generates a number of challenges for the public sector. International arrangements that were developed to foster free trade increasingly also have implications for the role of the state. Regional organisations such as the European Union play a double role in the global economy: on one hand, they represent an effort by the member states to compensate for their loss of ability to protect themselves against the excesses of globalisation; on the other, regional integration also deepens free trade among their members. The EU's role as a buffer against some of the effects of globalisation is particularly important because it is very difficult to establish organisations at the global level to handle the unintended consequences of globalisation, such as problems with the environment, migration and employment. The 2000s have witnessed an increase in the political contestation of both globalisation and European integration, as evident not only in the anti-globalisation and Euro-sceptic movements but also in some mainstream political parties.

The core theme in this book is that, in response to internal and external challenges, most liberal democracies have embarked on programmes to liberalise, modernise and privatise important aspects of public service delivery. Globalisation and regional integration set the scene for these developments, but they were also driven by political ideology, economic necessity and citizens' demands for better public services. Liberalisation and privatisation have been closely related, even though the sequence and emphasis has varied considerably, even among the EU member states. Across the board, however, liberalisation and privatisation have generated demands for more regulation. At the same time we have witnessed reforms in the services that remain at the core of the public sector, with a view to using aspects of the market logic to increase the efficiency of the public sector. This has involved separation of politics, administration and service delivery, as well as more use of competition and incentive mechanisms. Across the board, however, New Public Management reforms have prompted further debates on the role of market-type management techniques in the public sector. Independently of the public/private boundary, the increased complexity and uncertainty involved in delivering public services in sectors such as health care and education has given rise to the introduction of more non-hierarchical management and leadership structures. Over the years, the European states have developed a variety of new forms of hybrid governance structures as solutions to the challenges of public services delivery.

The development of the knowledge society continues to drive the development of the public sector and public service delivery in the direction identified and discussed in this volume – liberalisation and modernisation. Liberalisation has meant, and will continue to imply, extensive use of competition in the public sector and involvement of private actors in public service delivery. Modernisation has meant, and will continue to imply, more flexible, more user-oriented and more differentiated public services, provided by a plethora of public, semi-public and private organisations. The future development along both these trajectories looks set to be shaped by three aspects of the knowledge society: more demanding users; an overwhelming flow of information; and the proliferation of digital services (nearly 100 percent in some cases).

First, the knowledge society features more informed and demanding citizens, or users. We have already seen tendencies for public demand not only for more services, but also for better quality services and more differentiated services, tailored to the individual user. Privatisation, liberalisation and modernisation hardly satisfied this demand; it merely helped generate further demands for ever better services. Users can, and often will, be involved in the production or delivery of public services. User choice and complaints procedures are, in many cases, already well developed, and better informed users may well wish to take further advantage of these possibilities for participating and shaping public services in the future. The broad and easy availability of information makes it easier to compare services across localities and sectors. On-line access to the service provider makes feedback easier, and lowers the threshold for complaints. This increased contact between users and service providers also increases the overall demand on elected politicians for more and better services.

Second, the essence of the knowledge society is the overload of information that the 'information economy' generates. This, in turn, changes one of the core challenges of public sector management: from finding information to handling and selecting information. This problem manifests itself at all levels, from the citizen to the administrator and the policy-maker. From the citizen's perspective, the problem is the overwhelming information available about a range of services, and the difficulty of making a well-informed choice (for example, in choice of hospitals). For the administrator or service provider, the problem is two-fold: first in terms of selecting the information on which to base a decision, and second, in terms of allocating resources or advising an individual about available services. Political decision-makers face similar problems regarding how to select the appropriate information for decision-making. One solution to this problem (which is increasingly used) is to move the decision-making process down the hierarchy, in order that the decision be made as closely as possible to the final user of a service.

Third, the knowledge society entails ever greater use of digital systems, for the back-office functions of the public sectors as well as the front-line delivery of public services. With regard to public service delivery it is difficult to imagine that all users will have the capability to use digital systems. There will therefore always be a need for traditional service provision. The cost-savings generated by digital provision of service to the vast majority is freeing up resources to deal with the 'difficult cases', or even on new types of services. However, in most cases, the reorganisation of front-line services to digital format also requires substantial reorganisation and re-training for back-office operations. Digitalisation therefore involves initial costs in terms of re-organisation, but long-term savings because of automation. It also makes it easier to re-package services according to the user's need, and even to combine elements of public and private services. Although digitalisation was hardly an integral part of the New Public Management agenda, it has made many of the operations involved in NPM-type service provision much easier. In conjunction with stronger user involvement, therefore, digitalisation is generating a shift toward more individually oriented public services.

In short, the present trends in public management continue along the trajectory discussed in this book – the liberalisation and modernisation of public service provision. However, the development toward the knowledge society seems to indicate that the specific forms of governance and management in different countries and across sectors are diverging rather than converging. The New Public Management reform programmes suggested that public service provision in the Western liberal democracies might be converging, along the lines indicated by its core principles. Services would be disaggregated, subject to more competition, and incentives would be used more in public service production and provision. However, these have turned out to be broad themes in the development of the public sector – if anything, the last decade has witnessed an increase in the variety of organisations and leadership practices in the public sector. Even when public sector reforms are guided by comprehensive and coherent models, it is the political realities of the day and the local context that determine how public management is organised and carried out.

Bibliography

Andersen, S.S. (2001) 'Energy Policy: Interest Interaction and Supranational Authority', in S.S. Andersen and K.A. Eliassen (eds) *Making Policy in Europe: the Europeification of National Policy-Making* (London: Sage).

Andersen, S.S. and Eliassen, K.A. (2001) *Making Policy in Europe: the Europeification of National Policy-Making* (London: Sage).

Andersen, S.S. and Sitter, N. (2006) 'Differentiated Integration: What Is It and How Much Can the EU Accommodate?', *Journal of European Integration*, 28: 4, 313–30.

Aucoin, P. (1990) 'Administrative Reform in Public Management: Paradigms, Principles, Paradoxes and Pendulums', *Governance: An International Journal of Policy and Administration*, 3: 2, 115–37.

Balaam, D.N. and Veseth, M. (2005) *Introduction to International Political Economy* (Upper Saddle River: Pearson Education).

Baldwin, R. and Cave, M. (1999) *Understanding Regulation* (Oxford: Oxford University Press).

Bang, H. (1999) *Organisasjonskultur* (Lund: Studentlitteratur).

Bartle, I. (1999) 'Transnational Interests in the European Union: Globalisation and the Changing Organisation in Telecommunications and Electricity', *Journal of Common Market Studies*, 37: 3, 363–83.

Bass, B.M. (1960) *Leadership, Psychology and Organizational Behavior* (New York: Harper).

Bass, B.M. (1985) *Leadership Beyond Expectation* (New York: The Free Press).

Bass, B.M. (1990) *Handbook of Leadership: A Survey of Theory and Research* (New York: The Free Press).

Batley, R. and Stoker, G. (1991) *Local Government in Europe: Trends and Developments* (London: Macmillan).

Baylis, J. and Smith, S. (2005) *The Globalization of World Politics* (Oxford: Oxford University Press).

Becker, G. (1983) 'A Theory of Competition among Pressure Groups for Political Influence', *Quarterly Journal of Economics*, 98: 3, 371–400.

Belanger, F. and Hiller, J.S. (2006) 'A Framework for E-government: Privacy Implications', *Business Process Management Journal*, Special edition on e-government, 12: 1, 48–60.

Belbin, M.R. (1981) *Management Teams: Why They Succeed or Fail* (Oxford: Butterworth-Heinemann).

Bellamy, C. (2003) 'Moving to E-government: The Role of ICTs in the Public Sector in Public Management and Governance', in T. Bovaird and E. Löffler (eds) *Public Management and Governance* (New York: Routledge).

Bobbitt, P. (2002) *The Shield of Achilles: War, Peace, and the Course of History* (New York: Anchor Books).

Bogdanor, V. (2005) *Joined-Up Government* (Oxford: The British Academy/Oxford University Press).

Bohle, D. and Greskovits, B. (2007) 'Neoliberalism, Embedded Neoliberalism, and Neocorporatism: Paths towards Transnational Capitalism in Central-Eastern Europe', *West European Politics*, 30: 3, 443–66.

Borraz, O. and Le Galès, P. (2005) 'France: The Intermunicipal Revolution', in B. Denters and L.E. Rose (eds) *Comparing Local Governance: Trends and Developments* (London: Palgrave).

Boyen, R. (1997) 'French Statism at the Cross-roads', in C. Crouch and W. Streeck (eds) *Political Economy of Modern Capitalism* (London: Sage).

Bulmer, S. (1993) 'The Governance of the European Union: A New Institutionalist Approach', *Journal of Public Policy,* 13: 4, 351–80.

Bulmer, S. (1998) 'New Institutionalism and the Governance of the Single European Market', *Journal of European Public Policy*, 5: 3, 365–86.

Burley, A.M. and Mattli, W. (1993) 'Europe before the Court: A Political Theory of Legal Integration', *International Organization*, 47: 1, 41–76.

Burns, J.M. (1978) *Leadership* (New York: Harper & Row).

Carlyle, T. (1841) 'On Heroes, Hero-Worship and Heroic in History' reprinted in P. Davidsson and R. Griffin Ricky (eds) (2002) *Management, an Australasian Perspective* (Brisbane: John Wiley & Sons).

Checkel, J.T. (1999) 'Norms, Institutions, and National Identity in Contemporary Europe', *International Studies Quarterly*, 43, 83–114.

Christensen, T. (2004) 'Modern State Reforms', in K. Heidar (ed.) *Nordic Politics: Comparative Perspectives* (Oslo: Universitetsforlaget).

Christiansen, T. (2006) 'The European Commission: The European Executive between Continuity and Change', in J. Richardson (ed.) *European Union: Power and Policy-Making* (London: Routledge).

Christensen, T. and Lægreid, P. (2002) *New Public Management: The Transformation of Ideas and Practice* (Aldershot: Ashgate).

Christiansen, T., Jørgensen, K.E. and Wiener, A. (1999) 'The Social Construction of European Integration', *Journal of European Public Policy*, 6: 4, 528–44.

Chomsky, N. (2004) *Hegemony or Survival: Americas Quest for Global Dominance* (Allen & Unwin).

Cini, M. and McGowan, L. (1998) *Competition Policy in the European Union* (London: Macmillan).

Cloete, F. (2005) 'Introduction, Bridging the Public Administration Digital Divide', in F. Cloete (ed.) *Technologies in Public Administration* (Amsterdam: IOS Press).

Coase, R.H. (1937) 'The Nature of the Firm', *Economica*, 4: 16, 386–405.

Coen, D. and Héritier, A. (2000) 'Business Perspectives on German and British Regulation: Telecoms, Energy and Rail', *Business Strategy Review*, 11: 4, 29–37.

Cohn, T.H. (2005) *Global Political Economy: Theory and Practice* (Upper Saddle River: Pearson Education).

Colbjørnsen, T. (2004) *Ledere og lederskap: AFFs lederundersøkelser* (Bergen: Fagbokforlaget).

Conger, J.A and Kanungo, R. (1988) *Charismatic Leadership the Elusive Factor in Organizational Effectiveness* (San Francisco: Jossey-Bass).

Cooper, R. (2003) *The Breaking of Nations: Order and Chaos in the Twenty-First Century* (London: Atlantic Books).

Correljé, A. and van der Linde, C. (2006) 'European Supply Security and Geopolitics: A European Perspective', *Energy Policy*, 34: 5, 532–43.

Cram, L. (1994) 'The European Commission as a Multi-Organization: Social Policy and IT Policy in the EU', *Journal of European Public Policy*, 1: 2, 195–217.

Cram, L. (1997) *Policy-Making in the EU: Conceptual Lenses and the Integration Process* (London: Routledge).

Cram, L. (2001) 'Governance "to Go": Domestic Actors, Institutions and the Boundaries of the Possible', *Journal of Common Market Studies*, 39: 4, 595–618.

Cuervo, M.R.V. and López Menéndez, A.J. (2006) *A Multivariate Framework for the Digital Divide: Evidence for European Union-15* (Amsterdam: Elsevier).

Dahl, R.A. (1957) 'The Concept of Power', *Behavioral Science* 2, 201–18.

Dahl, R.A. (1961) *Who Governs? Democracy and Power in an American City* (New Haven: Yale University Press).

Dahl, R.A. (1971) *Polyarchy: Participation and Opposition* (New Haven: Yale University Press).

Davies, A. (1994) *Telecommunications and Politics: The Decentralised Alternative* (London: Pinter).

Denters, B. and Rose, L.E. (2005) *Comparing Local Governance: Trends and Developments* (London: Palgrave).

Dicken, P. (2003) *Global Shift: Reshaping the Global Economic Map in the 21st Century* (New York: Guilford Press).

Digital Divide.org (2007) *Ushering in the Second Digital Revolution* [Online] Available from URL: <http://www.digitaldivide.org/dd/index.html> [Accessed 18 January 2007].

Doern, G.B. and Wilks, S. (1996) *Comparative Competition Policy: National Institutions in a Global Market* (Oxford: Clarendon Press).

Downs, A. (1956) *An Economic Theory of Democracy* (New York: Harper & Row)

Downs, A. (1967) *Inside Bureaucracy* (Boston: Little, Brown & Co.).

Dunleavy, P. (1991) *Democracy, Bureaucracy and Public Choice: Economic Explanations in Political Science* (London: Harvester Wheatsheaf).

Dunleavy, P. and Hood, C. (1994) 'From Old Public Administration to New Public Management', *Public Money and Management*, July–September, 9–16.

Dunleavy, P. and Margetts, H. (2000) 'The Advent of Digital Government: Public Bureaucracies and the State in the Internet Age', APSA conference paper, www.governmentontheweb.org/downloads/papers/APSA_2000.pdf

Dunleavy, P. and O'Leary, B. (1987) *Theories of the State: The Politics of Liberal Democracy* (London: Macmillan).

Eliassen, K.A. and From, J. (2007) *The Privatisation of European Telecommunications* (Aldershot: Ashgate).

Esping-Andersen, G. (1990) *The Three Worlds of Welfare Capitalism* (Cambridge: Polity Press).

Esser, J. and Noppe, R. (1996) 'Private Muddling through as a Political Programme? The Role of the European Commission in the Telecommunications Sector in the 1980s', *West European Politics*, 19: 3, 547–62.

European Commission (2005) *Europe's Information Society: European Commission – Information society – eEurope 2005* [Online] Available from URL: <http://ec. europa.eu/information_society/eeurope/2005/index_en.htm> [Accessed 20 February 2007].

European Commission (2006) *White Paper on a European Communication Policy* (Luxembourg: Office for Official Publications of the European Communities).

Eyre, S. and Lodge, M. (2000) 'National Tunes and a European Melody? Competition Law Reform in the UK and Germany', *Journal of European Public Policy*, 7: 1, 63–79.

Eyre, S. and Sitter, N. (1999) 'From PTT to NRA: Towards a New Regulatory Regime', in K.A. Eliassen and M. Sjøvaag (eds) *European Telecommunications Liberalisation: Too Good to be True?* (London: Routledge).

Ferlie, E., Ashburner, L., Fitzgerald, L. and Pettigrew, A. (1996) *The New Public Management in Action* (Oxford: Oxford University Press).

Fiedler, F.E. (1967) *A Theory of Leadership Effectiveness* (New York: McGraw-Hill).

Flynn, N. (1997) *Public Sector Management* (Hemel Hempstead: Prentice Hall/ Harvester Wheatsheaf).

Friedman, T.L. (2000) *The Lexus and the Olive Tree: Understanding Globalization* (New York: Anchor Books).

From, J. (2001) 'Decision-Making in a Complex Environment', *Journal of European Public Policy*, 9: 2, 219–37.

Fukuyama, F. (1992) *The End of History and the Last Man* (New York: The Free Press).

Fukuyama, F. (2004) *State-Building: Governance and World Order in the 21st Century* (Ithaca: Cornell University Press).

Gabel, M. and Hix, S. (2002) 'Defining the EU Political Space: An Empirical Study of the European Elections Manifestos, 1979–1999', *Comparative Political Studies*, 35: 8, 934–64.

Gabriel, O.W. and Eisenmann, S. (2005) 'Germany: A NE Type of Local Government?', in B. Denters and L.E. Rose (eds) *Comparing Local Governance: Trends and Developments* (London: Palgrave).

Garrett, G. (1995) 'The Politics of Legal Integration in the European Union', *International Organization*, 49: 1, 171–81.

Garrett, G. and Tsebelis, G. (1996) 'An Institutional Critique of Intergovernmentalism', *International Organization*, 50: 2, 269–99.

George, S. (1985) *Politics and Policy in the European Community* (Oxford: Clarendon Press).

Gerber, D.J. (1998) *Protecting Prometheus: Law and Competition in the Twentieth Century* (Oxford: Clarendon Press).

Gerber, D.J. (2000) 'Preface to the Paperback Edition', in *Protecting Prometheus: Law and Competition in the Twentieth Century* (Oxford: Oxford University Press).

Giddens, A. (1990) *The Consequences of Modernity* (Cambridge: Polity Press).

Giddens, A. (1998) *The Third Way: The Renewal of Social Democracy* (Cambridge: Polity Press).

Gilpin, R. (2000) *The Challenge of Global Capitalism: The World Economy in the 21st Century* (Princeton: Princeton University Press).

Gilpin, R. (2001) *Global Political Economy: Understanding the International Economic Order* (Princeton: Princeton University Press).

Goetz, K. (2001) 'Making Sense of Post-Communist Central Administration: Modernization, Europeanization or Latinization', *Journal of European Public Policy*, 8: 6, 1032–51.

Graff, C. (1983) 'The Situational Leadership Theory: A Critical View', *Academy of Management Review*, 8, 285–91.

Grard, L., Vandamme, J. and van der Mensbrugghe, F. (eds) (1996) *Vers un service public europeen* (Paris: Editions Aspe Europe).

Haas, E.B. (1958) *The Uniting of Europe* (London: Stevens & Sons).

Haas, E.B. (1975) *The Obsolescence of Regional Integration Theory* (Berkeley: Institute of International Studies).

Hagen, K. (2006) 'EU "Soft Law" Social Policy: Sustainable State or Institutional Deficiency?', in J. From and N. Sitter (eds) *Europe's Nascent State? Public Policy in the European Union* (Oslo: Gyldendal Akademiske).

Hall, P.A. and Soskice, D. (2001) *Varieties of Capitalism: The Institutional Foundations of Comparative Advantage* (Oxford: Oxford University Press).

Hancher, L. (1996) 'The Regulatory Role of the European Union', in H. Kassim and A. Menon (eds) *The European Union and National Industrial Policy* (London: Routledge).

Hayek, F.A. (1944) *The Road to Serfdom* (Chicago: University of Chicago Press).

Hayes-Renshaw, F. and Wallace, H. (1997) *The Council of Ministers* (New York: St. Martin's Press).

Heeks, R. (2006) *Implementing and Managing eGovernment: An International Text* (London: Sage).

Held, D. (1995) *Democracy and the Global Order: From the Modern State to Cosmopolitan Governance* (Cambridge: Polity Press).

Held, D., McGrew, A., Goldblatt, D. and Perraton, J. (1999) *Global Transformations: Politics, Economics and Culture* (Stanford: Stanford University Press).

Hemphill, J.K. and Coons, R.E. (1957) 'Development of the Leader Behavior Description Questionnaire', in R.M. Stogdill and R.E. Coons (eds) *Leader Behavior: Its Description and Measurement Columbus* (Columbus: Bureau of Business Research, Ohio State University).

Héritier, A. (1999) *Policy-Making and Diversity in Europe: Escape from Deadlock* (Cambridge: Cambridge University Press).

Hermerijck, A., Keune, M. and Rhodes, M. (2006) 'European Welfare States: Challenges and Reforms', in P.M. Heywood, E. Jones, M. Rhodes and U. Sedelmeier (eds) *Developments in European Politics* (London: Palgrave).

Hersey, P. and Blanchard, K. (1988) *Management of Organizational Behavior* (Englewood Cliffs New York: Prentice Hall).

Hix, S. (1994) 'Approaches to the Study of the EC: The Challenge to Comparative Politics', *West European Politics*, 17: 1, 1–30.

Hix, S. (1998) 'The Study of the European Union II: The "New Governance" Agenda and Its Rival', *Journal of European Public Policy*, 5: 1, 38–65.

Hix, S. (1999) *The Political System of the European Union* (London: Macmillan), second edition 2005.

Hobbes, T. (1651) *The Leviathan* (London: Andrew Crooke).

Hoffmann, S. (1966) 'Obstinate or Obsolete? The Fate of the Nation-State in the Case of Western Europe', *Daedalus*, 95, 862–915.

Hood, C. (1991) 'A New Public Management for All Seasons', *Public Administration*, 69, 3–19.

Hood, C. (1998) *The Art of the State: Culture, Rhetoric and Public Management* (Oxford: Oxford University Press).

Hood, C. (2005) 'The Idea of Joined-Up Government: A Historical Perspective', in V. Bogdanor (ed.) *Joined-Up Government* (Oxford: Oxford University Press).

Hood, C., James, O. and Scott, C. (2000) 'Regulation of Government: Has it Increased, Is it Increasing and Should it Be Diminished?', *Public Administration*, 18: 2, 283–304.

Hood, C., Rothstein, H. and Baldwin, R. (2001) *The Government of Risk: Understanding Risk Regulation Regimes* (Oxford: Oxford University Press).

Horn, M.J. (1995) *The Political Economy of Public Administration: Institutional Choice in the Public Sector* (Cambridge: Cambridge University Press).

House, R.J. (1977) 'A 1976 Theory of Charismatic Leadership in Organizations: Perceived Behavioural Attributes and Their Measurement', *Journal of Organizational Behaviour*, 15, 439–52.

House, R.J. and Mitchell, T.R. (1974) 'A Path – Goal Theory of Leadership Effectiveness', *Administrative Science Quarterly*, 7, 323–52.

Howarth, D. (2006) 'Internal Economic and Social Policy Developments', *Journal of Common Market Studies*, 44, Annual Review, 81–100.

Hughes, O.E. (2003) *Public Management & Administration: An Introduction* (London: Palgrave).

International Telecommunication Union (2006) *World Telecommunication/ICT Development Report 2006: Measuring ICT for Social and Economic Development.* [Online] Available from URL: <http://www.itu.int/wsis/index.html> [Accessed 20 February 2007].

Jachtenfuchs, M.J. (1995) 'Theoretical Perspectives on European Governance', *European Law Journal*, 1: 2, 115–33.

James, O. (2000) 'Regulation insider Government: Public Interest Justifications and Regulatory Failures', *Public Administration,* 18: 2, 327–43.

Kassim, H. (1994) 'Policy Networks, Networks and European Union Policy Making: A Sceptical View', *West European Politics*, 17: 4, 15–27.

Kassim, H. and Menon, A. (1996) (eds) *The European Union and National Industrial Policy* (London: Routledge).

Katzenbach, J.R. and Smith, D.K (1993) *The Wisdom of Teams* (Boston: Harvard Business School Press).

Kelemen, R.D. and Tarrant, A. (2007) 'Building the Eurocracy: The Politics of EU Agencies and Networks', paper presented at the European Union Studies Association conference, Montreal, 17–19 May.

Keohane, R.O. and Hoffman, S. (1991) 'Conclusions: Community Politics and Institutional Change', in W. Wallace (ed.) *The Dynamics of European Integration* (London: Pinter).

Kerr, St. and Jermier, J. (1978) 'Substitutes for Leadership: Their Meaning and Measurement', *Organizational Behaviour and Human Performance*, 22, 375–403.

Keynes, J.M. (1936) *The General Theory of Employment, Interest and Money* (London: Macmillan).

Klein, N. (2001) *No Logo: The Age of Anticorporate Activism* (London: Flamingo, Harper Collins Publishers).

Kohler-Koch, B. (1996) 'Catching UP with the Change: The Transformation of Governance in the European Union', *Journal of European Public Policy*, 3: 3, 359–80.

Kohler-Koch, B. and Eising, R. (1999) *The Transformation of Governance in the European Union* (London: Routledge).

Kooiman, J. (2000) 'Societal Governance: Levels, Models and Orders of Social-Political Interaction', in J. Pierre (ed.) *Debating Governance: Authority, Steering, and Democracy* (Oxford: Oxford University Press).

Kooiman, J. (2003) *Governing as Governance* (London: Sage).

Kotter, J.P. (1988) *The Leadership Factor* (New York: The Free Press).

Kotter, J.P. (1990) *A Force for Change: How Leadership Differs From Management* (New York: The Free Press).

Krasner, S.D. (1999) *Sovereignty: Organized Hypocrisy* (Princeton: Princeton University Press).

Lane, J.E. (2000) *New Public Management* (London: Routledge).

Lawson, N. (1992) *The View from No. 11* (London: Bantam Press).

LeGrand, J. (2003) *Motivation, Agency and Public Policy: Of Knights & Knaves, Pawns & Queens* (Oxford: Oxford University Press).

Levi-Faur, D. (2006) 'Europe and the New Global Order of Regulatory Capitalism', in J. From and N. Sitter (eds) *Europe's Nascent State? Public Policy in the European Union* (Oslo: Gyldendal Akademiske).

Lijphart, A. (1984) *Democracies: Patterns of Majoritarian and Consensus Government in Twenty-One Countries* (New Haven: Yale University Press).

Likert, R. (1961) *New Patterns of Management* (New York: McGraw Hill).

Lindberg, L.N. (1963) *The Political Dynamics of European Economic Integration* (Stanford: Stanford University Press).

Lindblom, C. (1977) *Politics and Markets* (New York: Basic Books).

Lodge, M. (1999) 'Competing Approaches to Regulation', in K.A. Eliassen and M. Sjøvaag (eds) *European Telecommunications Liberalisation* (London: Routledge).

Lodge, M. (2002) *On Different Tracks: Designing Railway Regulation in Britain and Germany* (Westport: Praeger).

Lodge, M. (2008) 'Regulation, the Regulatory State and European Politics', *West European Politics,* forthcoming special issue on regulation.

Majone, G. (1994) 'The Rise of the Regulatory State in Europe', *West European Politics,* 17: 3, 77–101.

Majone, G. (1996) *Regulating Europe* (London: Routledge).

Majone, G. (1997) 'From the Positive to the Regulatory State', *Journal of Public Policy,* 17: 2, 139–67.

Mantel, S.J., Meredith, J.R., Shafer, S.M. and Sutton, M.M. (2005) *Core Concepts: Project Management in Practice* (Hoboken: John Wiley & Sons).

Manz, C.C. (1992) *Mastering Self-Management: Empowering Yourself for Personal Excellence* (Englewood Cliffs: Prentice Hall).

Manz, C.C. and Sims, H.P. (1980) 'Self-Management as a Substitute for Leadership: A Social Learning Perspective', *Academy of Management Review,* 5, 361–7.

March, J.G. and Olsen, J.P. (1989) *Rediscovering Institutions: The Organizational Basis of Politics* (New York: The Free Press).

Markellos, K., Markello, P., Panayiotaki, A. and Tsakalidis, A.A. (2007) 'Semantic Web Mining for Personalized Public E-services', in L. Al-Hakim (ed.) *Global E-government: Theory, Application and Benchmarking* (London: Idea Group Publishing).

Marks, G., Hooghe, L. and Blank, K. (1996) 'European Integration from the 1980s: State-Centric v. Multi-Level Governance', *Journal of Common Market Studies,* 34: 3, 341–77.

Marks, G., Scharpf, F.W., Schmitter, P.C. and Streeck, W. (eds) (1996) *Governance in the European Union* (London: Sage).

Martin, S. (1998) *Competition Policies in Europe* (Amsterdam: Elsevier).

McCubbins, M.D. and Schwartz, T. (1984) 'Congressional Oversight Overlooked: Police Patrols and Fire Alarms', *American Journal of Political Science,* 28, 165–79.

McCubbins, M.D., Noll, R. and Weingast, B. (1987) 'Administrative Procedures as Instruments of Political Control', *Journal of Law, Economics and Organization,* 3, 243–79.

McGowan, F. and Wallace, H. (1996) 'Towards a European Regulatory State', *Journal of European Public Policy,* 3: 4, 560–76.

McGowan, L. and Wilks, S. (1995) 'The First Supranational Policy in the European Union: Competition Policy', *European Journal of Political Research,* 28, 141–69.

McLaughlin, K., Osborne, S.P. and Ferlie, E. (eds) (2002) *New Public Management: Current Trends and Future Prospects* (London: Routledge).

Megginson, W.L. and Netter, J.M. (2001) 'From State to Market: A Survey of Empirical Studies on Privatization', *Journal of Economic Literature,* 39: 2, 321–89.

Micklethwait, J. and Wooldridge, A. (2003) *The Company: A Short History of a Revolutionary Idea* (New York: The Modern Library).

Milward, A. (1984) *The European Rescue of the Nation State* (London: Routledge).

Milward, A. (1992) *The European Reconstruction of Western Europe 1945–51* (London: Routledge).

Mitrany, D. (1946) *A Working Peace System* (London: the Royal Institute of International Affairs).

Moran, M. (2002) 'Review Article: Understanding the Regulatory State', *British Journal of Political Science,* 32, 391–413.

Moravcsik, A. (1991) 'Negotiating the Single European Act: National Interests and Conventional Statecraft in the European Community', *International Organization*, 45: 1, 19–56.

Moravcsik, A. (1998) *The Choice for Europe: Social Purpose & State Power from Messina to Maastricht* (Ithaca: Cornell University Press).

Mossialos, E. and LeGrand, J. (1999) *Health Care and Cost Containment in the European Union* (Aldershot: Ashgate).

Muller, D.C. (2003) *Public Choice III* (Cambridge: Cambridge University Press).

Newbery, D.M. (1999) *Privatization, Restructuring and Regulation of Network Utilities* (Cambridge: Massachusetts Institute of Technology Press).

Newman, J. (2001) *Modernising Governance: New Labour, Policy and Society* (London: Sage).

Niskanen, W. (1971) *Bureaucracy and Representative Government* (Chicago: Aldine-Atherton).

Niskanen, W. (1973) *Bureaucracy: Servant or Master* (London: Institute of Economic Affairs).

Nugent, N. (2006) *The Government and Politics of the European Union* (London: Palgrave).

OECD (Organisation for Economic Co-operation and Development) (2003) *Promise and Problems of E-Democracy: Challenges of Online Citizen Engagement* (Paris: OECD Publications).

Ogus, A.I. (1994) *Regulation: Legal Form and Economic Theory* (Oxford: Oxford University Press).

Ogus, A.I. (2002) 'Regulatory Institutions and Structures', *Annals of Public and Comparative Economics*, 73: 4, 627–48.

Ohmae, K. (1995) *The End of the Nation State: The Rise of Regional Economies* (New York: The Free Press).

Olivero, G., Bane, D.K. and Kopelman, D. (1997) 'Executive Coaching as a Transfer of Training Tool: Effects on Productivity in a Public Agency', *Public Personnel Management*, 26: 4, 461–70.

Olson, M. (1965) *The Logic of Collective Action: Public Goods and the Theory of Groups* (Cambridge: Harvard University Press).

Olson, M. (1982) *The Rise and Decline of Nations: Economic Growth, Stagflation and Social Rigidities* (New Haven: Yale University Press).

Olson, M. (1993) 'Dictatorship, Democracy and Development', *American Political Science Review*, 87: 3, 567–76.

Olson, M. (2000) *Power and Prosperity: Outgrowing Communist and Capitalist Dictatorships* (New York: Basic Books).

Osborne, D. and Gabler, T. (1992) *Reinventing Government* (New York: Addison-Wesley).

Pareto, V. (1906) *Manuale d'Economia Politica* (Milan: Societa Editrice Libraria).

Peltzman, S. (1989) 'The Economic Theory of Regulation after a Decade of Deregulation', *Brookings Papers on Economic Activity* (Washington, DC: Brookings Institution).

Pettinger, R. (2002) *Introduction to Management*, third edition (New York: Palgrave).

Pfeffer, J. (1981) *Power in Organizations* (Marshfield: Pittman).

Phelps, E. (1985) *Political Economy: An Introductory Text* (New York: W. W. Norton & Co.).

Pierre, J. (2000) *Debating Governance: Authority, Steering, and Democracy* (Oxford: Oxford University Press).

Pierson, C. and Castle, F.G. (2000) *The Welfare State Reader* (Cambridge: Polity Press).

Pierson, P. (1996) 'The Path to European Integration: A Historical Institutionalist Analysis', *Comparative Political Studies*, 29: 2, 123–63.

Pierson, P. (2004) *Politics in Time: History, Institutions, and Social Analysis* (Princeton: Princeton University Press).

Pollack, M.A. (1996) 'The New Institutionalism and EC Governance: the Promise and Limits of Institutional Analysis', *Governance*, 9: 4, 429–58.

Pollack, M.A. (1997) 'Delegation, Agency and Agenda Setting in the European Community', *International Organization*, 51, 99–135.

Pollitt, C. (2000) 'Is the Emperor in His Underwear? An Analysis of the Impact of Public Management Reform', *Public Management*, 2: 2, 181–99.

Pollitt, C. (2003) *The Essential Public Manager* (Maidenhead: Open University Press).

Pollitt, C. and Bokhaert, G. (2000) *Public Management Reform* (Oxford: Oxford University Press), second edition 2004.

Przeworski, A. (1991) *Democracy and the Market: Political and Economic Reforms in Eastern Europe and Latin America* (Cambridge: Cambridge University Press).

Putnam, R. (1988) 'Diplomacy and Domestic Politics: The Logic of Two-Level Games', *International Organization*, 42: 3, 427–60.

Quirk, P.J. (1988) 'In Defense of the Politics of Ideas', *Journal of Politics*, 50, 243–77.

Ravenhill, J. (2005) *Global Political Economy* (Oxford: Oxford University Press).

Rawls, J. (1971) *A Theory of Justice* (Cambridge: Harvard University Press).

Rho, S.Y. (2007) 'Digital Public Sphere: Rhetoric or Reality', in L. Al-Hakim (ed.) *Global E-government: Theory, Application and Benchmarking* (London: Idea Group Publishing).

Rhodes, R.A.W. (1996) 'The New Governance: Governing without Government', *Political Studies,* 44: 652–67.

Rhodes, R.A.W. (1997) *Understanding Governance* (Buckingham: Open University Press).

Rhodes, R.A.W. (2000) 'Governance and Public Administration', in J. Pierre (ed.) *Debating Governance: Authority, Steering, and Democracy* (Oxford: Oxford University Press).

Rhodes, R.A.W. and Dunleavy, P. (1995) *Prime Minister, Cabinet & Core Executive* (London: Macmillan).

Rhodes, R.A.W. and Marsh, D. (1992) *Policy Networks in British Government* (Oxford: Clarendon Press).

Richards, D. and Smith, M.J. (2002) *Governance and Public Policy in the UK* (Oxford: Oxford University Press).

Richards, D. and Smith, J. (2004) 'The "Hybrid State": Labour's Response to the Challenge of Governance', in S. Ludlam and J. Smith (eds) *Governing as New Labour: Policy and Politics under Blair* (London: Palgrave).

Richardson, J. (1996) 'Policy-Making in the EU: Interests, Ideas and Garbage Cans of Primeval Soup', in J. Richardson (ed.) *European Union: Power and Policy-Making* (London: Routledge).

Richardson, J.J. and Jordan, G.A. (1979) *Governing under Pressure: Policy Process in a Post Parliamentary Democracy* (Oxford: Basil Blackwell).

Rocheleau, B. (2005) *Public Management Information Systems* (Hershey: Idea Group Publishing).

Rosamond, B. (2000) *Theories of European Integration* (London: Macmillan).

Rose, L. (2004) 'Local Government and Politic', in K. Heidar (ed.) *Nordic Politics: Comparative Perspectives* (Oslo: Universitetsforlaget).

Ross, G. (1995) *Jacques Delors and European Integration* (Cambridge: Polity Press).

Sandholtz, W. (1993) 'Institutions and Collective Action: The New Telecommunications in Western Europe', *World Politics*, 45, 242–70.

Sandholtz, W. and Zysman, J. (1989) '1992: Recasting the European Bargain', *World Politics*, 41: 1, 95–128.

Sassoon, D. (1996) *One Hundred Years of Socialism: The West European Left in the Twentieth Century* (London: I. B. Tauris).

Savas, E.S. (1987) *Privatization: the Key to Better Government* (Chatham: Chatham House Publishers).

Sbragia, A. (1992) *Euro-Politics: Institutions and Policymaking in the 'New' European Community* (Washington, DC: The Brookings Institution).

Sbragia, A. (2000) 'The European Union as Coxwain: Governance by Steering', in J. Pierre (ed.) *Debating Governance: Authority, Steering, and Democracy* (Oxford: Oxford University Press).

Scharpf, F.W. (1997) *Games Real Actors Play: Actor-Centred Institutionalism in Policy Research* (Boulder: Westview Press).

Scharpf, F.W. (1999) *Governing in Europe: Effective and Democratic?* (Oxford: Oxford University Press).

Schattschneider, E.E. (1960) *The Semisovereign People: A Realist's View of Democracy in America* (Chicago: Holt, Rinehart & Winston).

Schein, E.H. (1993) 'On Dialogue, Culture, and Organizational Learning', *Organizational Dynamics*, 22: 2, 40–51.

Schein, E.H. (2004) *Organizational Culture and Leadership,* third edition (San Francisco: Jossey-Bass).

Schmidt, S.K. (1997) 'Sterile Debates and Dubious Generalisations: European Integration Theory Tested by Telecommunications and Electricity', *Journal of Public Policy*, 16: 3, 233–71.

Schmidt, S.K. (1998) 'Commission Activism: Subsuming Telecommunications and Electricity under European Competition Law', *Journal of European Public Policy*, 5: 1, 169–84.

Schmitter, P.C. (1974) 'Still the Century of Corporatism?', *Review of Politics*, 36, 85–131.

Scholte, J.A. (2000) *Globalization: A Critical Introduction* (London: Palgrave).

Sedelmeier, U. (2001) 'Comparative Politics, Policy Analysis and Governance – A European Contribution to the Study of the European Union?', *West European Politics*, 24: 3, 173–82.

Seldon, A. (2001) *The Blair Effect: The Blair Government 1997–2001* (London: Little, Brown & Co.).

Seldon, A. and Kavanagh, D. (2005) *The Blair Effect: The Blair Government 2001–5* (Cambridge: Cambridge University Press).

Shepsle, K. and Bonchek, M.S. (1997) *Analyzing Politics: Rationality, Behavior and Institutions* (New York: W. W. Norton & Co).

Sims, H.P. and Gioia, D. (1986) *The Thinking Organization* (San Francisco: Jossey-Bass).

Smith, A. (1776) *An Enquiry into the Nature and Causes of the Wealth of Nations* (London: W. Strahan & T. Cadell).

Smith, J. (2004) 'Conclusion: Defining New Labour', in S. Ludlam and J. Smith (eds) *Governing as New Labour: Policy and Politics under Blair* (London: Palgrave).

Snellen, I. (2005) 'Technology and Public Administration: Conditions for Successful E-Government Development, Some Introductory Observations', in F. Cloete (ed.) *New Technologies in Public Administration* (Amsterdam: IOS Press).

Stacey, J. (2003) 'Displacement of the Council via Informal Dynamics? Comparing the Commission and Parliament', *Journal of European Public Policy,* 10: 6, 936–55.

Stern, J.P. (1998) *Competition and Liberalization in the European Gas Market: A Diversity Model* (London: The Royal Institute of International Affairs).

Stewart, J. (2003) *Modernising British Local Government: An Assessment of Labour's Reform Programme* (London: Palgrave).

Stigler, G.J. (1971) 'The Theory of Economic Regulation', *Bell Journal of Economics and Management Science*, 6: 2, 3–21.

Stiglitz, J.E. (2003) *Globalization and its Discontents* (New York: W. W. Norton & Co.).

Stiglitz, J.E. and Charlton, A. (2005) *Fair Trade for All* (Oxford: Oxford University Press).

Stirton, L. and Lodge, M. (2001) 'Transparency Mechanisms: Building Publicness into Public Services', *Journal of Law and Society*, 28: 4, 471–89.

Stoker, G. (1991) 'Introduction: Trends in Western European Local Government', in R. Batley and G. Stoker (eds) *Local Government in Europe: Trends and Developments* (London: Macmillan).

Stoker, G. (1998) 'Governance as Theory: Five Propositions', *International Social Science Journal*, 155, 17–28.

Stoker, G. (2000) 'Urban Political Science and the Challenge of Urban Governance', in J. Pierre (ed.) *Debating Governance: Authority, Steering, and Democracy* (Oxford: Oxford University Press).

Strom, K. (1990) 'A Behavioral Theory of Competitive Political Parties', *The American Journal of Political Science*, 34: 2, 565–98.

Taylor, P. (1991) 'The European Community and the State: Assumptions, Theories and Propositions', *Review of International Studies*, 17, 109–25.

Taylor, P. (1996) *The European Union in the 1990s* (Oxford: Oxford University Press).

Thatcher, M. (1997) 'The Development of Regulatory Frameworks: The Expansion of European Community Policy-Making in Telecommunications', in S. Stavridis, E. Mossialos, R. Moran and H. Machin (eds) *New Challenges to the European Union: Policies and Policy-Making* (Aldershot: Dartmouth).

Thatcher, M. (1988) 'The European Family of Nations', the 'Burgues speech' of September 1988, reprinted in M. Holmes (ed.) (1996) *The Eurosceptical Reader* (London: Macmillan).

Thomson, D.J. (1967) *Organizations in Actions: Social Science Bases of Administrative Theory* (New York: McGraw-Hill).

Torres, L., Pina, V. and Basilio, A. (2006) 'E-Governance Developments in European Union Cities: Reshaping Government's Relationship with Citizens', *Governance*, 19: 2, 277–302.

Tranholm-Mikkelsen, J. (1991) 'Neo-Functionalism: Obstinate or Obsolete? A Reappraisal in the Light of the New Dynamism of the EC', *Millennium*, 20: 1, 1–22.

Traunmüller, R. and Wimmer, M. (2004) 'E-Government: A Roadmap for Progress', in J.M. Mendes, R. Soumi and C. Passos (eds) *Digital Communities in a Networked Society: E-Commerce, E-Business, and E-Government (The Third IFIP Conference on E-Commerce, E-Business, and E-Government)* (Boston: Kluwer Academic Publisher).

Tsebelis, G. (1990) *Nested Games: Rational Choice in Comparative Politics* (Berkeley: University of California Press).

Tsebelis, G. (1994) 'The Power of the European Parliament as an Agenda Setter', *American Political Science Review*, 88, 128–42.

Tsebelis, G. and Garrett, G. (2000) 'Legislative Politics in the European Union', *European Union Politics*, 1: 1, 9–36.

Tullock, G. (1965) *The Politics of Bureaucracy* (Washington: Public Affairs Press).

UN (United Nations), Department of Economic and Social Affairs (2005) *UN Global E-government Readiness Report 2005, From E-government to E-inclusion* (United Nations Publications) [Online] Available from URL: < http://www.unpan.org/egov-ernment5.asp> [Accessed 16 January 2007].

Van Wart, M. (2005) *Dynamics of Leadership in Public Service* (New York: M.E. Sharpe).

Vickers, J. and Yarrow, G. (1988) *Privatization: An Economic Analysis* (Cambridge: MIT Press).

Wallace, H., Wallace, W. and Webb, C. (1983) *Policy Making in the European Community* (London: John Wiley).

Walsh, K. (1995) *Public Service and Market Mechanisms: Competition, Contracting and the New Public Management* (London: Macmillan).

Weaver, R.K. and Rockman, B.A. (1993) *Do Institutions Matter? Government Capabilities in the United States and Abroad* (Washington, DC: The Brooking Institution).

Weber, M. (1922/1947) *Wirtschaft & Gesellschahft* (Tubingen: J.C.B. Mohr); in English translation 1947 as *The Theory of Social and Economic Organization* (New York: The Free Press).

Weiler, J.H.H. (1991) 'The Transformation of Europe', *The Yale Law Journal*, 100: 8, 2405–83.

Weller, P. (2000) 'In Search of Governance', in G. Davis and M. Keating (eds) *The Future of Governance* (Allen & Unwin).

Wessels, W. (1997) 'An Ever Closer Fusion? A Dynamic Macropolitical View on Integration Processes', *Journal of Common Market Studies*, 35: 2, 267–99.

Wilks, S. (1996) 'Regulatory Compliance and Capitalist Diversity in Europe', *Journal of European Public Policy*, 3: 4, 536–59.

Wilks, S. (1999) *In the Public Interest: Competition Policy and the Monopolies and Mergers Commission* (Manchester: Manchester University Press).

Wilks, S. (2005) 'Agency Escape: Decentralisation or Dominance of the European Commission in the Modernization of Competition Policy?', *Governance*, 18: 3, 431–52.

Wilks, S. (2007) 'The European Competition Network: What has Changed?', paper presented at the European Union Studies Association conference, Montreal, 17–19 May.

Wilson, D. (2005) 'The United Kingdom: An Increasinglty Differentiated Polity?', in B. Denters and L.E. Rose (eds) *Comparing Local Governance: Trends and Developments* (London: Palgrave).

Wilson, G.K. (1990) *Business and Politics: A Comparative Introduction* (London: Macmillan).

Wilson, J.Q. (1989) *Bureaucracy: What Government Agencies Do and Why They Do It* (New York: Basic Books).

Wincott, D. (1996) 'The Court of Justice and the European Policy Process', in J. Richardson (ed.) *European Union: Power and Policy-Making* (London: Routledge).

Winham, G. (2005) 'The Evolution of the Global Trading Regime', in J. Ravenhill (ed.) *Global Political Economy* (Oxford: Oxford University Press).

Wise, M. (2000) 'The Role of Competition Policy in Regulatory Reform', in *The OECD Review of Competition Law and Policy in Denmark* (Paris: OECD).

Yalom, I.D. (1995) *The Theory and Practice and Group Psychotherapy* (New York: Basic Books).

Young, H. (1989) *One of Us: Life of Margaret Thatcher* (London: Macmillan).

Yukl, G. (2006) *Leadership in Organizations* (Upper Saddle River: Pearson Prentice Hall).

Index

business practices 30–1, 115–20, 122, 126
  see also global companies

C2G *see* Government to Citizens
    *e*Government
Cabinets, EU 40
capitalism, models of 56, 62–70, 72–3
Carlyle, T. 152
cartels 77, 82
Cassis de Dijon ruling 46
Cave, M. 92
Central Asia 125
Central European states 64
centre-left politics 7, 9–10, 100, 103–6
centre-right politics 59, 100, 104, 137
charismatic leadership 153–4
charismatic legitimacy 94
Chicago School 5, 80, 83
choice *see* user choice
citizen participation 126–9
civil service 94–8, 102
classical economic theory 3–5, 83
  see also Chicago School
'climber' bureaucrats 96
Clinton, Bill 7, 9, 65
coaching 164–6
Coase, R.H. 99
co-creating leadership 155
co-decision procedure, EU 39, 42
Coen, D. 79
Cold War 16, 21–2, 34
College of Commissioners, EU 40, 90
Commission of the European Communities
    see European Commission
Committee of Permanent Representatives
    (Coreper) 46
common market regimes 30
communication 151, 155–7, 160–7
communism, collapse of 16, 22, 48
'communitarian' approach 138
comparative studies 37–8, 81–8
*Comparing Local Governance: Trends and
    Developments* (Denters and Rose) 147
competencies, bureaucracies 94
competition viii, 1
  liberalisation 61, 67–8, 73
  markets 22–3, 75–8, 83–4, 102–3
  modernisation with little/no 140–1
  organisational design 132, 140–4
  public administration 102–3, 106
  purchaser–provider arrangements 142–4
  regulation for 80, 81–3
competition policy 75–92
  comparative study 81–8
  European Union 40, 43, 47, 50, 52–3,
    69–70, 85–8

competitive tendering 65, 102–3, 105, 107,
    137, 144
complexity, public sector 57–9
Compulsory Competitive Tendering 137, 144
  see also competitive tendering
consensual model of capitalism 63–4,
    67–8, 73
  see also social democracy
Conservative Party 66
  see also Thatcher
'conserver' bureaucrats 96
Constitutional Treaty 39, 48
constructivist approach 37
consultation 39, 41, 127
consumption 77, 147
contracts 103–4
control mechanisms
  bureaucracies 96, 99, 101–2
  governance 108–9
  institutional governance 132, 134,
    135, 144–7
co-operation procedure, EU 39, 41, 46
coordination 108–9
copyright protection 129
Coreper *see* Committee of Permanent
    Representatives
corporatisation of utilities 60–1
corporatist model of capitalism 56, 63–4, 73
cost-based charging 134–5
costs of regulation 145–6
  see also finance
Council of Ministers, EU 36–7, 39–41, 43,
    45–6, 48, 51
counter control 96
cross-subsidies 77–8
Cuervo, M.R.V. 126
cultural globalisation 21–2
culture of organisations 151, 155, 156–7
Custom Resource Management 119

de facto monopolies 141
*Debating Governance: Authority, Steering and
    Democracy* (Pierre) 111–12
decentralisation 11, 131–41
deepening European integration 44–6, 48
defence sector 21, 90
'Delaware effect' 50
delegation 140
delivery of services 131–48, 169–73
demand for regulation 78–80
democracy 18, 113, 126–9, 155–6
  see also liberal democracies; social
    democracy
*Democracy, Bureaucracy and Public Choice:
    Economic Explanations in Political Science*
    (Dunleavy) 111

democratic deficit 18
de-monopolisation 65
Denmark 48–9, 84, 141–4
    see also Scandinavia
Denters, B. 147
deregulation 65–6, 72–3, 91
developing countries 25, 27–8,
    119, 122, 125–6
devolution programmes, UK 137, 141
DG Competition 86, 88, 89–90
DGs *see* Directorates General
Dicken, P. 33
digital divide 115, 123–4, 125–6
digital revolution 113, 114–16, 121, 170
digitalisation vii–viii, 2, 16–17, 23, 32
    boundary permeability 20
    eGovernment 113–30
    knowledge society 170, 172
direct elections 42
Directorates General (DGs) 40, 86, 88, 89–90
dirigiste system 86–7
disaggregation, public administration 101–2
discussion forums 127–8
dispute settlement procedures 25
division of labour 94–5
division management 157
Doern, Bruce 75
Doha Round 26–7
Downs, Anthony 5, 8, 95–7
Dunleavy, P. 8, 14, 111
Dutch models *see* Netherlands
Dynamics of Leadership in Public Service
    (Van Wart) 168

eBusiness 115, 118, 126
ECJ *see* European Court of Justice
ECN competition policy 88
eCommerce 115–16
Economic and Monetary Union (EMU) 49
economics
    competition policy 83–4, 86–7
    eGovernment 115–16
    EU policy 44
    globalisation 21, 30–1
    information economy 170–1
    liberalisation/privatisation 63–4, 67
    political economy 2–7
    public administration 93, 97–9, 100
    public sector efficiency 57–9
    regulation 76–7
e-consultation 127
ECSC *see* European Coal and Steel
    Community
e-democracy 127–8
education 132, 136–9, 141, 145–6
    see also schools

EEA *see* European Economic Area
EEC *see* European Economic Community
eEconomy 115–16
eEnterprises 115–16
eEurope strategy 117, 126
effective competition 143–4
effectiveness, public administration 93, 100
effects, action concept 162–3
efficiency quest 1, 7, 56–62, 93, 100, 141–2
EFTA *see* European Free Trade Association
egoistic motivations 111
eGovernment 113–30
    accountability 147
    concepts/strategies 116–20
    definition 117
    democracy 113, 126–9
    implementation problems 124–5
    maturity levels 119–20, 127
    solutions/use 122–3
eGovernment Organization 116
El-Agraa, A.M. 54
elderly care 132, 141
electoral politics 79–80
electricity provision 56, 69, 71–2, 89, 146
elite theory 4–5
empowering leadership 154–5
'empty chair' crisis, EU Council 45–6
EMU *see* Economic and Monetary Union
energy sector 71–2, 89, 90
    see also electricity provision
environmental problems 22, 76
EP *see* European Parliament
e-participation 127–8
e-readiness criteria 117, 125
Esping-Andersen, G. 63
The Essential Public Manager (Pollitt) 148
EU *see* European Union
Euratom 36, 46
European Coal and Steel Community
    (ECSC) 29, 36, 46
European Commission 39–40, 46, 49–50
    competition policy 85–6, 87–8, 90
    e-democracy 128
    ECJ relationship 42–4
    EP relationship 42
    power 37
    scope expansion 47
    utilities liberalisation 70–1
European Council 40–1, 43, 46
European Court of Justice (ECJ) 35, 37,
    42–5, 47, 51–3
European Economic Area (EEA) 48
European Economic Community (EEC) 36,
    44, 45–6
European Free Trade Association
    (EFTA) 29, 48

micro-level change vii–viii, 85, 87, 91, 131
migration effects 21
military matters 21
Mitrany, D. 36
mixed ownership of utilities 60
mobile networks 122–3
modernisation 1–14
   competition lack 140–1
   governments 113–30
   knowledge society 169–72
   organisational structures 131, 144, 147
   public administration 93–112
   social democracy 7–11
Modernising Governance: New Labour, Policy and Society (Newman) 14
monopolies 22–3
   EU policy 47
   organisational design 141
   privatisation/liberalisation 65, 70–3
   public administration 102
   regulation 76–7, 81–2
Moravcsik, A. 37, 62
most-favoured-nation (MFN) principle 25, 26
motivation
   bureaucrats 96
   leadership 151, 155, 160, 166
   New Public Management 110–11
Motivation, Agency and Public Policy: Of Knights & Knaves, Pawns & Queens (LeGrand) 112
motorway charges 135
multilateral free trade 88–9
multi-level governance 37, 105–6
mutual power-dependence 108

nation states vii, 32–3, 89
National Health Service 102–3
national-level change vii, 12
   budget decentralisation 137
   globalisation effects 27–31
   governance 106, 108
   regulation 91
National Regulatory Agencies (NRAs) 89, 90
natural monopolies 76, 81
   see also monopolies
NDPB *see* Non-Department Public Bodies
negative externalities 76
'negative' instruments 81
'negative' integration 50–1
negotiation 109
neo-functionalism 36, 37, 44–5
neo-liberalism 20, 59
Netherlands
   institutional governance 133
   liberalisation/privatisation 62–3, 67–8
   organisational design 140

Netherlands *cont.*
   public sector efficiency 57, 59
   Third Way politics 10, 11
network utilities 56, 76, 81
   see also utilities
networks
   definition 159
   eGovernment 122–3
   team leadership 161
new institutionalism 8, 38
New Labour 9–10, 105
   see also Blair, Tony
The New Public Management in Action (Ferlie et al.) 111
New Public Management (NPM) 13, 93–112
   digitalisation 172
   eGovernment 121–2
   European Union 49
   user choice 131, 132–3, 138
New Right 2–7, 97–9, 103
Newbery, D.M. 92
Newman, J. 14, 105–6
Niskanen, William 6, 97–8
Non-Department Public Bodies (NDPB) 134
non-hierarchical organisations 151, 161, 162–6, 170–1
Nordic countries *see* Scandinavia
Norway 141–3
   see also Scandinavia
NPM *see* New Public Management
NRAs *see* National Regulatory Agencies
Nugent, N. 54

OECD *see* Organization for Economic Co-operation and Development
OFSTED inspections 138, 145–6
O'Leary, B. 14
Olson, M. 6, 78–80
OMC *see* open method of coordination
one-stop-shops 119
open method of coordination (OMC) 51, 53, 106, 108
operative management 157, 158
'ordo-liberal' system 86
organisational structures vii–viii, 13, 131–48
   competition 140–4
   eGovernment 120–3
   management/leadership 151, 158–62
organised interest groups 78–80
   see also interest groups
Organization for Economic Co-operation and Development (OECD) 56–7, 62, 88–9, 100–1, 103, 130
Organizational Culture and Leadership (Schein) 168

Osborne, D. 73, 100
ownership issues 60, 133, 134
   see also state ownership

Pareto optimality 4, 76, 77
participation 126–9
performance management 156
Perraton, J. 33
personal power 155
Pettigrew, A. 111
Pettinger, R. 168
physical restrictions, competition 142–3
Pierre, J. 111–12
pluralist theories 4–5, 38, 43, 78, 95–7
police-patrol control systems 99
policy 'drift' 98
policy-making
   civil service 102
   competition policy 75–92
   European Union 37–40, 43–54
   globalisation effects 27–8
   governance 106–7, 109
Policy-Making in the European Union
   (Wallace et al.) 54
political economy 2–7
The Political System of the European Union
   (Hix) 54
politics
   electoral 79–80
   European Union 35–9, 50–4
   globalisation of 19, 30–2
   interest groups 78–9
   management tools 149–50
   public choice analysis 5–7
   public sector efficiency 58–9
   see also individual political groups/theories
The Politics of Regulation: Institutions and
   Regulatory Reforms for the Age of
   Governance (Jordana and Levi-Faur) 92
Pollack, M.A. 54
Pollitt, C. 107, 111, 148
pollution regulations 76
positional power 155
'positive' instruments 81
'positive' integration 50
positivist theories 78
postal services 56, 69, 72
power
   European Union 37
   governance 108, 109–10
   leadership 153–4, 155–6
PPP *see* Public-Private Partnerships
practical restrictions, competition 142
price-fixing 77, 82
principal–agent theory 98–9
privacy issues 128–9

private goods 76, 79
private schools 143
private sector
   boundary-blurring 107, 134, 169
   management 149–50
privatisation vii–viii, 1, 12–13, 55–74
   definition 59–60, 61
   efficiency quest 56–62
   European Union 51–2
   globalisation 22–3
   knowledge society 169–71
   patterns of 62–70
Privatization, Restructuring and Regulation of
   Network Utilities (Newbery) 92
process, leadership 151
procurement methods 118
product liability laws 77
production globalisation 16, 17
profit motive 60, 156
prohibition-based competition policy 82, 84, 87
Promise and Problems of E-Democracy:
   Challenges of Online Citizen Engagement
   (OECD) 130
property rights 76
Protecting Prometheus: Law and Competition
   in the Twentieth Century (Gerber) 91
provider–purchaser arrangements 142–4
public administration
   accountability 146–7
   competition 102–3
   eGovernment 119
   governance 104–11
   modernisation 93–112
   New Right 97–9, 103
   pluralist theories 95–7
   reorganisation 101–2
   Weber's model 94–5, 99
public choice analysis 5–11, 38, 58, 97
public goods 76, 79
public governance 15–33
Public Management & Administration: An
   Introduction (Hughes) 147
Public Management Information Systems
   (Rocheleau) 130
Public Management (PUMA) reports 100
Public Management Reform (Pollitt and
   Bokhaert) 111
Public-Private Partnerships (PPP) 107,
   135, 142
public sector
   boundary-blurring 107, 134, 169
   efficiency questions 57–9
   management tasks 156–8
   management tools 149–50
   see also public administration; public
     governance; public services